TEACHING ENVIRONMENTAL ETHICS

TEACHING
ENVIRONMENTAL ETHICS

EDITED BY

CLARE PALMER

BRILL
LEIDEN · BOSTON
2006

This book is printed on acid-free paper.

Library of Congress Cataloging-in-Publication Data

Teaching environmental ethics / edited by Clare Palmer.
    p. cm.
  Includes bibliographical references and index.
  ISBN 90-04-15005-6 (pbk. : alk. paper)
   1. Environmental ethics—Study and teaching. 2. Environmental education.
I. Palmer, Clare, 1967-

GE42.T43 2006
179'.1071—dc22

2006042506

ISBN: 90 04 15005 6

PRINTED IN THE NETHERLANDS

CONTENTS

LIST OF CONTRIBUTORS

Dane Scott, dane.scott@mso.umt.edu

Owen Goldin, owen.goldin@marquette.edu

Kevin de Laplante, kdelapla@iastate.edu

Jim Sheppard, sheppardj@umkc.edu

Raymond Benton, rbenton@luc.edu
Christine Benton, christinebenton@earthlink.net

David Takacs, David_Takacs@csumb.edu
Daniel Shapiro, daniel_shapiro@csumb.edu

Lisa Newton, LHNewton@mail.fairfield.edu

Emily Brady, emily.brady@ed.ac.uk
Alan Holland, a.holland@lancaster.ac.uk
Kate Rawles, Kate@outdoorphilosophy.co.uk

Richard A. Baer Jr., rab12@cornell.edu
James A. Tantillo, jat4@cornell.edu
Gregory E. Hitzhusen, geh23@cornell.edu
Karl E. Johnson, kej3@cornell.edu
James R. Skillen, jrs76@cornell.edu

Dorothy Boorse, dorothy.boorse@gordon.edu

Jame Schaefer, schaeferj@marquette.edu

Michael Nelson, mpnelson@uidaho.edu

Philip Cafaro, cafaro@lamar.colostate.edu

Roger Gottlieb, gottlieb@wpi.edu

Hugh Mason, hugh.mason@port.ac.uk

INTRODUCTION TO
TEACHING ENVIRONMENTAL ETHICS[1]

Clare Palmer

Introduction

In 1971-2, at the University of Wisconsin-Stevens Point, J. Baird Callicott taught what appears to have been the first university course called *Environmental Ethics*.[2] Since then the teaching of environmental ethics has grown substantially. Courses of this name (or with closely related names such as *Environmental Philosophy*) are widely available in colleges and universities in the US and—though to a lesser extent—in Canada, Europe, Australasia and South Africa. (The instructors, locations and syllabi of a number of these courses are available at the website of the Environmental Ethics Syllabus Project.)[3] Such courses are taught at both undergraduate and graduate level; and although an impressionistic survey indicates that most are run from philosophy departments, they may also be linked to, or located wholly within, departments such as theology and religious studies, environmental studies, conservation and forestry. Environmental ethics may also form an explicit part of the syllabus in more general applied ethics courses as well as, for example, contributing to courses in environmental policy, conservation biology and environmental economics.

On reflection, this expansion in the teaching of environmental ethics is not surprising. Indeed, a strong case can be made that the explicit teaching of environmental ethics and values should be central to environmental education of all kinds. After all, fundamental questions as to why environmental issues might be thought to *matter*, and what constitutes an environmental *problem* are inevitably premised on some kind of judgment about what is valuable. As James Proctor (1997: 133) argues: "terms such as 'crisis' are evaluative judgments, not statements of fact. Thus we should consider that thinking of environmental ethics as a *response* to environmental crisis is not wholly correct, that indeed at some level an ethic informs and hence *precedes*

Clare Palmer (Ed.), *Teaching Environmental Ethics*, 1-11.
© *2006 Koninklijke Brill NV. Printed in the Netherlands.*

the ways we make sense of [for example] anthropogenic climate change." Environmental education in the classroom—in environmental science, geography and so on—that does not explicitly discuss underlying value positions (about, for instance, what *makes* the present situation a crisis) is likely to *assume* that particular beliefs and practices just are good or bad. And (apart from anything else) in making such an assumption, an educational opportunity to deepen students' understanding, and to develop their analytic and evaluative abilities is lost.[4] Equally, though, the teaching of environmental ethics allows students to reflect explicitly not only on the kinds of values embedded in talk of "environmental crisis," but also on the kinds of environmental value assumptions with which they are constantly surrounded elsewhere in the curriculum, as well as, of course, outside the classroom. As David Orr (1992: 20) one of the great modern exponents of environmental education argues "All education is environmental education"; or, more broadly as the title of the Benton's paper in this collection so neatly captures, one answer to the question "Why teach environmental ethics?" is "Because we already do".

The Role of Advocacy in Teaching Environmental Ethics

To argue that teaching environmental ethics explicitly is important and worthwhile, however, says nothing about the aims, methods or principal concerns of such teaching. And here, views about what teaching environmental ethics entails or should entail diverge quite significantly, in particular with respect to whether the teaching of environmental ethics should be seen as in any sense a practice of advocacy. Indeed, several different broad orientations with regard to the role of advocacy in environmental ethics teaching can be identified (most are represented in this book). Of course, this identification can be contested; there are, undoubtedly, many different ways of carving up the territory of teaching environmental ethics, even in terms of approaches to advocacy. And it might be that there are areas of overlap, approaches to advocacy that fit none of these orientations, and teachers that move between different orientations when running an environmental ethics course. However, I hope that the kinds of division I suggest may, at least, be helpful in thinking about what might be going on in environmental ethics teaching.

One orientation might be called "pure intellectualist" environmental ethics teaching. Here, such teaching is seen purely as an intellectual project, aiming to develop students' ethical reasoning abilities with respect to the environment. It introduces them to ethical issues raised by the environment, and outlines a range of different ethical approaches and values that are potentially relevant to thinking about those issues. Students are encouraged to think critically, to analyse arguments and to consider the evidence for claims, to develop their own consistent arguments and to offer sound reasons for advancing them, and successful students do so. "Pure intellectualist" environmental ethics teaching, though, does not aim to influence students' own beliefs, values and practices (although they *may* change as a result of what they learn.) Nor does it aim to promote any kind of environmental protection. This kind of environmental ethics teaching fits the model of many other academic subjects. There is no attempt at advocacy of any kind; the course is regarded as an intellectual exercise.[5]

A second orientation might be called "ethical advocacy" environmental ethics teaching. It, too, introduces possible ethical issues raised by the environment, and outlines a range of potentially relevant approaches and values. As with the "pure intellectualist" model, students are encouraged to think critically, to analyse arguments and to consider the evidence for claims, to develop their own consistent arguments and so on. However, the "ethical advocacy" model, alongside the straightforwardly intellectual aim, also aims to help students in working through what is ethical in an environmental context, with a view that they should endorse it. Such an approach is likely to encourage students critically to consider, and to be prepared to revise, their own beliefs, values and practices with respect to the environment. The "ethical advocacy" then, consists of an additional aim to encourage students to consider what *is* ethical, and to live an examined and ethical life with respect to the environment. But no particular content to this examined and ethical life is presupposed. It might be that a student provides cogent arguments presented in good faith that (for instance) the environment carries only instrumental value, and that this means its exploitation even for relatively trivial human interests is acceptable. For the purposes of "ethical advocacy" environmental ethics teaching, a student adopting such a view would have fulfilled the aim of critically scrutinising his or her own environmental values, beliefs and practice in the light of what has been learned in the class.

Others take an "environmental advocacy" orientation in teaching
environmental ethics. (This is the majority view in this book, and
perhaps the majority view in environmental ethics teaching as a
whole, as de Laplante suggests in his paper.) Ethical issues about
the environment are generally raised in the context of environmental
crisis—an environmental crisis understood to have been produced
by misguided values. These mistaken values—emphasising consumerism
and consumption and understanding the environment as a resource—
are seen as tightly bound into what Sterling (1996: 20) calls the
"dominant social paradigm". Given the dominant social paradigm
(DSP) and the urgency of the environmental crisis, the teaching of
environmental ethics is regarded as both vital (in putting forward
new values) and counter-cultural (in exposing, and opposing, the
DSP). Courses that interpret teaching environmental ethics in this
way, of course, retain intellectual aims. But there are major additional aims. Not only does such teaching aim to produce students
who live ethical, examined lives with respect *to* the environment; it
also aims to produce students who live ethical examined lives with
respect *for* the environment. (Indeed, this kind of teaching is sometimes known as education *for* the environment.) Students are challenged and encouraged to move from holding views congruent with
the DSP to adopting a new environmental ethic. Although such an
environmental advocacy approach may take different shapes and be
more or less "radical", frequently it endorses non-anthropocentrism,
adheres to an idea of intrinsic value in nature, and advocates respect
and care for the environment. Further, in aiming to change the values of students, such teaching aims also to change their behaviour
(for instance as consumers, as political actors, and, where relevant,
in their professional lives). However, such environmental advocacy
should not necessarily be interpreted as steering students towards a
particular environmental ethic. Such an approach to teaching environmental ethics may be pluralist in terms of philosophical or religious underpinning (for instance "respect" may follow from Christianity
or Buddhism for example)[6] and pluralist in terms of the working-out
of respect (the land ethic, biocentrism and so on). What matters is
that students emerge with an orientation towards, and a commitment to, respecting or caring for nature, though this respect may be
underpinned by different worldviews and have several possible prin-
cipled manifestations.

Fourthly, some adopt a "specific advocacy" orientation to environmental ethics teaching: that is, they focus on, and advocate, one

particular form of environmental ethic (such as, for instance, the land ethic). Courses of this kind often direct student concern to a range of environmental issues particularly relevant to the ethic at stake. A number of different kinds of ethical responses to those problems may be outlined, but the one flowing from the specific environmental ethic advocated is argued to be the most successful. Good reasons and arguments for the desired ethical position are put forward; other views may be discussed but are seen ultimately as unsuccessful challenges. (It should be noted that such approaches to teaching often arise when the course is being taught in relation to a particular *concern*, such as forestry or land management.) In most cases the "specific advocacy" approach to teaching environmental ethics is also "environmental advocacy," inasmuch as the aim is to persuade students to adopt beliefs, values and practices of respect for the environment (though filling out "respect" here with a specified content.) But this is not necessarily the case. A specific advocacy position might aim to persuade students that the only kind of environmental ethic that needs to be adopted is one where the environment would be best used for the benefit of present human beings. This would still be advocating a particular ethical position, even though it could not easily be described as being advocacy *for* the environment.

Methods of Teaching in Environmental Ethics

Environmental ethics teaching not only manifests a diversity of orientations and attitudes towards advocacy, it also manifests a diversity of teaching methods. A number of contributors to this book claim that the nature of their environmental ethics teaching requires them to adopt specific methods that—in relation to teaching in higher education as a whole—might be seen as unusual or unorthodox. Some of these methods seem to emerge from the nature of environmental ethics as a subject. Others arise from the ways in which educators orient their environmental ethics teaching with regard to advocacy.

Dealing with multidisciplinarity and interdisciplinarity, for example, is part of the nature of environmental ethics—even where teaching is located wholly within a philosophy department. Most obviously, acquaintance with some basic material—both factual and conceptual—in various sciences, including biology, ecology and atmospheric chemistry is usually required; some understanding of technological development is helpful; there may also be issues arising from wildlife

management, urban planning, forestry and so on. Yet teaching that
involves drawing on a number of disciplines is not straightforward
for a variety of reasons. Members of academic disciplines and professions tend to cohere into "disciplinary cultures", sharing disciplinary
assumptions about, for instance, ways of understanding the world,
ways in which knowledge about the world can be discovered or produced, and validated; concerns about the most important objects for
scholarly attention, and, indeed, beliefs concerning the learning
processes by which students can most effectively graduate to full
membership of the disciplinary community.[7] If multidisciplinary teaching dominates—where different disciplines are juxtaposed but not
directly related to one another—it can be difficult for students to
work with the resulting contrast in approaches to knowledge and
learning. Interdisciplinarity—where different disciplines are actively
interrogated by one another and some kind of integration, often at
a problem-focused level is attempted—is more difficult to achieve
but may be more rewarding for students. Consequently, many educators
in environmental ethics consciously attempt to develop interdisciplinarity. Some methods that can be adopted include paying conscious
attention to the contrasting intellectual cultures of different academic disciplines, involving members of different disciplines actively in
the design and delivery of courses, and including visitors to the course
from other academic disciplines or from professional environmental
practice. These visitors can be questioned about the nature of their
discipline or professional practice, on what bases they make knowledge-
claims within this discipline or profession, and what kinds of value
assumptions tend to underpin their academic or professional work.[8]
The Interdisciplinary Minor in Environmental Ethics at Marquette
University, discussed by Schaefer in this book, provides an example
of just such an attempt to achieve interdisciplinarity.

A number of educators in environmental ethics—including some
in this book—also argue that since environmental ethics is about the
environment, some teaching at least should actively *engage with* the
environment, rather than wholly being book learning. To do this,
some environmental ethics teachers adopt methods involving *experiential education*. This may entail the organisation of field trips to particularly interesting or important environments (as with the field trip
to the island of Rum discussed in this book); venturing into local
environments to consider environmental problems and values at stake
there; or even just attention to and awareness of the classroom envi-

ronment itself. Actively engaging with an environment in these ways may have a variety of purposes. It may, for instance, allow students to understand and appreciate qualities (in particular aesthetic qualities such as sublimity) difficult to grasp from books and discussions. It may also be based on the thought that actively experiencing a situation in person brings home the impact of ethical decision-making in ways that learning in the classroom cannot. Experiential methods of teaching environmental ethics are, obviously, particularly appropriate in a context of advocacy of any kind: the impact is likely to be felt on an individual's own beliefs and values as part of their examined life, as well having an effect on their purely academic work.

And, indeed, it is the advocacy aims—whether ethical, environmental or specific—of much teaching in environmental ethics that give rise to many of the concerns for method displayed in the papers in this book. Where there is some intent in a course to encourage students to examine their own lives, ethical beliefs and practices, one might expect reactions from students that are not "purely academic". A number of papers consider how to build students' emotional reactions into the methods adopted in teaching classes, anticipating that student responses to learning about environmental problems or to changing their own environmental values will include—*inter alia*—pessimism, depression, powerlessness, frustration, anger, confusion and uncertainty. Dealing with these kinds of responses (discussed, for instance, in Sheppard's and Gottlieb's papers) may require carefully tailored teaching and learning methods, ones that are, perhaps, unusual in higher education.

Subject Concerns in Environmental Ethics Teaching

The potential subject matter of environmental ethics is, of course, vast. For this reason, environmental ethics educators must of necessity select particular *subject concerns* around which their courses focus. Some may emphasise geographical, place-based concerns.[9] These concerns may, literally, focus on the character of, and environmental issues raised by, the local environment (Cafaro's paper in this book illustrates how a course in environmental ethics may use local and regional environments as a focus). But place may also be important inasmuch as it reflects a particular political culture. For example, genetically modified organisms, or foot-and-mouth disease, having

been the focus of recent political debate in Europe may seem particularly key topics for European environmental ethics courses, but
be of less immediate prominence in other parts of the world.

Equally, though, the pedagogic concerns selected for attention may
reflect both the background of the instructor and the constituency
of the students being taught. Some instructors have qualifications in
biology rather than in philosophy and teach students who are science majors; this is reflected in the concerns on which they focus
(see, for instance, Boorse's paper on non-indigenous invasive species
in this book). Others, whether with philosophical backgrounds or
not, teach environmental ethics to non-specialist students from a
range of different backgrounds (for instance Mason, Gottlieb and
Nelson in this book); teaching non-specialist students certainly affects
the kinds of material one might choose to include in a syllabus. The
subject concerns of environmental courses are also likely to reflect
the approach to environmental ethics adopted by the educator (even
where there is not an intention to advocate such an approach).
Environmental pragmatists, for example, are more likely to construct
their courses around policy issues; those committed to deep ecology
are more likely to emphasise wilderness (whether or not they are
geographically located in proximity to wilderness). Yet others may
shape their subject concerns in teaching environmental ethics through
the lenses of broader socio-political commitments (such as feminism,
animal welfare and bioregionalism).

In subject concern, then, as well as in method and orientation
towards advocacy, environmental ethics courses can be extremely
diverse. The papers in this book effectively illustrate this diversity.
What they also illustrate is that my original plan for the book—to
have one section on theoretical questions in teaching environmental
ethics, and a second section showcasing courses in practice—was
misconceived. The practical discussions of courses rested on theoretical principles about appropriate orientations, aims and methods;
while many of the more theoretical papers used particular courses
to illustrate their points. So in the end, the book was organised
broadly along a spectrum from the more theoretical to the more
practical, but no clear divide between the two could—or, on reflection,
should—be established. As should surely be the case, the aim is to
have theory informing practice, and practice informing theory.

Conclusion: A worry about advocacy in an educational context

I want to conclude this introduction with one worry—admittedly of a controversial nature—concerning the kind of environmental ethics teaching that adopts an orientation of "environmental advocacy" or "specific advocacy" (or indeed, some combination of the two). Of course, there are good reasons why so many in higher education adopt these approaches to teaching environmental ethics. In particular, it might be argued, the intensity of the environmental crisis is now so pressing that what is important is that students acquire—and pass on—new environmental values. Environmental ethics education should be education *for* the environment—acting as a counterweight to those other educational pressures, both formal and informal, that have such very different understandings of environmental value.

Yet it is precisely this understanding of the role of education, especially in a university context, that might generate uneasiness. Increasingly, work in educational theory has emphasised the importance of critical thinking to students' education. Critical thinking can be defined in many different ways, but one leading definition proposes that it is "centrally concerned with giving reasons for one's beliefs and actions, analysing and evaluating one's own and other people's reasoning, devising and constructing better reasoning. Common to these activities are certain distinct skills, for example, recognizing reasons and conclusions, recognizing unstated assumptions, drawing conclusions, appraising evidence and evaluating statements, judging whether conclusions are warranted" (Thomson 1996: 2). Encouraging students to develop these skills and abilities, to become autonomous thinkers in their own right, seems to be fundamentally important to any educational undertaking. Yet it also seems to be in tension with any strong sense of education *for* the environment. In the not dissimilar context of "education for sustainable development", Jickling (1992: 8) asks, "Should education aim to advance a particular end such as sustainable development? Is it the job of education to make people behave in a particular way?" and concludes with a strongly argued negative. "Education for sustainable development, education for deep ecology (Drengson 1991), or education for anything else is inconsistent with that criterion [enabling people to think for themselves]." (Jickling 1992: 8). This, then, is precisely my concern about the apparent dominance of environmental advocacy, and specific advocacy of a particular environmental ethic, in the environmental ethics classroom. Students may be encouraged to become passive learners, accepting what they are being taught and revising their views accordingly, rather than developing the critical skills of recognising assumptions, evaluating and criticising arguments and learning to think for themselves. Educationally, this is surely less beneficial to the student than developing their critical thinking, even if by doing so the student ends up with a less environmentally-respectful environmental ethic.

But there is a further issue to consider here. A passive learner is likely to be a passive learner in all situations; an active critical thinker likewise. If a student is accustomed to passive acceptance of values, it is unlikely to be those values absorbed from a few hours in the environmental ethics classroom that persist, but rather those derived from the much longer and greater exposure to the world outside the classroom. And, in the long term, these are unlikely to be the kinds of environmental values that those adopting an environmental advocacy position would defend. But similarly, the student who has become a critical thinker, who has learned to argue, to worry at value questions, to accept nothing at face value, is less likely to be overwhelmed by those values from outside the classroom, but to subject them to critical scrutiny. Of course, what kinds of environmental ethic such a critical thinker might end up adopting cannot be predicted or guaranteed. But such an ethic is likely to be rigorous, defensible and backed up by evidence. And even though refraining from environmental advocacy in the classroom may seem to be a risk (since one is not helping students to any ethical position with respect to the environment), it seems to be a risk worth taking. If threats to the environment are as many and as severe as many environmentalists think, then even the most critical of reasoners is likely, on reflection, to adopt an active environmentally-protective ethic. And such an ethic—unlike that adopted by more passive learners—is unlikely to be overwhelmed by the strongly represented but weakly supported environmental values outside the classroom.

NOTES

1. Acknowledgements: I would like to thank Jim Sheppard and Quentin Merritt for comments on earlier drafts of this introduction.

2. Callicott makes this claim in several places and it does not appear to be contested. See http://www.phil.unt.edu/faculty/vjbc.html

3. See http://www.appliedphilosophy.org/syllabusproject/index.html (This website is becoming a little outdated, but it is still useful).

4. Admittedly, this view may have to be argued for in some college and university contexts, where the teaching of environmental ethics can be viewed with suspicion, as Sheppard points out (pers.comm.).

5. Sheppard (pers.comm.) suggests that some would argue that just to teach environmental ethics theoretically (without any attempt at advocacy) could be seen as a form of environmental activism. This follows the kind of claim made by Callicott (1992: 3) that "because of the academic debate about intrinsic value in nature, the concept of intrinsic value in nature has begun to penetrate and reshape the discourse of environmental activists and environmental agency personnel". If one accepts this claim, the category of "pure intellectualism" in environmental ethics teaching may not hold water; or one might want to divide intellectualist environmental ethics teaching into two kinds.

6. This is the kind of pluralism Naess seems to endorse in his form of deep ecology (see Naess 1993, Light 2000).

7. See Becher and Huber (eds.) (1990) and Jones, Merritt, and Palmer (1999a).

8. For further discussion on interdisciplinarity in environmental higher education, see Jones, Merritt and Palmer (1999b).

9. I am grateful to Jim Sheppard for highlighting a number of the following points in a response to an earlier draft of this introduction.

REFERENCES

Becher, T. and L. Huber (eds). 1990. "Disciplinary Cultures". Special issue of the *European Journal of Education*, 25: 3 235-240.

Callicott, J. Baird. 2002. "The Pragmatic Power and Promise of Theoretical Environmental Ethics: Forging a New Discourse". *Environmental Values* 11: 12-25.

Jickling, B. 1992. "Why I don't want my children educated for sustainable development". *Journal of Environmental Education* 23: 45-8.

Jones, Peter; Merritt, Quentin and Clare Palmer. 1999a. "The Case for Values Awareness in Environmental Higher Education" in IGU Commission on Geographical Education. *Geography and Environmental Education: International Perspectives*. Institute of Education, London. 11-13th April 1999. Proceedings.

———. 1999b. "Critical Thinking and Interdisciplinarity in Environmental Higher Education: the case for epistemological and values awareness." *Journal of Geography in Higher Education* 23: 3 249-357.

Light, Andrew. 2000. "Callicott and Naess on Pluralism" in Katz, Light and Rothenberg (eds) *Beneath the Surface: Critical Essays in the Philosophy of Deep Ecology*. Cambridge: MIT Press, pp. 125-148.

Naess, Arne. 1993. "The Deep Ecology Movement: Some Philosophical Aspects" in Zimmerman *et al.* (eds) *Environmental Philosophy*. New Jersey: Prentice Hall, pp. 193-212.

Orr, David. 1992. *Ecological Literacy*. New York: SUNY.

Proctor, James. 1997. "*Earth's Insights*: A Geographer's Perspective on its Rationale and Method." *Worldviews: Environment, Culture, Religion* 1: 2 131-138.

Sterling, Stephen. 1996. "Education in Change" in J. Huckle and S. Sterling (eds) *Education for Sustainability*. London: Earthscan, pp. 18-39.

Thomson, Anne. 1996. *Critical Reasoning. A Practical Introduction*. London: Routledge.

TRANSFORMING THE "MARKET-MODEL UNIVERSITY": ENVIRONMENTAL PHILOSOPHY, CITIZENSHIP AND THE RECOVERY OF THE HUMANITIES

Dane Scott

Abstract
This paper addresses the problem of the declining status of philosophy and the humanities in higher education. These events have given rise to discussions of the "corporatization" of higher education and the dominance of the "Market-Model University." In the Market-Model University the chief goals are to teach marketable skills and develop marketable innovations. In responding to these developments, my thesis is that practical philosophy, exemplified by environmental philosophy, offers direction for positive reforms that will revitalize philosophy and the humanities. (While my comments focus on philosophy, I believe much of what is said can apply to other fields in the humanities.) More specifically, they point to a "Citizen-Model University" as a positive alternative to the Market-Model. In the Citizen-Model University the chief goal is education for "citizenship". This focus in education will allow democratic societies to better meet the challenges of the twenty-first century. Such challenges are increasingly characterized by difficult decisions involving environmental problems (e.g., global warming) and technological developments (e.g., biotechnology). These kinds of problems cannot be left to the "invisible hand" of the market. They require democratic citizens capable of moral deliberation, leading to intelligent choices.

Keywords: higher education, "Market-Model University," citizenship, practical philosophy, environmental philosophy, environmental education

Introduction

The complexity of our present troubles suggests as never before that we need to change our present conception of education. Education is not properly an industry, and its proper use is not to serve industries, either by job training or by industry subsidized research. Its proper use is to enable citizens to live lives that are economically, politically, socially, and culturally responsible. This cannot be done by gathering or "accessing" what is now called "information"—which is to say facts without context and therefore without priority. A proper education enables young people to put their lives in order, which means knowing what things are more important than other things; it means putting first things first. (Wendell Berry 2001: *Thoughts in the Presence of Fear*)

Clare Palmer (Ed.), *Teaching Environmental Ethics*, 12-34.

Over the last thirty years higher education in the United States has undergone changes of great consequence. The goals of the university are increasingly conceived in economic terms.[1] This trend has created what Engell and Dangerfield have termed the "Market-Model University" (Engell and Dangerfield 1998). Under the Market-Model politicians, business leaders and university administrators see the social role of higher education in terms of its capacity for supporting economic growth. This model is now institutionalized at major universities and through powerful organizations. For example, the University of California advertises itself as "a powerful engine for economic growth—training California's skilled workforce, developing new technologies, sparking regional prosperity (UC Impact Report 2002)."[2] On the national level, the Business-Higher Education Forum, whose members include the presidents of prestigious universities and the CEOs of powerful transnational corporations, asserts: "Higher education and business are increasingly interdependent: Educational institutions produce human resources that corporations apply to the production of goods and services (Business-Higher Education Forum)."

In the business ethos of the Market-Model University subjects that are well suited to supply human resources and generate profitable innovations are thriving, while those less well suited are in decline. This means an ever-diminishing role for philosophy, and the humanities in general. For example, during the rise of the Market-Model University the percentage of students majoring in philosophy, history, foreign languages, English and literature has gone from a high in the late sixties of nearly 18% to approximately 8% in 2002 (Initiative for the Humanities 2004: 28). Over the same period there has been rapid growth in "marketable" degrees. For instance, majors in computer and information sciences and protective services have grown by a factor of 5 to 10 (Engell & Dangerfield). The most popular major is now business, outnumbering English by 4 to 1 (Ibid.). In addition, since the 1960s the percentage of faculty members in the liberal arts has halved (Ibid.). Finally, it is well documented that instructors and adjuncts, rather than tenured professors, are increasingly teaching courses in the humanities due to lack of adequate funding.

The decline in the status of the humanities is also evident in faculty salaries and moneys spent on programs. In comparison to fields that generate marketable degrees and innovations, professors in the humanities earn "thousands or tens of thousands of dollars" less (Ibid.).

Between 1976 and 1996 the gap between the average starting pay
for assistant professors in business to those in the humanities grew
to over $20,000 (Ibid.). Given the symbolic and practical significance
of faculty salaries, the implications of this trend are clear. Finally, a
recent study of internal university financing "found that humanities
departments consistently ranked among the lowest in cost per student (Initiative for the Humanities 2004: 29)."

Under a thoroughgoing market-model this decline threatens the
survival of some humanities programs. To illustrate, one prominent
state university system requires degree programs to graduate a min-
imum of ten majors a year; this requirement makes no qualitative
distinctions between subject areas.[3] If a program does not meet this
numerical standard of production, an administrator must argue for
its continued existence. The logic of this system of valuation is obvious: students/customers are seeking marketable degrees based on
expectations of the needs of industry; if there is insufficient "cus-
tomer" demand for a product/degree then it should be discontin-
ued. This logic and system of valuation supports Langdon Winner's
contention that education has been redefined as "a commodity for
sale in the market at a competitive price" and "'students' are redefined
as 'customers' (Winner 1997: 4)."

While this data could obviously be more specific and complete,
the direction over the last 30 years is clear: the evolution of a two-
tiered system in higher education where departments that readily
serve economic ends are thriving, while those that do not are declining.

How should supporters of philosophy and the humanities confront
these developments? A natural response is to be angry, defensive and
reactionary. However, a more positive response is to adapt through
progressive reforms. Bill Readings asserts that reactionary reforms to
stop the anti-humanities "corporatization" of the university are inadequate. Rather, the task is much larger; it involves rethinking "the categories that have governed intellectual life for over two hundred years"
(Press and Washburn 2000). In the same vein, Langdon Winner writes:

> There is a distinct danger that we could find ourselves in the ulti-
> mately futile position of being hunkered down, defending a citadel
> under siege. What is needed to sustain us in the long battles ahead is
> a renewed vision of what education is about and what its relationship
> to the larger society ought to be (Winner 1997: 10).

The goal of this paper is to suggest a "renewed vision" for philosophy, and the humanities, which is better adapted to the new social realities. Toward that end, my thesis is that practical philosophy, exemplified by environmental philosophy, provides direction for positive reforms. (While the following comments focus on philosophy, I believe much of what is said can apply to other fields in the humanities.) More specifically, practical fields such as environmental philosophy provide the foundation for a Citizen-Model University, as a positive alternative to the Market-Model. In sum, the Citizen-Model University will allow democratic societies to better meet the challenges of the twenty-first century, which are increasingly characterized by difficult decisions involving environmental problems (e.g., global warming) and technological developments (e.g., biotechnology). These kinds of problems cannot be left to the "invisible hand" of the market. They require democratic citizens capable of deliberation, leading to intelligent choices.

In pursuing my thesis this paper will be divided into a description of the problem, a diagnosis, and a suggested line of treatment. More specifically, Part I will briefly describe and diagnose the problem: the rise of the Market Model University and the decline of the humanities. Part II will articulate a program of rehabilitation: the Citizen-Model University.

Part I: The Creation of the Market-Model University

What is creating this new environment in higher education? One important factor is a change in the way universities are funded: public funding has decreased while funds from private corporations have increased. These changes were initiated in the 1980s with the rise of the Reagan revolution's philosophy of free-market individualism. So, I believe there is some truth in saying that both the decline of pubic support, due to the anti-tax movement, and the "corporatization" of higher education are twin consequences of the ascendancy of this "anti-public", free-market philosophy.

This claim is supported by the focused effort to reorganize the academy in the 1970s and 1980s. More specifically, in the early 1980s a group of politicians, industry leaders and university administrators set out to make science a more efficient engine of economic growth. During this period there was a sense that U.S. industry was falling behind. The problem was diagnosed as a failure of "American industry to maintain an innovative climate and make use of scientific breakthroughs" (Krimsky 1999: 20). The cure was to forge a closer relationship between industry and the academy. Toward that end, Congress passed a series of acts aimed at removing barriers between these institutions. The consequence was major restructuring in academic science, and the academy in general.[4]

The Effects of Bayh-Dole

The most important of these laws is the Bayh-Dole Patent and Trademark Amendment, which allows U.S. universities to patent and license discoveries made from publicly funded research.[5] Gordon Rausser, a defender of private/public alliances and former Dean of UC Berkeley's College of Natural Resources, notes that the "motivation" behind this Act, "is the linkage between discovery and innovations at research universities and the capture of commercial market value that ultimately promotes U.S. economic growth" (Rausser 1999: 3). Rausser summarizes the consequences of these changes: "universities have responded . . . [by] expanding their technological transfer activities . . . They have become a bit more like private companies" (Ibid.: 1).

So the consequence of Bayh-Dole is to change the university environment by making research an important source of revenue. For example, in the five years from 1991 to 1996 there was a 75% increase in the number of "licenses executed by universities" (Ibid.: 7). Further, during this period the patent royalties more than doubled, from $248 million in 1992, to $611 million in 1997 (Ibid.). The latest survey by the Association of University Technology Managers (AUTM) indicates that the business of U.S. universities continues to grow despite a sluggish economy. For the 2001 fiscal year the AUTM survey (for which 222 institutions submitted data) shows that, "Sponsored research expenditures are up 16.6%, invention disclosures are up 14.8%, U.S. patent applications are up 13.6%, licenses and options are up 15.2%, license-related income is up 11.9% and new products are up 58.9%" (AUTM 2003). This translates to 9,454 patents and $827 million in royalties—a greater than one-third increase since 1997.[6] This data to some degree explain why "economic pressures and rewards have transformed American higher education in the last 30 years" (Engell and Dangerfield).

The Changing Value of Knowledge and the Market-Model

In order to better understand why these changes have led to an inhospitable environment for the humanities it is important to see how they have transformed the way knowledge is valued in higher education. For instance, in his argument supporting university/industry "joint ventures," Gordon Rausser asserts that the distinctions between public research goods and private research goods (that is, the distinction between basic and applied research) should be dissolved (Rausser 1999: 6).[7] The theory behind rejecting these distinctions follows from a rejection of a commonly held model that sees a linear flow from publicly funded, basic science to privately funded, applied science. In place of this model is one that sees basic science driven by applied science and the desire for marketable technologies. To support his point, Rausser refers to a book by Terence Kealey, *The Economic Laws of Scientific Research*. In that book Kealey presents historical arguments to support the claim that basic science is driven by marketable technologies. Kealey's radical thesis is for the abolition of "public science." In other words, *science* would do better if market forces, rather than public bureaucracies governed it.

What is significant here is that marketable technologies are not seen as a windfall consequence of basic science. Rather basic science is done with potential products in view. There is no doubt truth to the idea that the relationship between basic and applied science is complex, and often flows in both directions, from basic to applied, and vice versa. However, the significance of this social philosophy of science leads to fundamental changes in the way knowledge is valued in higher education.

To bring this point into relief it will be helpful, for heuristic purposes, to use to classical categories of knowledge, specifically with reference to Aristotle. Broadly speaking, the model Rausser is rejecting holds sharp distinction between *epistēmē* and *technē*. To explain: in one sphere is *epistēmē*, which refers to pure theory, disinterested knowledge as an end in itself (Ostwalt 1962: 307). It is in the broadest sense theoretical science. In another sphere is *technē*, which refers to know-how, the kind of knowledge needed to produce a product. *Technē* is not valued as an end in itself, but as a means to other ends. It is in the broadest sense applied science (Ibid.). In the traditional university *epistēmē* is valued over *technē*, basic science is held in higher esteem than applied science. However, in the Market-Model

University the relationship between *epistēmē* and *technē* is inverted. Perhaps more accurately, theory is valued to the extent that it is likely to enhance marketable skills and generate profit-making technologies.

Diagnosis

This last point leads to an obvious explanation for the decline of the humanities. The recent trend to prioritize *technē* over *epistēmē* devalues philosophy and the humanities, because philosophy, and I assume the other humanities, primarily conceives of its activities as focusing on theory, *epistēmē*. However, unlike computer science or biochemistry, for instance, knowledge (*epistēmē*) in these fields does not have a relationship with any *technē*. The profitable interplay between pure science and applied science does not have a parallel in the liberal arts. Philosophical theories rarely lead to, or can be driven by, the potential for developing marketable products. Further, philosophical education is seen as *not* teaching skills that can be *directly* marketed to employers.[8]

Part II: The Revitalizing Philosophy and the Humanities

Given the way knowledge is valued in the Market-Model University, how can philosophy and the humanities be revitalized? How can these fields avoid being relegated to second-class status in the twenty-first century's university? The positive task, recalling the words of Langon Winner, is to offer a "renewed vision of what education is about and what its relationship to the larger society ought to be" (Winner 1997: 10). The key here is to make the case that philosophy provides an essential social good that should be generously supported by the public.

The Conservative Reaction

As noted earlier, one common reaction to the decline of the humanities is an incredulous assertion that the study of knowledge (*epistēmē*) in the liberal arts is an intrinsic good, which cannot be converted into crude cost-benefit calculations. For example, the historian, Richard Hofstadter, an early critic of the instrumentalist view of higher education, argued that, "The ultimate criterion of the place of higher learning in America will be the extent to which it is esteemed not as a necessary instrument of external ends, but as an end in itself" (Press and Washburn 2000). This view represents a common reaction of those in the humanities who suddenly find themselves as second-class citizens in the university.

However, given the current state of affairs in higher education and society at large the intrinsic value argument is not likely to persuade. For example, Allan Bloom's call to return to the classical liberal arts, in his 1987 polemic, *The Closing of the American Mind*, generated much heat and sparks but little reform. According to David Orr, one reason for the failure of conservative reformers like Bloom is they do not offer a "coherent vision of the liberal arts relevant to our time" (Orr 1992: 100).

There seems to be a common sense, societal assumption that theory must, in some way, be connected to practice.[9] On the one hand, it is easy for people to see how scientific theories are related to society through the constant string of technologies that directly affect peoples' lives. Scientific theories produce tangible, societal goods. On the other hand, it is difficult for people to see how the pursuit of knowledge in philosophy, for example, is related to society. The reason for this is philosophy's overwhelming focus on theoretical issues. For example, Andrew Light and Avner de Shalit characterize academic philosophy as follows:

> When philosophers talk to one another at conferences, at universities, and through books and articles, they tend to generalize, theorize and express themselves in the abstract. They often ask questions that are purely hypothetical, about an ideal, theoretical world (Light and de Shalit 2003: 1).

As just noted, it is often hard to see how these discussions relate to society in general. Further, philosophers, more often than not, make no attempt to make such connections. In sum, philosophical *epistēmē* frequently stand aloof, indifferent to the concrete concerns of real people. There are, of course, many exceptions, but this is the dominant trend. Hence, to the outsider philosophy appears obtuse and irrelevant. This is likely contributing factor to its stagnation, or decline.[10]

Given all this, it is hard to see how the conservative, intrinsic value argument can move skeptical administrators, politicians and taxpayers to generously support philosophy and the humanities.

The Progressive Alternative

To repeat, the task is to provide a renewed vision of philosophy and the humanities, where these fields provide an essential social good, or in the words of David Orr, to provide a "coherent vision of the liberal arts relevant to our times" (Orr 1992: 100). This cannot be done as long as the Market-Model dominates higher education. The humanities, in a manner of speaking, do not have a parallel "applied humanities" with the economic potential of the applied sciences, that would allow it to thrive under this model. However, in the Citizen-Model University, educating citizens is the primary goal, while supporting the economy is secondary.[11] Practical philosophy, and the practical humanities in general, plays a crucial role in providing a social good: the training of citizens.

Broadly speaking, what I am calling the Citizen-Model University is part of a deep tradition in liberal education in which the goal is to develop citizens. However, the notion of a "citizen," like other important ethical/political goals, such as "freedom" or "justice," is contested. While it is not possible to develop and defend an exhaustive ideal of a "citizen" in this paper, I will present the basic outlines drawing on classical and contemporary sources, specifically Aristotle and John Dewey.

Aristotle, Citizenship, and Practical Wisdom

The Greek, *eleutheria*, freedom, is synonymous with citizen; it means to participate in the life of the *polis*, in contrast to slaves and foreigners. The key idea here is that a citizen is granted free choice (*prohairesis*). This notion of choice, *prohairesis*, means more than mere preference. Aristotle observes that, "It is a mistake to identify choice . . . with appetite, passion, wish or some other form of opinion (*Nicomachean Ethics* (*NE*) 1111b, 15). Hans-Georg Gadamer writes that *prohairesis* refers to the human capacity to "knowingly prefer one thing to another and consciously choosing among alternatives" (Gadamer 1986: 91). He continues: "The free decision takes its bearings by the order of preferences guiding one's life conduct, whether it be pleasure, or power and honor, or knowledge" (Ibid.: 91). Moreover, there is an excellence or virtue (*aretē*) associated with choosing, which is only "realized fully in the free status of the citizen in the polis" (Ibid.). This excellence in choosing is practical wisdom, *phronēsis*.

The philosopher Philippa Foot has articulated a simple but help-ful conception of practical wisdom (Foot, 1978: 322-323). In her con-ception, wisdom consists of two parts: the first is to know the right means to acquire certain good ends (Ibid.). The second is to know what a particular end is worth. This is to be distinguished from a clever person who knows how to acquire ends, but cannot discern their value. For example, a wise person understands that, in very broad terms, pleasure is desirable and knows the best means to acquire pleasure. But a wise person also knows that health is of greater value than pleasure. Hence, that person will subordinate the pursuit of pleasure to that of health when they conflict.

So the moral ideal of a "good citizen" is one that possesses prac-tical wisdom. Aristotle writes that such people "have the capacity of seeing what is good for themselves and for mankind, and these are, we believe, the qualities of men capable of managing households and states (*NE*, 1140b, 10)." The point to see here is the connection between freedom, citizenship and making choices as guided by prac-tical wisdom. In sum, the good citizen is one who makes wise choices on both the personal and social levels.

Moreover, *phronēsis* is a third sphere of knowledge, to be distinguished from theoretical knowledge, *epistēmē*, and practical know-how, *technē*. Gadamer writes: "Practical knowledge (*phronēsis*) is another kind of knowledge, [distinguishable from *epistēmē*, which aims at the true]. Primarily, this means that it is directed toward concrete situations (Ibid.: 93)." Further, practical wisdom is not "merely master technical expertise (Ibid.)." Therefore, the kind of education that would help students become good citizens aims to develop practical wisdom (*phronēsis*), the study of which is the province of practical philosophy.

Dewey, Citizenship, and Intelligent Choice

In this discussion, John Dewey is important for distinguishing the notion of a free-person, or citizen, being used here, from that of classical Liberalism. This distinction is particularly important since classical Liberalism is the antecedent of the contemporary free-market individualism, which underwrites the Market-Model University.

Dewey notes that there is a fallacy in the political and economic theories of classical Liberalism. He writes of its founders that:

> They thought of individuals as endowed with an equipment of *fixed and ready-made* capacities, the operation of which if unobstructed by external restriction would be freedom, and freedom which would almost automatically solve political and economic problems (Dewey 1928: 270, emphasis added).

The reason the Market-Model University can subordinate or largely ignore the need for training to citizenship is because the social and political philosophy behind it presupposes a negative conception of freedom. That is, "in a state of nature" people possess the necessary equipment for citizenship: the rational and moral capacity for exercising the power of free choice. Given this view, the task of creating a free society is removing political and economic obstacles to free choice. While this may be something of a caricature of classical Liberalism, nonetheless, Dewey is right in terms of focus. The focus is on removing obstacles to free choice rather than developing the capacity for making free choices.

In contrast, Dewey argues for a positive conception of freedom in which citizens acquire the ability to make *intelligent* choices. To explain: the significant choices one makes in the present affect, positively or negatively, the quality and/or quantity of future choices. The person who makes intelligent choices enlarges the realm of freedom. To get the idea here, one need just imagine a game of chess, where unintelligent choices lead to undesirable and limited options, and intelligent choices lead to desirable ones. Dewey writes that an intelligent choice "enlarges our range of actions, and this enlargement in turn confers upon our desires greater insight and foresight, and makes choice more intelligent (Ibid.: 276)." This is common sense; one who chooses intelligently, through prudent deliberation will, more often than not, create positive conditions for future choices.

More specifically, there are two main aspects to Dewey's notion of intelligent choice: The first is the observation that our present choices shape the environment in which future choices will be made. For example, the choices to take care of one's body and save for retirement create conditions for free choices when one is 70. This may mean, for example, cultivating a desire for certain foods and types of exercises. In contrast, one who chooses not do these things, preferring to fulfill other desires, is likely to have forced options at that age, due to failing health and limited finances.

The second aspect is that how we deliberate is to a large extent the function of intellectual habits. So if we critically reflect upon our habits of deliberation we can move toward making better choices in the future. In contrast, those who do not reflect on their habits of arriving at choices are destined to repeat bad habits. Sooner or later such people will create conditions at odds with their desires. For example, many people habitually make poor purchasing decisions leading to large credit card debt. If they do not intelligently reflect on how they are making their household decisions, they will ultimately relinquish their freedom to creditors.

In sum, of course, there are no guarantees that intelligent choices will always enhance freedom; the unexpected, luck, etc., is always in play. However, people who develop the habits of careful, self-critical deliberation will, more often than not, enhance their freedom as far as possible. This idea of intelligent choice can be applied to the aggregate choices of free societies. If collectively a society does not cultivate habits intelligent choice, that society will diminish the realm of freedom.

While much more needs to be said, particularly about the moral component of choices, the above should provide a sketch of the idea of a citizen. In sum, it is centered on the acquired ability of a person to make free choices. Free choices require an excellence as described by Dewey's notion of intelligent choice and Aristotle's notion of practical wisdom. Both thinkers see the virtue of making wise or intelligent choices as the product of developing habits of reflective, self-critical moral judgment and habits of deliberation, within a social context. This positive conception of freedom and citizenship is in contrast to the negative conception in classical Liberalism, which is the antecedent of the free-market individualism that underwrites the Market-Model University.

Practical Philosophy and the Citizen-Model University

So how does practical philosophy go about the task of education for citizenship? To begin, in general terms the Citizen-Model University explicitly focuses on courses that develop deliberative skills and moral judgment. In both the traditional university and the Market-Model practical wisdom is largely taken for granted. For example, in the traditional university *epistēmē* is of chief value and *technē* is subordinate; *phronēsis* is not an explicit focus. Allan Bloom, for instance, seems to believe that studying the classics produces wisdom as a sort of byproduct. In the Market-Model *technē* is the primary focus and *epistēmē* is

seen in terms of its relevance to developing marketable skills and
technologies. Here too there is little explicit focus on *phronēsis*, as it
is relegated to the odd elective in applied ethics. In the Citizen-
Model University the chief focus is *phronēsis*, which is brought into
close relationship with *epistēmē* and *technē*. The relationship might be
visualized as follows: *Epistēmē* ↔ *Phronēsis* ↔ *Technē*. In simplistic terms,
in the Citizen-Model University students will study, for example, the
theory behind cloning and the technology of cloning, but most importantly they will deliberate over the concrete, practical question:
"Should we clone?" One might object that such questions are already
discussed. However, the real issues are emphasis, priorities and how
such questions are approached.

Turning to the question of emphasis and priorities, in the Citizen-
Model University practical philosophy is moved from the periphery
to the center. In some ways this is already starting to happen with
the proliferation of courses in applied ethics, ethics centers and professional organizations devoted to "applied philosophy". There would,
of course, be strong objections to making practical issues the main
focus of philosophical research and education, particularly from academic philosophers. As noted earlier, the field is dominated by theoretical problems. Applied philosophy is a subspecialty. In his essay,
"The Recovery of Practical Philosophy," Stephen Toulmin responds
to this objection. He writes:

> Nowadays, then, philosophers are increasingly drawn into public debates
> about environmental policy, medical ethics, judicial practice, or nuclear
> politics. Some contribute to these discussions happily; others fear that
> engaging in applied philosophy prostitutes their talents and distracts
> them from their proper concern with quantification theory, illocution-
> ary force, possible worlds, or the nature of *Erlebnis*. For these purists,
> I have a special message. These practical debates are no longer "applied
> philosophy": they are philosophy itself (Toulmin 1988: 345).

Toulmin has spent a career providing arguments to support this "special message" to academic philosophers, most recently in his book,
Return to Reason (Toulmin 2001a), and in the essay cited above. Hence,
to save space I will merely refer to these works. Nonetheless, a line
of argument has already been established: either philosophers engage
in these public debates or continue to drift into social irrelevance.

There is a second criticism of the increasing trend toward "applied
philosophy", articulated by Christina Sommers. Addressing this criticism provides the opportunity to contrast "applied philosophy" with

"practical philosophy." In her essay, "Teaching the Virtues," Sommers' goal is to criticize an educational system that creates students who are "dogmatically committed to moral relativism" (Sommers 1991: 671). She believes that the way ethics is taught on university campuses is contributing to this problem. Sommers writes: "The current style of ethics teaching, which concentrates so much on social policy, is giving students the wrong ideas about ethics. Social morality is only half of the moral life; the other half is private morality" (Ibid.: 670). On the one hand, I think Sommers' criticism of *the way* "applied ethics" is taught is on target. On the other, it misses the mark by identifying the emphasis on social policy as part of the problem.

As a student of Aristotle, Sommers would no doubt agree that it is a mistake to make too strong a distinction between private morality and social morality. As was seen above, people who possess practical wisdom tend to make intelligent, ethical choices in whatever context. Further, according to Alasdair MacIntyre, one of the pathologies of modern life is the "liquidation" of the moral-self into discrete life segments, particularly through the distinctions of the private-self and the public-self. MacIntyre comments that, "The liquidation of the self into a set of demarcated areas of role-playing allows no scope for the exercise of dispositions which could genuinely be accounted as virtues (MacIntyre 1984: 205)." The primary virtue of citizenship is *phronesis*, which is a predicate of a whole life. Hence, a course in social morality has direct implications for private morality, and vice versa. Both should help the student develop practical wisdom, or their capacity for intelligent choice. There is no public/private distinction in terms of the disposition toward making wise/intelligent choices.

This is why I believe environmental philosophy serves as an exemplar within practical philosophy for promoting the virtues of citizenship. Specifically, the essential linkage between social and private morality is everywhere apparent in environmental ethics. This point can be illustrated with a brief reference to what might be called the foundational parable of environmental ethics, Garrett Hardin's "The Tragedy of the Commons" (Hardin 1968). In Hardin's parable each herdsman makes the private, economic/moral choice to add an *extra* cow to the common pastureland. This "private" choice is based entirely on a morality of rational self-interest. However, since all rational, self-interested individuals are making the same choice, the result is a social and ecological catastrophe. The common pasture is destroyed due to the effects of overgrazing. In environmental ethics,

one's private morality cannot be separated from the whole social
and ecological cloth. This realization is a basic element of what
David Orr calls "ecological literacy." Orr writes: "Ecological literacy . . . implies a broad understanding of how people and societies
relate to each other and to natural systems, and how they might do
so sustainably" (Orr 1992: 92). Importantly, Orr believes those who
become ecologically literate will develop into "global citizens."

So, for the above reasons, I believe Sommers misses the mark by
identifying the current emphasis on social ethics as part of the problem.[12] However, as indicated, I believe she is on target with her criticism of the way these courses are taught. A typical course in applied
ethics begins with a critical survey of different moral theories. Next,
essays that apply these various theories to both sides in the social
debates are critically examined. Sommers concludes from personal
experience that, "the atmosphere of argument and counterargument
was reinforcing the ideas the *all* moral questions have at least two
sides, i.e., that all of ethics was controversial (Sommers 1991: 671).

It seems that an unfortunate side effect of the standard approach
to teaching applied ethics is to encourage students to become pyrrhon-
ist. That is, it implicitly teaches the pyrrhonian belief that every
argument can be balanced by an equally strong counterargument.
The result is agnosticism and ambivalence toward the idea of a right
(or best) course of action. But in many social debates, for example,
the one of global warming, inaction is a course of action. It is a
vote for the status quo. However, as David Orr asserts, an education "ought to change the way people live, not just how they talk"
(Orr 1992: 91).

There are also problems with research in applied philosophy. A
growing number of environmental philosophers, such as Byron Norton
and Andrew Light, have begun to criticize applied environmental
philosophy. In their recent book, Light and Avner de-Shalit note a
lack of connection between environmental philosophy and environmental activism and policy. Their observations are drawn directly
from activists who say that, "environmental philosophy was a far cry
from what was needed in practice" (Light and de Shalit: 50). Moreover,
Light and de Shalit continue: "Environmental activists have often
pointed to a need for an environmental philosophy constructed in
language and argument accessible to wider audiences (Ibid.)."

One possible reason for this disconnect between "applied philosophy" and practical action is that applied philosophy follows a logic

that people rarely use when making choices. Byron Norton provides the following contrast between the logic of "applied philosophy" and that of "practical philosophy." On the one hand, applied philosophy is the "application of general philosophical principles in adjudication among policy goals or options (Norton 1996: 107)." By starting with ethical theory, research in applied philosophy follows the same pattern as courses in applied ethics. Universal principles are derived from that theory. These principles are then applied with deductive rigor to particular, "narrowly circumscribed hypothetical cases (Ibid.)."[13] On the other hand, practical philosophy "derives theories (if needed) from the problem context itself (Norton 1996: 108)." Norton states that, "practical philosophy . . . is more problem-oriented; its chief characteristic is an emphasis on theories as tools of understanding, tools that are developed to resolve specific policy controversies (Ibid.)."

One solution to the problems of applied philosophy is for philosophers to use a model of reasoning that better fits the deliberative process people actually use when making choices. This of course would focus attention on practical philosophy and practical reasoning. One area of research in practical philosophy is to study normative models of practical reasoning. Below is such a model, which has been modified from the work of the Canadian philosopher Douglas Walton (Walton 1998: 154-155). The idea here is that this model for practical reasoning could overcome the shortcomings in teaching and research in applied ethics. In practical reasoning the end of the argument is an imperative for action. Thus it requires students to choose a course of action. Moreover, because it does not start with abstract ethical theories, it should more easily provide a common language with a wider audience.

To explain the model, practical reasoning starts with a goal. The fact that people frequently share goals, sometimes for different reasons, means theoretical debate can often be avoided. This is a distinct advantage over the logic of applied philosophy. As Light and Katz point out, applied philosophy "requires a commitment to a theory prior to its application (Light and Katz 1996: 10)." With practical philosophy there is no need to engage these difficult-to-agree-upon theoretical debates as long as people agree upon the goal. People do not need to reach consensus over the right ethical theory. It is enough that they agree on the goal, for whatever reason. As Norton has demonstrated, people do not have to share the same theoretical, environmental ethics to share the same practical, environmental goals (Norton 1991). That is, people with different "worldviews" often converge on the same policy goals.[14] However, sometimes people do disagree about whether a particular goal should be pursued or how various goals should be prioritized. At this point theoretical debates about ethical theories have their place, but it is only in connection to real disputes as they arise in policy deliberation.

Once a goal is agreed upon, the right or best means needed to realize the goal must be chosen. So the next step in practical reasoning is to make an open-ended list of possible ways of achieving the goal. This list acknowledges the fact that there is often more than one way to realize a goal. Also, because it is open-ended, it makes room for alternatives not yet considered or sufficiently developed at the present time. Next, in deciding upon the best means to achieve a goal a list is made of the *practical obstacles* that might prevent reaching the goal through each selected means. Also, a list of possible *side-effects* is made for each alternative listed. The conclusion takes these factors into account to arrive at the best means for achieving the goal.

This model does not avoid the need to debate theoretical issues; however they are only discussed as needed in the context of concrete problems in real-life deliberations. For example, there is the problem of how much moral weight to assign to *potential* side effects. The recent intense discussion over the "precautionary principle", which roughly says we should error on the side of precaution when there is potential for irreversible environmental harm, shows how theoretical issues in ethics and philosophy of science are engaged in the deliberative process. Also, the existence of practical obstacles may imply the need for radical social and political change in order to reach a goal through a particular means. This requires social and political philosophy to be discussed.

Given this model, the following kinds of questions should be asked in teaching and research (Walton 1998: 155). First, is the goal adequately understood and agreed upon? Second, how should this goal be prioritized in relation to other goals? Third, have all possible alternatives been listed and adequately evaluated? Fourth, have all practical obstacles been considered and thoroughly evaluated? Fifth, have all significant side effects been anticipated and appraised? Finally, is the selected means really the *best* alternative? Or, should we reexamine the list of alternatives?

In the classroom context, because this approach is focused on arriving at decisions, students cannot be ambivalent. Also, because it uses technical, philosophical vocabulary only when needed, it should allow philosophers to better communicate with a wider audience. Moreover, when theoretical philosophical issues are engaged it is within the context of policy deliberation. This should make it easier for the non-philosopher to see their importance.

Conclusion

The task of building the Citizen-Model University begins with two facts. The first fact is that the day when philosophy and the humanities did not need to justify their existence is gone. The second is that the modern university is driven by science, engineering, medicine and technology. The second fact provides the key to addressing the first through the new practical fields in the humanities, such as environmental philosophy. These fields show the way toward the Citizen-Model University.

In the twentieth century it became clear that our commitment to science and technology as *the* way to improve human life comes with serious health and environmental side effects, as well as deeply troubling ethical dilemmas. This awareness gave birth to the practical fields in the humanities, such as philosophy of medicine, philosophy of technology, and environmental philosophy, to name but a few. As indicated above, over the last few decades, new fields in the practical humanities have developed in response to the social and ethical issues arising from the massive growth of science and technology. However, these fields have had less effect than they might have had due to the dominance of the method of applied philosophy. The move to practical philosophy should make philosophy more relevant.

Practical philosophy is highly integrative in character. It must combine an understanding of the latest scientific and technological developments with a deep understanding of the traditional humanities. Students being educated in these fields must exhibit a high degree of sophistication to deal with complex issues such as global warming, which do not respect traditional disciplinary boundaries. It is by working though such complex issues that the possibility arises for students to develop the mental attitudes of responsible citizenship.

Such a possibility can be seen by looking at what is required to deal with environmental issues such as global warming, using the model of practical reasoning described above. To begin, students must clarify the social and ethical goals associated with the global warming issue. There is some agreement on social goals, as most countries agree something should be done to reduce the rate of anthropogenic input of greenhouse gases. However, there is wide disagreement on how this goal should be prioritized in relation to other goals. Dealing with the complexities of identifying the goal requires a working understanding of the potential social and environmental consequences of climate change. This must be combined with the moral sophistication needed to ethically assign value and prioritize various goals. Also, there is disagreement over the right means for pursuing the goal of reducing greenhouse gases. So students are challenged to learn the basic science involved in global warming and various alternative solutions. This requires a sophisticated understanding of science and philosophy of science. This ethical, social, scientific and political knowledge would be used to list and judge the side effects and practical obstacles for various alternatives. Finally, students are challenged to take this information and deliberate with each other with the *requirement* of reaching conclusions. In sum, students in such a practical, environmental philosophy course are encouraged to develop the capacity to intelligently and ethically deliberate in a social context: to become citizens. Moreover, this is done in a way that is directly connected to the pressing problems that as citizens they are already forced to confront.

In sum, what then would it take to move away from the Market-Model University and toward the Citizen-Model? First, we should rethink the categories that govern higher education in light of new practical fields in the humanities that deal with such pressing issues in the areas of the environment, medicine, and science and technology. At present, these are seen as minor subspecialties within the older disciplines. They should be pushed to the fore as the avant-garde of the Citizen-Model University. Second, there must be a reorientation of values among *all* university administrators and faculty. Their first loyalty should be to the ideal of a democratic society consisting of responsible citizens. Their various loyalties to business and professional organizations must be subordinated to this ideal. Finally, the trend toward making universities directly accountable to business must stop. This does not mean that academy cannot complement industry by offering useful training programs and developing marketable innovations. However, higher education's first loyalty is to the ideal of the citizen and democracy. This will require the taxpaying public to realize that to preserve a quality democratic ethos, they must supply adequate funding if universities are to gain independence from industry.

Notes

1. While my comments will be confined to the US, there are signs of similar changes taking place in Canada, Europe, and elsewhere.

2. The UC Impact report claims that the UC system contributes up to $16 billion to California's gross state product. Further, it predicts that between 2002-2011 UC will contribute productivity gains of 104,000 new jobs and $5.2 billion (Ibid.).

3. This is the policy in the University of North Carolina system.

4. An outline of this legislation is as follows: (1) The 1980 Steven-Wydler Technological Transfer Act encouraged interaction between public scientists and private industry; (2) In the same year, the Bayh-Dole Patent and Trademark Laws Amendment allowed universities to patent and license discoveries made from publicly funded research. This legislation was, and remains, highly controversial. For instance, Krimsky notes that, "Some in Congress argued that granting private companies the rights to publicly funded research amounted to an enormous giveaway to corporations"; (3) In 1981 Congress passed the Economic Recovery Act, which gave companies "a twenty-five percent tax credit for sixty-five percent of their direct funding to universities for basic research"; (4) The Federal Technological Transfer Act of 1986 "expanded science-industry collaboration to laboratories run by the federal government" (Krimsky 1999: 21).

5. In their *Atlantic Monthly* article Press and Washburn comment on the effects of the Bayh-Dole Act, which they see as revolutionizing the university-industry relationship. They write: "From 1980 to 1998 industry funding for academic research expanded at an annual rate of 8.1 percent, reaching $1.9 billion in 1997". Moreover, "before Bayh-Dole, universities produced roughly 250 patents a year (many of which were never commercialized); in the fiscal year 1998, however, universities generated more than 4,800 patent applications" (Press & Washburn 2000).

6. It is important to note that many European countries have either enacted or are considering some version of Bayh-Dole. Gitte Meyer, of the Danish Centre for Bioethics and Risk Assessment, writes that, "[Bayh-Dole] has now been copied in Denmark." She goes on to note striking similarities between the attitudes of current European politicians to those of their American counterparts that gave rise to Bayh-Dole (Meyer 2003).

7. In 1998 Berkeley's College of Natural Resources (CNR) made a "strategic alliance" with the transnational, Swiss based biotech company Novartis (now Sygenta). The arrangement brought $25 million to the Department of Plant and Microbial Biology over five years to fund basic research. In exchange the company received "first right to negotiate licenses on approximately a third of the department's discoveries—including the results of research funded by state and federal sources" (Press & Washburn 2000). Moreover, it granted the company an unprecedented two of the five seats on the department's research committee, which determines project funding. There was much faculty opposition to the agreement on the Berkeley campus. The administrator who was the "chief architect of the Novartis deal," Gordon Rausser, argued that faculty resistance was due to ignorance about the "changing economic realities of higher education" (Press & Washburn 2002). As noted earlier, part of these new economic realities are the decline in public funding and the increase in funding from corporate sources. However, another part of the new economic reality is the reconceived role of research at public universities as an engine for economic growth. For example, Rausser comments: "New growth theorists argue that up to 50% of all U.S. economic growth over the last 50 years is due to investment in R & D. Future growth will depend on future research and investment" (Rausser 1999: 7). Obviously, new growth theorists see the immense research capacities of public universities in terms of the potential to create wealth. In sum, the theory behind Berkeley's agreement with Novartis is that marketable technologies should drive basic research. This is evident in the structure of the agreement. Rausser writes that what is ground-breaking about the relationship between Novartis and Berkeley is that it starts, "on the front end, not the back end, after some discovery has occurred" (Rausser).

8. It is important to note that while industry has no doubt always exerted influence on the academy, over the last thirty years there has been an explicit program to merge these institutions. Accompanying these changes is a collapsing of the distinctions between public science and private science, basic research and applied research.

9. Another problem, which I will not pursue here, might be due to the effects of postmodernism's deconstruction of the idea of humanistic *epistēmē*. In sum, postmodern theories of theory, if you will, may be undermining the credibility of humanistic research.

10. Again, I believe what is said here of philosophy is likely to apply to other fields in the humanities.

11. It should be noted that what I'm suggesting here does not deny the importance of higher education for economic development. Universities should train skilled workers and develop marketable technologies. The issue is one of prioritizing goals. The goal of education for citizenship should be primary, supporting economic growth secondary. There is a distinct drift in the Market-Model University that neglects or subordinates what should be the primary goal. In order to sustain a thriving, democratic society both skilled workers and good citizens are necessary, but training of citizens is comes before producing a skilled work force. Moreover, mastering a narrow, technical skill does not contribute to the development of the qualities of a good democratic citizen. The totalitarian states of the 20th century trained many first class technicians.

12. Conversely, nothing in these comments would discourage teaching courses on issues that could more readily be called private morality.

13. One needs to ask if people reason this way in making important personal or political decisions? Do people start by deciding whether or not they are Kantians, Utilitarians, Deep Ecologists, etc.? Next, do they derive universal principles from that theory and apply the relevant principle to the particular controversy, thus arriving at a course of action consistent with their theoretical commitments?

14. Also, Light has argued for a pragmatic, "metatheoretical compatibilism". Needless time is spent arguing ethical theory, when people are in basic agreement on environmental problems that urgently need to be addressed (Light 1996: 161).

REFERENCES

Aristotle. 1962. *Nicomachean Ethics*. Trans. Ostwalt, M. New York: Macmillan Publishing Company.

Association of University Technology Managers. "Press Release". 2003. http://www.autm.net. (accessed: 7/10/04).

Berry, W. 2001. *In the Presence of Fear*. Orion Society.

Business-Higher Education Forum, http://www.acenet.edu/programs/bhef/about.cfm (accessed: 6/24/04).

Engell, J. and A. Dangerfield. 1998. "The Market-Model University: Humanities in the Age of Money". *Harvard Review*, May-June. http://www.harvard-magazine.com/issues/mj98/forum.html. (accessed: 6/25/04)

Dewey, J. 1989. *Freedom and Culture*. Buffalo, NY: Prometheus.

———. 1928. "Philosophies of Freedom," in Gouinlock, J. (ed.) *The Moral Writings of John Dewey* 1995. Ameherst, NY: Prometheus Books, pp. 261-287.

Foot, P. 1978. "Virtues and Vices". in Sommers and Sommers 2001: pp. 319-334.

Gadamer, H-G. 1986. *Reason in the Age of Science*. Trans. Lawrence, F.G. Cambridge, MA: The MIT Press.

———. 1989. *Truth and Method*. 2nd edn. Trans. Weinsheimer, J. & Marshall, D.G. New York: Crossroad.

Hardin, G. 1968. "The Tragedy of the Commons". *Science* 162: 1243-46.

Initiative for the Humanities 2004. "Project Update", *Bulletin of the American Academy*, Spring: 26-29.

Krimsky, S. 1999. "The Profit of Scientific Discovery". *Chicago-Kent Law Review* 75(15): 15-35.

Light, A. 1996. "Compatibilism in Political Ecology," in Light and Katz 1996.

Light, A. and A. de-Shalit. 2003. "Introduction: Environmental Ethics—Whose Philosophy? Which Practice?" in Light and de-Shalit (eds) *Moral and Political Reasoning in Environmental Practice*. Cambridge, MA: The MIT Press.

Light, A. and E. Katz. 1996. *Environmental Pragmatism*. London: Routledge.

MacIntyre, A. 1984. *After Virtue*. 2nd edn. Notre Dame, IN: Notre Dame University Press.

Meyer, G. 2003. "Research policy with side-effects" Danish Center for Bioethics and Risk Assessment. www.bioethics.kvl.dk. (accessed: 5/10/04)

Norton, B. 1991. *Toward Unity Among Environmentalists*. New York: Oxford University Press.

———. 1996. "Integration or Reduction: Two Approaches to Environmental Values," in Light and Katz 1996, pp. 105-138.

Orr, D. 1992. *Ecological Literacy*. Albany: State University of New York Press.

Ostwalt, M. 1962. "Glossary of Technical Terms" in Aristotle. *Nichomachean Ethics*. Trans. Ostwalt, M. New York: Macmillan Publishing Company, pp. 308-316.

Press, E. and J. Washburn. 2000. "The Kept University," *Atlantic Monthly*, March. http://www.theatlantic.com/issues/2000/03/press.html. (accessed: 7/10/04).

Rausser, G. "Public/Private Alliances". *AgBioForum*. 2: 5-10.

Sommers, C. 1991. "Teaching the Virtues," in Sommers and Sommers 2001, pp. 670-681.

Sommers, C. and F. Sommers (eds). 2001. *Vice and Virtue in Everyday Life*. 5th edn 2001. Harcourt.

Toulmin, S. 2001a. *Return to Reason*. Cambridge MA: Harvard University Press.
———. 1988. "The Recovery of Practical Philosophy," *The American Scholar* 57.
   337-352.
University of California Impact Report, http://universityofcalifornia.edu/startshere/
   main.html (accessed: 7/9/04)
Walton, D. 1998. *The New Dialectic: Conversational Contexts of Argument*. Toronto:
   University of Toronto Press.
———. 1990. *Practical Reasoning: Goal-Driven, Knowledge-Based, Action-Guiding Argumentation*.
   Savage, MD: Rowman & Littlefield.
Winner, L. 1997. "Draft of a chapter, Resisting Technoglobalists' Assault on
   Education," in M. Moll (ed.) 1997. *Tech High: Globalization of the Future of Canadian
   Education*. Ottawa: Frenwood. http://www.rpi.edu/~winner/queens2.html. (accessed:
   6/22/04).

ENVIRONMENTAL EDUCATION
AND METAETHICS[1]

Owen Goldin

Abstract

Contrā Dale Jamieson, the study of the metaethical foundations of environmental ethics may well lead students to a more environmentally responsible way of life. For although metaethics is rarely decisive in decision making and action, there are two kinds of circumstances in which it can play a crucial role in our practical decisions. First, decisions that have unusual features do not summon habitual ethical reactions, and hence invite the application of ethical precepts that the study of metaethics and ethical theory isolate and clarify. Second, there are times in which the good of others (including organisms and systems in the natural world) may well be given greater weight in one's ethical deliberations if theory has made clear that the good to be promoted is ontologically independent of one's own good.

Keywords: Environmental ethics, environmental education, environmental value, metaethics, Dale Jamieson

Introduction

Classes in environmental ethics are increasingly common at the college level. Often, these classes focus on the question of the metaphysical status of the value or goodness to be ascribed to entities and systems in the natural world.[2] Is value inherent in Nature? Does it originate and exist in the mind of the one who recognizes the value? Are there other possibilities?

Here I would like to discuss the role that such questions play in environmental education. The study of environmental philosophy is meant to stimulate critical reflection on the relationship between human beings and the natural environment. We may well think that this reflection will lead to better attitudes and actions in regard to the environment. Is this a reasonable belief? More specifically, does exploring philosophical questions concerning the source and ontological basis of value contribute to what many take to be the central task of classes in environmental ethics: cultivating the attitudes that lead to appropriate action in regard to the natural world?[3]

An ethical theory clarifies the good to be promoted and identifies what a moral agent is obligated to do in the pursuit of this good.

Clare Palmer (Ed.), *Teaching Environmental Ethics*, 35-47.

A metaethics grounds and justifies this ethical theory on the basis
of an account of rationality, human nature and the larger world of
which it is a part. A metaethics often employs a metaphysics, which
discusses the underlying structures and realities that are responsible
for the obligations that the ethical theory presents. But despite the
fact that many Western ethical theories are grounded in metaphysical theory, the thesis that metaphysics can or should make a
difference in the morality of our action is by no means uncontro-
versial. Dale Jamieson in particular has argued against this.[4] I think
that he is right to de-emphasize the importance that metaphysical
metaethics plays in people's actual decisions and ways of life. I do
however think that there are important exceptions to Jamieson's view,
and that one of these is environmental ethics, an area in which
Jamieson has specialized.

The question of the metaphysical basis of value has had an important role to play in the emerging field of environmental ethics. Much
ink has been spilt trying to show that natural things and systems
have value in and of themselves, not to be understood as a means to
the actualization of some other good, and not to be taken as always
derived from a mental or emotional attitude that people take towards
them, in order to show that there is a moral obligation to preserve
them, regardless of whether they contribute to human interests.[5]
Given the philosophical temper of our times, such speculation is wont
to seem metaphysically extravagant, out of sync with the hard sciences and smacking of mysticism. One might think "if environmental ethics rests on such dubious foundations, so much the worse for
environmental ethics." This is why Jamieson, with his special interest in the field, takes it upon himself to argue that environmental
ethicists can be spending their time more productively than by arguing over metaphysics. I argue here that there are special features to
the field of environmental ethics that give special importance to
theorizing concerning the conceptual and ontological underpinnings
of ethics. One need not explicitly engage in metaethics or metaphysics in order to have a worthy ethical attitude towards the natural world. But in this area, at any rate, such speculation has the
potential for making a decisive difference in our *praxis*.

Metaphysics and Ethics

Metaphysics and ethics have long been intertwined. Ethical theory often explicitly rests on a metaphysical foundation, and the data of ethics are among the givens that form the raw material of metaphysical analysis. But to what extent is metaphysics involved in ethical deliberation and action? It seems that it has an important role to play only insofar as it has an essential role in ethical theory, and insofar as ethical theory plays an essential role in ethical judgment and decision making. But must one engage in ethical theory in order to act ethically? Perhaps only Plato, the Stoics and Kant set the bar so high. It is well known how Plato makes philosophy necessary for right action. From the earlier dialogues to the *Republic*, Socrates insists that one must have a special knowledge of the good, in order to achieve what is good. For the Stoics, right action is possible only for the sage, whose mind penetrates the underlying logos of the cosmos. For this reason, Stoics were forced to admit that almost all, if not all, human beings were fools and acted accordingly. Kant, on the other hand, was more optimistic concerning the abilities of unschooled everyday reason. For Kant, ethical action is rational action, and necessarily involves an application of the Categorical Imperative, but this is not an application of theory and does not require of the agent any excursion into metaethics. Other Western ethical philosophical traditions also seem less committed to the role played by ethical theory and its metaphysical foundation as prerequisites for ethical action. To be sure, Aristotle tells us that a theoretical account of the human good gives us a target at which to aim (NE I.2), but this may be a glance at either the political implications of the ethics (since a leader needs to clearly see the *telos* of the community) or Book 10's encouragement of the contemplative life, neither a fundamental part of the everyday morality of the private citizen. Rather, for most people the moral life comes through the ethical habituation that results from obeying the law and following the example of the *phronimos*, the person of practical wisdom. This is similarly the case in Natural Law theory, whose underlying metaphysics is more involved and has a more explicit role to play in ethical theory than that of Aristotle's ethics from which it is largely derived. Finally, ethical theories such as that of Hume or classical utilitarianism which ground ethics on human sentiment hold that the study of ethical theory may refine our sentiments and render them consistent with each other, but cannot serve to instill the core sentiments of fellow-feeling that underlie morality. Such theories often explicitly dispense with metaphysical speculation, since the core moral sentiments are taken as empirically given and not to be justified by any more basic account.

For this reason, it appears that Jamieson is battling something of a straw man; to dissuade us from overemphasizing the issue of the metaphysical foundations of value in nature, he writes that ethical realists understand metaethics "as some immaculate conception that sits in judgment of our practices" or "part of a reforming philosophical project . . . philosophy run amok."[6] Jamieson tells us that "philosophy, understood as the appreciation of, and reflection on, our practices, leaves the world alone. It may inform and incline our thoughts, but it cannot determine them."[7] Platonists, Cynics, and Stoics aside, no major figure in the Western philosophical tradition has thought otherwise (except insofar as the activity of philosophy itself is taken to be constitutive of the good life). Engaging in metaethics or metaphysics has rarely been taken to be required for living in a decent manner. More particularly, it would be astonishing to claim that a class in environmental ethics is a prerequisite for the cultivation of ecologically responsible habits.

However, even if one can act perfectly morally without expertise in metaphysics, I can imagine three kinds of cases in which people's actions can be affected by virtue of engaging in ethical theory and metaethics. These are worth mentioning, even though in the first two kinds of cases it is not philosophical thought as such that is decisive, and hence these do not dislodge Jamieson's point concerning the impracticality of theories concerning the ontology of value.

(1) If we antecedently assume that consistency is a good for which we should strive, ethical theory is useful in making sure that our judgments are consistent. We may give up or alter an ethical judgment when we see that it is inconsistent with other judgments or beliefs to which we are committed. This is the stuff of Socratic elenchus, and at their best we see this sort of thing in our introductory ethics classes. Students who are committed to certain ethical principles can be led to see that they implicitly clash with certain judgments they make. This can lead people to revise these judgments and to make different choices. But typically in such a case the students come to isolate and apply foundational ethical precepts, and to identify certain goods and duties at a general level. Discussion

need not extend to the level of metaphysical analysis, explaining what it is about the world that makes these goods desirable and gives these duties their binding character.

For example, one might be led to see that the right to life entails a right to a modicum of health care, and one's political allegiances could conceivably change as a result of such an argument. But how would this depend on a metaphysical account of human nature that explains what it is about human beings that gives them a right to life? Similarly, students who already take cruelty to animals to be a moral evil can be shown that certain practices in factory farming, or even purchasing food that derives from such practices, is inconsistent with their initial assumptions. Those who already value biodiversity can be shown that this ethical commitment is incompatible with the typical American lifestyle. But such reflection does not rest on investigating the theoretical foundations of value. To show consistency or inconsistency in a set of views does not depend on any particular theoretical grounding of ethics—all that is required is an account of principles and basic precepts, and the ability to think logically.

(2) An ethical theory may have certain pragmatic value that is to a certain extent independent of its philosophical value. It was Plato, in the *Laws*, who first suggested that philosophy is not only for philosophers—the very fact that an already respected authority presents a logos (argument) in support of a rule makes a citizen more inclined to follow and uphold that rule, even though he or she is not capable of fully understanding that argument.[8] In this way, a priest might argue for a certain moral view on the basis of Natural Law theory. The argument may be only half-understood by his congregants, but the very fact that the argument is there may give the position greater weight than it would have had only on the basis of the priest's personal or ecclesiastical authority. Similarly, the Talmud rests on a metaphysics (not all of which can be supported on strictly philosophical grounds). As an observant Jew, my study of Talmud can motivate me in adhering to Jewish law with greater diligence than I would simply on the basis of rabbinical authority unsupported by argument. This is so in spite of the rudimentary nature of my understanding of Talmudic reasoning. This is because *arguing* for a conclusion is a powerful rhetorical device for persuading others of that conclusion. The fuller the argument (that is, the greater the extent that it is based only on agreed-upon premises), and the more it is adequately understood, the more convincing the argument is. This is so, even

if, as is always (or nearly always) the case, the argument is not fully grasped, from its foundations through its intervening steps.

If I understand Jamieson correctly, it is here that one finds metaethics to have some pragmatic value. Ontological claims are made in order to provide foundations and fill in the gaps found in ethical argumentation. An argument containing as an unsupported premise the claim that others ought to value some entity or state of affairs is less full than one that grounds this premise in some general ontology. In so arguing, we speak in a way that reifies our act of valuing and presents the value found as something independent of that act, and accordingly as something to be considered in everyone's ethical deliberations, regardless of perspective or interests. We do this as a rhetorical ploy, to get others to act as we would like them to, for we are suggesting that the value is "out there," available for them too to recognize, if only they would see. An ethical theory, which pretends to take this value as its object and study it apart from the psychological and social conditions of the acts of valuing that give rise to it, is part of this same rhetorical enterprise.[9] Thus, Jamieson writes: "In everyday life, we commit acts of metaethics when reflective thought, unreflective argument, or the simple pressure of serious disagreement takes us to the brink of a rhetorical abyss. At such moments we employ metaethical strategies in the service of our practical ends."[10] It cannot be denied that discussion of the metaphysical bases of ethical theory can play this role, sometimes effectively. In cases of this kind, too, it is not the metaphysics behind the theory that gives it its practical import, except insofar as those argument fragments that are comprehended make the whole account more persuasive. In this way, a student might only half-understand the arguments behind the land ethic, but the air of authority and the persuasive manner of a teacher of environmental ethics who lays out the theoretical foundations of the land ethic may predispose the student to accept it, and the parts of the argument that the student *does* understand may be decisive in her coming to say to herself "Makes sense to me." She may come to call herself an adherent of the land ethic, something that might never have happened had she not sat through lectures and discussions covering material she inadequately grasps. This may well be decisive in later leading the student to avoid applying pesticides on her lawn, and so forth.

(3) I should not omit to mention the kind of thing that we see in Plato's dialogues, and that hopefully goes on in our classes, including

those in environmental ethics. Through leading students to engage in the activity of philosophical reflection (including metaethical reflection) students can learn for themselves that this activity is intrinsically valuable, and it may come to form part of their conception of the good life. This may indeed lead to some practical decisions: from the decision to join a philosophy reading group to devoting one's life to metaphysics. But, on the face of it, this does not seem different from the practical implications of being introduced to fine French cuisine. To show otherwise requires the sort of theoretical argumentation whose practical value is at issue.

(4) There is one more kind of case in which a metaphysical metaethics can conceivably lead to the making of new and more enlightened decisions. I suspect that it is this sort of case that both the champions and detractors of the practicality of metaphysical metaethics have in mind in their disputes. One may accept an ethical theory, with all of its metaphysical framework, on the merits of supporting arguments, which are indeed adequately understood. Then one may come to make certain ethical judgments on account of the fact that this theory demands it. The theory itself may be responsible for ethical choices. Thus an argument based on an ethical theory may lead to an unanticipated conclusion—it is at least imaginable that a slaveowner may have seen the error of his ways as a result of reading Kant closely and carefully. Further, when ethical obligations come in conflict, a theory can help prioritize ethical demands. An example might be an intricate argument applying the Thomistic doctrine of double effect to an ethical dilemma. It is my contention that this happens rarely, with important exceptions. One exception is the area of environmental ethics.

I do not here set for myself the task of proving the negative claim, concerning the rarity of case number 4. Nietzscheans and other anti-theorists are better able to do this than I am. Besides, as I have mentioned, few such cases are attested within the Western philosophical tradition. Here I aim to argue that the area of environmental ethics has distinctive characteristics, so that the sort of metaphysical reflection that is invited by ethical thought experiments may be decisive in the formulation of new ethical judgments.

Metaphysical Reflection and Environmental Ethics

I begin with a thought experiment that has become something of a chestnut in the area of environmental ethics. I lay it out not in order to adequately evaluate whether it is successful in isolating a "metaphysical intuition" concerning the value of the natural world (I think it is) but in order to explore its purported role as foundational to an environmental ethics that makes a real difference in practice.

The thought experiment I would like to consider was formulated by Richard Routley at the dawn of environmental philosophy as such.[11] Imagine a last man, who takes it in his head to destroy the living things and ecosystems that would otherwise survive him. Our immediate unreflective response would be to say that there would be something very wrong about this. Thus, Routley argues, our thought experiment shows that nonhuman beings have inherent value. There is a goodness to them that is not dependent on the thought processes of an evaluator; for, in the situation under consideration, the evaluator is absent from the scene. Routley argued that, insofar as traditional Western ethics is not able to account for this value, it is deficient, and ethics needs a new foundation. Thus environmental ethics as a distinctive discipline is born.

There are various ways of countering Routley's claim, and various ways in which it can be defended, some of which Routley himself offered to critics both potential and actual. I have much to say on this, which I hope to soon offer the community of environmental ethicists. But I here avoid such ontological speculation, since my present task is to wonder what effect such exploration has on actual conduct. More specifically, what effect could a college philosophy class in which such metaphysical argumentation plays a dominant role have on the actual behavior of students taking it? Could it conceivably lead to a more environmentally responsible life, after the examinations and paper assignments are long forgotten?

Suppose that someone finds Routley's argument philosophically convincing. What has happened? A thought experiment shows that certain things are good independent of human valuation and hence shows the inadequacy of a metaethics that denies this. Accordingly, an alternative ethical theory is required, which gives some ontological status to such goodness. This theory both posits value outside of the human realm (a move with which Jamieson and Callicott have no objection) and takes the source of that value to lie outside of the human realm (which these two authors deny). Hence, one adopts the new ethical theory and its metaphysical commitments because it has greater explanatory power than its rivals.

The metaphysical speculation at issue is not a prerequisite for finding noninstrumental value in nature. Rather, the thought experiment is prior to such speculation, and shows that we do find such value in nature, regardless of any metaphysical thought or theorizing concerning the source of this value. In everyday life, we may well have made decisions to preserve such value, whether through practicing organic gardening, keeping on the trails to prevent erosion, or giving money or time to an environmental cause. But such decisions could well have been made in the interests of human beings: who is clear about his motives? The thought experiment is meant to provide some clarity here, by postulating a case in which the decision cannot be made for the sake of people who take an actual interest in the bearers of goodness, since by hypothesis there are no people to take such an interest. Yes, this is an extreme case, of a sort that people will not encounter in their day to day decision making, the sort of science fiction example to which teachers of introductory ethics too often resort. But these cases have their use: they provide what the real world does not, ways of imaginatively abstracting decisions from surrounding circumstances. If one is trying to prove that a certain factor X is (or can be) decisive in ethical decision-making, one strains to set up an example where another factor Y, which is often taken to be decisive, cannot be not operative. (For example, in our introductory ethics classes we set up implausible examples where using another as a mere means, through the infliction of pain, would without question be for the greatest good for the greatest number, an evaluation always questionable in the real world, in order to prove the Kantian principle that one ought not use another rational being merely as a means.) Here, a principle to be demonstrated is that natural beings have value or worth that is not dependent or derivative on the activity of valuing, and this is done by setting up the example in such a way that the possibility of an evaluator is excluded. To be sure, even if one accepts the results of the thought experiment, the theory that one is committed to is somewhat minimal. All that has been shown is that there is value in the natural world that is not dependent on the activity of valuing. It is left to further theorizing to say what the bearer of this value is (individual organisms? ecosystems?), and what it is about the world that is responsible for it. The nature of value

is unclear, and nothing is revealed concerning its relation to naturalistic
properties. Similarly nothing is said about our epistemological access
to them. Still, the existence of such value is an ontological claim,
one that is quite explicitly a piece of metaphysics. Admittedly, the
thought experiment raises a swarm of further metaphysical and epistemological problems, but metaphysical accounts need to start somewhere, and the existence of value that is neither anthropocentric nor
anthropogenic, indicated by the kind of thought experiment that
Routley explores, is at least a possible metaphysical principle.

   I claim that in this case, when a new ethical theory is in place,
with the metaethical commitment to value in nature ontologically
independent of human valuation, judgments will be made that would
otherwise not have been made. This has a real effect in regard to
our personal decisions and public policy decisions. Consider for example public policy debates concerning wilderness preservation. It is
true that one does not need a metaphysical account of value as
inherent in natural systems and the living things within them, in
order to see that wilderness preservation can be a good thing. One
may find pleasure in the knowledge that a bit of wilderness exists,
apart from any theorizing. Wilderness can be valued on instrumental grounds: it is good for the psychological wellbeing of a country's citizens, it provides an irreplaceable kind of pleasure that would
rank high on the kind of qualitative scale we see in Mill, it pre-
serves species that may have unanticipated uses, it is good for clean
air, clean water, and so forth. But on such an account the question
of how much wilderness to preserve quickly becomes one of balancing these goods with other goods whose value arises from human
thought and desire. To be sure, such prudential balancing would be
required even if we were to recognize value that things in the natural world have in themselves, regardless of whether or not their
worth is recognized or recognizable by evaluators. But in those cases
in which we know that there are few people with enough awareness
to enable us to say that they truly value what is at issue (for example, vast stretches of the Arctic National Wildlife Reserve, which for
most people exist only as blank areas on a map) citizens may well
make different decisions, by virtue of their new explicitly theoretical
commitments. The matter at hand may call to mind the principle
that wilderness has value, and that it follows that public policy must
take account of this. The situation stands in contrast to a public
policy matter that concerns human beings alone. There we are on

more familiar ethical ground. Our desires to clothe the poor and feed the hungry are familiar responses to certain kinds of situations, as are our desires to inculcate self-reliance and practice fiscal responsibility. How to balance competing ethical demands is a matter of prudential judgment. But an explicit ethical theory, with all of its metaphysical underpinning, will rarely be the occasion for the judgments made here. This is because the situations are not so unusual or unfamiliar as to immediately call to mind the ethical theorizing to which one has been exposed, in however fragmentary a form.

A similar sort of example is that which concerns citizens and policymakers in the areas of food and reproductive technologies. Ought crops to be genetically modified? To be sure, such cases lend themselves to standard consequentialist analyses. Is the food safe? What will happen as the variety of seed stock is diminished? But some who consider the prospect of a tomato with the genes of a pig, say, may initially experience revulsion, and this may occasion the realization that living things belong to kinds with an integrity that has non-instrumental value. To be sure, revulsion is notoriously unreliable as a moral guide. More often than not it arises from prejudice and superstition, rather than a sensitive moral compass. Again, my question is not whether a line of metaphysical metaethical thinking is sound, but whether it can have a real role to play in our practical decisions. It seems clear to me that the sort of revulsion that many have in considering the prospect of so-called "Frankenfoods" can be the occasion for explicitly metaphysical thinking concerning the value of biological species, and how this is to be understood from an ecological perspective. One is led to reflect on whether we ascribe goodness to individuals that belong to certain kinds, or to the kind itself, or the ecosystem in which it plays a role, given some ontological standing. This kind of metaphysical thinking *can* be decisive in one's rejection of less dramatic forms of genetic alteration in agriculture. Were one to start by considering the issue of the ethical permissibility of altering a crop to make it less susceptible to drought, one would probably find it permissible. It is the imaginative thought experiment of the unusual case that focuses attention on the metaphysical thesis concerning the value of biological kinds, and such attention leads to a moral precept that is adopted and employed in all cases that one takes to be applicable.[12]

Now in this case an anti-metaphysical "out" is available: one could always say in response to the revulsion occasioned by certain products of genetic engineering or other reproductive technologies that all that our feelings show is that we do not like these things.[13] Accordingly, one could argue that the disvalue or evil that we think is present is merely a matter of our own distress. Routley sets up his thought experiment to try to render such a suggestion inapplicable. Again, whether he does so successfully is controversial, and it is not my present task to defend him here. I merely want to maintain the practical value of his work. The metaphysical implications of Routley's ethical thought experiment are clearer than those that rest on imaginative explorations of monstrosities brought about by genetic engineering. Even those who share a moral revulsion at the prospects of various forms of genetically engineered organisms are in principle able to account for them as *their* feelings, worthy of moral consideration only as feelings among other feelings, and hence such as can be counterbalanced by the preferences of others. But if an argument effectively concludes that living things and the natural systems of which they form a part have intrinsic value that is not ontologically dependent on the valuer, one who follows that argument is less likely to take this value to be outweighed by the preferences of others.

Conclusion

I conclude that although the sort of metaphysical accounts that underlie ethical theorizing are rarely decisive in decision-making and action, there are two kinds of circumstances in which such accounts can play a crucial role in practical decisions. First are those decisions that have unusual features that do not summon habitual ethical reactions and hence invite the application of theoretical ethical precepts that the study of metaethics and ethical theory isolate and clarify. Second, there are times in which the good of others (including organisms and systems in the natural world) is not to be analyzed as one's own good. In such a case, this good may well be given greater weight in one's ethical deliberations. This is why, contra Jamieson, students who study the purported ontological foundations of environmental ethics may well come to live in a more environmentally responsible manner. Metaphysics is not a perquisite for the recognition of ethical obligations to the natural world for its own sake. But it can help.

Notes

1. Acknowledgments: I am grateful for the incisive comments of Dale Jamieson and an anonymous referee, and to Arun Iyer for editorial help.

2. See the Environmental Ethics Syllabus Project at http://appliedphilosophy. mtsu.edu/ISEE/

3. My focus here is whether *individual* reflection, of the sort encouraged by classes in philosophical ethics, has an effect on individual conduct. This question is different from (though related to) the question of the extent to which a society's *general* philosophical or cultural outlook determines or influences the actions of members of that society. Yi-Fu Tuan has expressed scepticism on the latter issue, see Tuan 1971.

4. I focus on Jamieson 2002: 225-43.

5. For the debates on this issue, see for example Rolston 1989, Callicott 1985 and the papers collected in *The Monist* 1992, Vol. 75, No. 2: *The Intrinsic Value of Nature*.

6. Ibid.: 232.

7. Ibid.: 243.

8. At *Laws* 721e-723d, the Athenian Stranger argues that laws ought to be prefaced by preludes which give the reasoning behind the law, so as to better persuade the citizens that they are to be obeyed. The preludes are to be written even though they may delve into abstruse metaphysics (as is the case for the long theological prelude of *Laws* 10) and, as the Stranger recognizes, most of the citizenry will be unable to fully understand the reasoning they present (722b). On this, see Bobonich 1999.

9. Jamieson 2002: 235-6.

10. Ibid.: 232.

11. Routley and Routley 1980.

12. Cf. the "heuristics of fear" discussed in Jonas 1984.

13. Such an identification of nonhuman bearers of value, which falls short of moral realism, may well have *some* impact on moral judgment but, I am arguing, when it is given some ontological grounding it is afforded significant protection against being outweighed by the moral consideration of human desires.

References

Aristotle *Nicomachean Ethics*. Trans. Crisp, Roger. Cambridge: Cambridge University Press. 2000.
Bobonich, Christopher. 1999. "Persuasion, Compulsion and Freedom in Plato's *Laws*," in G. Fine (ed.) *Plato 2: Ethics, Politics, Religion and the Soul (Oxford Readings in Philosophy)*. Oxford: Oxford University Press, pp. 373-403.
Callicott, J. Baird. 1985. "Intrinsic Value, Quantum Theory, and Environmental Ethics," *Environmental Ethics* 7: 257-275.
Jamieson, Dale. 2002. *Morality's Progress: Essays on Humans, Other Animals, and the Rest of Nature*. Oxford: Clarendon Press.
Jonas, Hans. 1984. *The Imperative of Responsibility*. Chicago: University of Chicago Press.
Rolston, Holmes. 1989. "Are Values in Nature Subjective or Objective?" in *Philosophy Gone Wild*. Buffalo, NY: Prometheus Books, pp. 91-117.
Routley, R. and V. Routley. 1980. "Human Chauvinism and Environmental Ethics," in D.S. Mannison, M.A. McRobbie, and R. Routley (eds) *Environmental Philosophy*. Canberra: Australian National University, pp. 96-189.
Tuan, Yi-Fu. 1971. "Environmental Attitudes," *Science Studies* 1: 215-24.

CAN YOU TEACH ENVIRONMENTAL PHILOSOPHY WITHOUT BEING AN ENVIRONMENTALIST?

Kevin de Laplante

Abstract
The orthodox conception of environmental philosophy is of an applied or practical philosophical discipline in the service of the ethical, social and political aims of the environmental movement. In this essay I show that there is a coherent alternative conception of the subject matter of environmental philosophy—what I call an "ecological" conception—that can be defined *independently* of environmentalist concerns. I argue that, as a framework for advancing both the theoretical and applied aims of environmental philosophy, the ecological conception of environmental philosophy has a number of advantages over the orthodox conception. I conclude with some remarks on the implications of adopting the ecological conception for teaching courses in environmental philosophy.

Keywords: ecology, environmental ethics, environmental philosophy, teaching, environmental education

Introduction

I would wager that any academic who self-identifies as an environmental philosopher will also self-identify as an environmentalist, or at least as someone with strong sympathies with the broad aims of the environmental movement. The association is natural, given that environmental philosophy as an academic discipline arose in the 1970s in response to a perceived need for intellectual support for the ethical, social and political commitments of environmentalism. I have never met an environmentalist nor an environmental philosopher who did not believe that environmental problems were not a serious threat to the long-term welfare of both human and nonhuman nature on this planet, and that this threat did not demand anything less than a substantial restructuring of humanity's relationship with the natural world.

What does this association between environmental philosophy and environmentalism imply for our understanding of the *subject matter* of environmental philosophy? Can a person do *research* in environmental philosophy that is not motivated in some way by environmentalist

Clare Palmer (Ed.), *Teaching Environmental Ethics*, 48-62.

concerns? Can a person *teach* environmental philosophy without endorsing some form of ethical or political environmentalism?

I believe that the right answer to both questions is "yes". The orthodox conception of the discipline treats environmental philosophy as, in essence, the *intellectual handmaiden* of environmentalism, as an applied or practical philosophical discipline in the service of environmentalism. I show in this paper that there is a coherent alternative conception of the subject matter of environmental philosophy—what I call an "ecological" conception—that can be defined *independently* of environmentalist concerns. I argue that the ecological conception of environmental philosophy has greater potential as a framework for advancing both the theoretical and applied aims of environmental philosophy than the orthodox conception.

The first two sections of the paper introduce and contrast the orthodox and ecological conceptions of environmental philosophy. The third section discusses the advantages of the ecological conception over the orthodox conception. The fourth section considers a possible objection to the ecological conception based on the worry that it may hurt the environmentalist cause by distancing environmental philosophy too much from real-world environmental concerns. The fifth section discusses the significance of the ecological conception for teaching environmental philosophy.

1. *The Orthodox Conception of Environmental Philosophy*

How is the subject matter of environmental philosophy generally conceived by its practitioners? The central themes of environmental philosophy, as the discipline is currently understood and practiced, revolve around two related but distinct sets of questions:

(1) Do human beings have moral obligations to protect or preserve the natural environment? If so, what are they, and to whom, or what, are they owed? How are such obligations justified?

(2) What are the root causes of contemporary attitudes and practices with respect to the natural environment, and how can we change them?

These two sets of questions identify two broad, partially overlapping sub-disciplines of environmental philosophy. Answers to the first set of questions effectively define the field of "environmental ethics". It is within the context of these questions that students are introduced to the important distinction between anthropocentric (human-centered) and nonanthropocentric (nonhuman-centered) approaches to grounding moral obligations toward the natural environment.[1] Answers to the second set of questions effectively define the field variously known as "political ecology", "radical ecology", or "radical environmental philosophy". It is within the context of this second set of questions that one encounters the various schools of deep ecology, ecofeminism, social ecology, socialist ecology, etc.

As presented, these two sets of questions do not make explicit reference to environmental problems or the normative aims of the environmental movement. These problems and aims are universally recognized, however, as the motivating context for the whole enterprise.[2] The 1960s saw the rapid growth of information concerning a diverse array of environmental threats, including overpopulation and its relation to poverty and famine, the depletion of non-renewable resources, and the harmful effects to human and nonhuman welfare caused by chemical pollutants. The result was the birth of modern *environmentalism*, a socio-political movement predicated on the belief that current attitudes and practices toward the environment are at best imprudent, and at worst, gravely immoral, to other human beings and perhaps to nature itself. "Environmental philosophy" as an academic discipline arose in the early 1970s in response to a perceived need for intellectual support and defence of the ethical and political commitments of environmentalism.

It is important to see that on the orthodox conception, the subject matter of environmental philosophy is not only historically tied to environmentalism, it is *conceptually* tied as well. Consider: *What reason would there be to pursue answers to the two sets of questions noted above if there were no environmental crisis, if human beings actually lived in sustainable harmonious relationships with the natural world*? Why would anyone worry about justifying ethical practices toward the environment if our practices were already ethical? Why would anyone be concerned about understanding the root causes of environmental attitudes and practices if there was no felt need to change them? If we accept the orthodox conception of the subject matter of environmental philosophy, there would be little reason to pursue the philosophical projects that currently occupy the vast majority of environmental philosophers. At the very least, it is entirely unclear what the subject matter of environmental philosophy would be under such circumstances.

2. *The Ecological Conception of Environmental Philosophy*

I can imagine that many environmental philosophers would happily admit that environmental philosophy is predicated on environmentalism, and that in the absence of any need for such a movement, there would be no reason for the existence of a distinct philosophical discipline dedicated to the problems of environmental ethics and radical political ecology as outlined above. This is just to acknowledge that environmental philosophy is an *applied* or *practical* philosophical discipline occasioned by contingent historical circumstance, that it was never intended to be anything more than that.

I can also imagine, however, that some environmental philosophers would resist the dissolution of environmental philosophy simply on the grounds that it wasn't "needed" anymore. Surely, they might say, we have gained many insights into human nature, culture, and our relationship to the broader physical and biological world through the sustained efforts of environmental philosophers. Environmental ethicists have challenged traditional conceptions of moral value, and developed new ways of thinking about the origins and justification of ethical norms. Deep ecologists, ecofeminists and other radical environmental philosophers have developed original and insightful critiques of the "self" as a theoretical entity, and drawn scholarly attention to what may be called the "ecological dimensions" of human economic, social and political activity.[3] Surely, it might be argued, these sorts of investigations are worthwhile and can be continued with or without the motivating context of a looming environmental crisis.

This is certainly my own view (though one can reasonably debate the case-by-case merits of the contributions of environmental philosophers on these various topics). It remains unclear, however, how to salvage a distinct identity for environmental philosophy under the orthodox conception of the discipline. We must consider what it is that such investigations have in common that warrants regarding them as falling within the domain of a distinct branch of philosophy for which the adjective "environmental" is informative.

I submit that what the diverse investigations of environmental philosophers have in common, when divorced from their relationship to environmentalism, is their focus on *the difference that environment makes* in understanding a particular phenomenon, i.e. they involve examination of a system or phenomenon at some focal level of description (the mind, the body, the self, interpersonal relations, economic activity, social organization, technological development, institutional change, etc.), and investigate the role that relationships between the focal system and its surrounding environment play in explaining, constituting or otherwise influencing the phenomenon at that focal level. This sort of investigation is naturally called "ecological".

More generally, one can characterize this "ecological" conception of environmental philosophy as *the study of the scientific, metaphysical, epistemological and normative dimensions of human-environment relations*. The ecological conception of environmental philosophy thus involves many areas of physical, biological and social science, as well as the core areas of philosophy. This definition may appear overly general, but it acquires content via its self-conscious focus on ecological relationships. The philosophical problems of environmental philosophy on this conception would include the core conceptual and methodological issues that structure the discourse of a host of human ecological sciences. On this conception, foundational investigations in ecological approaches to perception and action in the cognitive sciences (e.g. Gibson [1976] 1986; Reed 1996), or environmental history (e.g. Tainter 1988; Diamond 1997) or ecological economics (e.g. Costanza and Wainger 1991), or ecological anthropology (e.g. Abel 1998), or ecological/relational research traditions in metaphysics, epistemology and value theory (e.g. Rowlands 2003), would all count as research in environmental philosophy. Such investigations can be conducted with or without environmentalist concerns in mind. In my usage, the ecological conception of environmental philosophy is roughly synonymous with the *philosophy of human ecology*.[4]

What is the relationship of the domain of environmental philosophy on the orthodox conception to the domain of environmental philosophy on the ecological conception? It is the relation of *part* to *whole*; the philosophical problems of the orthodox conception are a *subset* of the broader domain encompassed by the ecological conception. What distinguishes the problems of the orthodox conception is their focus on the normative dimensions of the human-environment relationship in relation to contemporary environmental concerns. The domain of the ecological conception includes these, but also a broader array of non-normative philosophical problems. Thus, rather than constituting the *raison d'être* of environmental philosophy, the environmental crisis presents itself as an occasion for the *application* of philosophical thought on human-environment relations to the (very important and very difficult) problem of establishing a more harmonious and sustainable relationship between human beings and the natural world.

3. *Virtues of the Ecological Conception*

The ecological conception outlined above has virtues that, I believe, warrant its adoption in place of the orthodox conception. It encourages just the right kind of specialization and cross-disciplinary dialogue between related fields that can promote the advancement of environmental philosophy as both a theoretical and an applied discipline. Let me elaborate.

As a theoretical discipline, the ecological conception of environmental philosophy seeks to understand the difference that environmental relationships make to our general understanding of human nature and human activity in the world. At present, workers in the many subfields of human ecology that study these relationships often conduct their research in relative isolation from one another, and consequently fail to establish potentially productive interactions between these subfields. For example, there is a school of theoretical community and ecosystem ecology that is centered on the concept of "niche construction". Niche construction theorists have developed an expanded niche theory that entails a broadly co-evolutionary conception of genetic, organismal and environmental change, and have brought this theory to bear on a number of traditional problems of evolutionary biology and ecology, including human behavioural ecology and cultural evolution (Odling-Smee et al. 2003). Now, it turns out that the niche concept employed by niche construction theorists has many affinities with a conception of organism-environment relations advocated by *ecological psychologists*, who have been developing a version of ecological niche theory as a central feature of a general theory of the relationship between environmental information and the assembly and control of goal-directed behaviours in animals and humans (e.g. Heft 1989; Turvey 1992; Kadar and Effken 1994; Reed 1996).[5] These affinities suggest that there may be potential for productive dialogue between niche-construction theorists and ecological psychologists that could advance the research efforts of both camps. Unfortunately, the groups work in relative isolation from one another, scarcely noticing each other's existence. This isolation is due at least in part to the perception that niche-construction theorists are doing *ecology*, while ecological psychologists are doing *psychology*, an ostensibly different type of science altogether. But the research programs of *both* these groups explicitly fall within the domain of the ecological conception of environmental philosophy. The ecological conception

entails the view that these fields are part of a *common* theoretical
enterprise; consequently, promotion of the ecological conception may
encourage potentially fruitful theoretical interactions between otherwise isolated fields of study. This point applies to the whole array
of ecological subfields within the domain of human ecology.

Now, abstract theoretical problems of perception or cultural evolution may seem quite far from the concerns of orthodox environmental philosophers, but they are not. Many problems of orthodox
environmental philosophy turn on theoretical questions such as these.
Both deep ecologists and ecofeminists have advocated "ecological"
or "relational" conceptions of the self to which the research of ecological psychologists and others may offer theoretical support.[6] And
the ecological context of cultural evolution is a central topic for social
ecologists (Bookchin 1990). Most importantly, however, we must consider the foundational role that assumptions about human-environment
relations play in motivating the whole program of orthodox environmental philosophy. These involve assumptions regarding, among
others, i) the nature and severity of particular environmental threats
to human and nonhuman welfare, and the environmental crisis generally; ii) the nature of ecological limits to growth and resource consumption, and iii) the variety of ways in which human welfare may
be dependent on, and human nature conditioned by, the maintenance of certain relationships with local ecosystems and the global
biosphere. It is scepticism about these assumptions that remains, I
believe, the greatest source of resistance to environmentalist arguments.

Consider, for example, the debate between what may be called
"technocentric optimists" and "ecological pessimists" over human
population and limits to growth.[7] Before we can have a reasonable
discussion of how many people the earth *ought* to hold, we should have
at least some idea of how many people it *could* hold. Ecological pessimists understand natural resources primarily in material terms, as
fixed stocks of energy and matter in the environment that are drawn
down by human consumption and that have a slow or nonexistent
rate of renewal; they use this conception of resource use to argue
that human beings are at imminent risk of irreversibly degrading the
environmental resource base on which the welfare of current and
future generations depends. Technocentric optimists, on the other
hand, understand natural resources in a fundamentally different way,
not as material stocks of energy and matter in the environment, but
as *modes of use* of such stocks for particular *purposes*. This view emphasizes

the functional aspects of the resource concept, and highlights the capacity for *substitution* of resources, and even creation of *new* resources where none had existed before (see Simon 1981: 42-52). Technocentric optimists use this conception of resources to argue for policies that encourage technological innovation that will effectively increase the carrying capacity of the natural resource base. Granted, there are often strong political differences between ecological pessimists and technocentric optimists, but a central aspect of this debate turns on the *meaning* of the concept "resource", and on the degree to which the distinctive characteristics of human beings permit or resist the application of population growth models that link environmental carrying capacity and resource use. Insofar as an element of the environment is considered a resource only in relation to the purposeful activity of some organism, then the concept of a resource is a paradigmatically *ecological* concept, and the problem of understanding human resource use is a problem for ecological science.

Thus, on the ecological conception of environmental philosophy, the development of an adequate theory of resource use applicable to human beings is, or ought to be, a central problem for environmental philosophers. It is not viewed as such by the majority of proponents of the orthodox conception. This fact points to an advantage of the ecological conception of environmental philosophy over the orthodox conception with respect to the resources it can bring to the intellectual defence of environmentalism. The ecological conception focuses attention directly on the important ecological problems and issues that lie at the core of the positive case for environmentalism. The orthodox conception of environmental philosophy focuses attention on normative problems that may only be peripherally related to this case.

4. But Will it Hurt the Cause?

Upon first exposure to the suggestion that environmental philosophy ought to define its subject matter independently of the practical aims of environmentalism, most environmental philosophers with whom I have discussed the matter have reacted with a certain degree of apprehension. Here I consider and respond to one of these concerns.

It has been argued that an undue preoccupation with abstract theoretical issues (such as the debate over the existence and nature of intrinsic moral value in nature) has handicapped the application of environmental philosophy to real-world environmental problems and policy concerns, and that the ethical, political and policy aims of environmentalism are better served by a conception of environmental philosophy that is *driven by* and *subordinated to* these practical aims.[8] A defender of the orthodox conception might worry that the ecological conception being proposed threatens to move environmental philosophy in exactly the wrong direction, away from greater engagement with practical concerns and toward an even greater emphasis on abstract theoretical investigations of no direct relevance or applicability to environmental practice.[9]

I take this objection seriously. If I believed that reconceptualizing environmental philosophy in the way suggested by the ecological conception would actually interfere with or hinder the development of environmental philosophy as a practical discipline, then I would consider this a sufficient reason not to adopt it. But I do not see why this should be an expected consequence of adopting the ecological conception.

As noted in section three, the relationship between the subject matter of the orthodox conception and the subject matter of the ecological conception of environmental philosophy is best viewed as a part-whole relation; the philosophical problems of the orthodox conception are a *subset* of the broader set of problems for the science and philosophy of human ecology. Consequently, the problems of the orthodox conception—*including the problems of developing environmental philosophy as a practical discipline*—are also problems for the ecological conception. Adopting the ecological conception of environmental philosophy does not demand any change in the methodological or normative aims of environmental philosophers who view their task primarily in applied or practical terms. On the ecological conception, environmental philosophy is and remains a pluralistic discipline, with the capacity to host many different theoretical and applied orientations. Thus, while I agree that the successful application of environmental philosophy to contemporary environmental issues demands that environmental philosophy develop as a practical discipline focused on real-world problem solving, and that for such purposes it is important that theoretical investigations be conditioned and even driven by the demands of practical applicability, such a position is entirely consistent with viewing environmental philosophy at the same time as a broader discipline with a subject matter that transcends these demands.

5. *Implications for Teaching*

I have argued that the ecological conception offers a superior framework for advancing environmental philosophy both as a theoretical and an applied discipline, but what implications does it have for teaching? How would a course in environmental philosophy differ if it were taught from the perspective of the ecological conception rather than the orthodox conception?

"Rather than" is misleading, of course, if we accept the view that the problems of the orthodox conception are really a subset of the problems of the ecological conception. That said, the ecological conception does encourage some differences in approach and attitude toward the teaching of environmental philosophy. I discuss two here.

1. *Environmental philosophy is more than environmental ethics*

In principle, this has always been acknowledged by the orthodox conception. In practice, most environment-related courses offered by philosophy departments are still titled "environmental ethics", and there is a general expectation on the part of students, instructors and university administrators that such courses will focus on ethical issues relating to our treatment of the natural world. In assigning teaching responsibilities, it is commonly assumed that someone whose research focus is moral or political philosophy is, all other things being equal, better-suited to teach environment-related courses than someone whose research focus is metaphysics, epistemology or the philosophy of science. These assumptions might make some sense under the orthodox conception of environmental philosophy, but they are not supported by the ecological conception. The ecological conception treats environmental philosophy as a second-order philosophical discipline (a "philosophy of X") that draws on and engages with core positions in metaphysics, epistemology, value theory and the natural and social sciences. On the ecological conception, courses on conceptual and philosophical issues in environmental science, or environmental and ecological economics, or human cognitive ethology (the study of the ecological and evolutionary roots of human cognitive abilities), or the philosophies of anti-dualist philosophers like John Dewey or Maurice Merleau-Ponty, would all count as courses in environmental philosophy, and each would require a different set of teaching competencies on the part of a prospective instructor.

2. *Environmental ethics is more than environmental ethics*

The reality is that environmental philosophy courses offered in under-graduate curricula are expected to address normative issues relating to contemporary attitudes and practices toward the environment. On the ecological conception there are many different approaches to teaching such a course that one might take, and these will depend to a great extent on the background and research interests of the instructor. One approach, of course, is to treat it just like any other environmental ethics course, using the usual sources and anthologies; such courses falls entirely within the scope of the ecological conception.

From my own perspective as a philosopher of science specializing in the history and philosophy of ecology, I am inclined to re-frame the standard topics in a way that highlight their connection to problems in the philosophy of the natural and social sciences. For example, I open my intro environmental philosophy course with the question "Is there an environmental crisis?". This topic provides an opportunity to introduce basic concepts and issues in ecology and environmental science that are central to environmentalist arguments (e.g. population growth models, the first and second laws of thermodynamics, the diversity-stability hypothesis, the concept of "ecosystem services", the predictions of global climate change models, etc.). It has been my experience that "selling" environmentalism to a mixed class of undergraduates—and consequently, setting up the context for the ethical and socio-political issues that dominate the environmental philosophy literature—is best achieved by first establishing the case that current environmental trends pose a real threat. That there is a need for basic education on environmental issues comes as no surprise to anyone who regularly teaches in this field, particularly in light of the growing influence of corporate- and industry-friendly news media that tend to downplay environmental concerns by characterizing them as ideologically motivated and/or based on weak or questionable science. I take pains to distinguish environmentalist claims that are well supported by the available scientific evidence from those that are more conjectural, so that common ground can be established that can function as a basis for subsequent discussions.

Once the basic environmentalist arguments have been established, I move on to consider different hypotheses that might *explain* contemporary attitudes and practices toward the environment. This allows the introduction of material on economics and environment, technology and environment, women and environment, and so on, that is central to a number of positions in environmental ethics and radical environmental philosophy, but I frame these issues primarily as problems in the philosophy of the *social sciences* (i.e. the philosophy of economics, psychology, history, technology, etc.). These often have a normative component to them, but just as often they do not. Consider, for example, the debate between deep ecologists and ecosocialists over the root causes of social change. Deep ecologists focus on how individual beliefs and values shape and condition social behaviour and institutional practices, while ecosocialists focus on how institutional practices—particularly economic, technological and social practices—shape and condition individual beliefs and values (thus reflecting a "materialist" view in the sense of Marx). Each has a different view of what factors are dominant in explanations of social change. This is a classic debate in the philosophy of social science, and in class I try to highlight this aspect of the debate. It becomes an occasion to discuss Marxist/materialist views of history and their status in contemporary social theory, and to introduce recent work on environmental history and ecological anthropology that bears on the debate.

These examples illustrate one way that teaching environmental philosophy on the ecological conception might differ from approaches that view environmental philosophy as essentially a branch of applied ethics. In general, the ecological conception encourages instructors to look at problems from different disciplinary perspectives and to cast their nets more widely in assembling teaching materials that might productively inform discussion of environmental issues. At the senior undergraduate and graduate levels, one should expect greater diversity in both the types of courses that are offered and in the backgrounds and interests of the students enrolled in such courses. Such developments would, I believe, have a salutary effect on environmental philosophy as a whole.

Conclusion

The orthodox conception of environmental philosophy focuses on the normative dimensions of the human-environment relationship. The ecological conception broadens this perspective to include the full range of scientific and philosophical issues that bear on a complete understanding of the human-environment relationship. I have argued that the ecological conception offers greater resources for advancing environmental philosophy as both a theoretical and an applied discipline, by encouraging productive dialogue between otherwise isolated subfields of human and nonhuman ecology, and by focusing attention on the ecological issues that lie at the core of the environmentalist argument for political and social change. Environmental philosophy includes but is not synonymous with environmental ethics; it is a second-order philosophical discipline whose core problems bear on foundational issues in metaphysics, epistemology, value theory, and the natural and social sciences. This is a view that puts conceptual distance between environmental philosophy and environmentalism, but I have argued that it should be encouraged if environmental philosophy is to become more effective in promoting environmentalist aims.

NOTES

1. Note that I include even strongly anthropocentric approaches to these problems as properly belonging to environmental ethics.
2. See for example the introductory essays in the anthologies by Van De Veer and Pierce (1998), Light and Rolston (2003) and Armstrong and Botzler (2004).
3. On the "ecological self" from a deep ecological perspective, see Fox (1990) and Mathews (1991); from an ecofeminist perspective, see Plumwood (1991). On the "ecological dimensions of economic, social and political activity", see Clark (1998).
4. Of course, the various subfields of human ecology draw upon and overlap the various subfields of more traditional ecological and evolutionary sciences that focus on nonhuman organisms; "human ecology" merely indicates a focus of investigation, not a strict isolation from nonhuman ecology. For a defense of an expansive conception of ecological science that spans both the natural and social sciences, see de Laplante (2004).
5. Note that I am using the term "ecological psychology" to refer to a particular branch of perceptual and cognitive psychology that has no direct connection to that branch of *therapeutic* psychology that goes by the same name. Therapeutic ecological psychology asserts that the physical and psychological well-being of human beings is strongly dependent on meaningful interactions with natural environments (e.g. Roszak et al. 1995).
6. Compare, for example, Mathews 1991 and Plumwood 1991 with Heft 1989 and Kadar and Effken 1994.
7. See for example the debate between Julian Simon and Norman Myers in Myers and Simon (1994). Note that my use of the term "ecological" in this context is not tied to my use of the term in the phrase "ecological approach to environmental philosophy". Here I am using the term merely to indicate that pessimism regarding limits to growth and resource scarcity is often motivated by a presumed analogy between constraints governing human resource use and the constraints that typically limit population growth in nonhuman organisms. Note also that in this context the term (and the argument) is neutral with respect to the debate over whether nature has intrinsic or merely instrumental value (that is, "ecological" should not be read as "ecocentric" in any normative sense).

8. This view is most strongly identified with the movement known as "environmental pragmatism"; see Light and Katz (1996).

9. An anonymous referee noted that some environmental pragmatists may object to the suggestion that they are "defending orthodoxy", if orthodoxy requires a commitment to some fixed set of normative ends with respect to human-environment relationships. They would argue that pragmatism encourages a provisional and experimental attitude toward ends as well as means (see Norton 2003). But the orthodox conception of environmental philosophy, as I have defined it, requires no commitment to a fixed set of normative ends, whether anthropocentric or nonanthropocentric. All that it requires is a commitment to the view that environmental philosophy is, or ought to be, an intellectual discipline that is primarily concerned with ameliorating the relationship between human beings and the natural world. I would be surprised to find an environmental pragmatist who would not agree to this.

REFERENCES

Abel, T. 1998. "Complex Adaptive Systems, Evolutionism, and Ecology within Anthropology: Interdisciplinary Research for Understanding Cultural and Ecological Dynamics". *Georgia Journal of Ecological Anthropology* 2: 6-29.

Armstrong, S.J. and R.G. Botzler (eds). 2004. *Environmental Ethics: Divergence & Convergence*. 3rd edn. New York: McGraw-Hill.

Bookchin, M. 1990. *The Philosophy of Social Ecology: Essays on Dialectical Naturalism.* Montreal: Black Rose Books.

Clark, J. 1998. "Political Ecology: Introduction" in Zimmerman et al (eds) *Environmental Philosophy: From Animal Rights to Radical Ecology*. 2nd edn. pp. 345-63.

Costanza, R., and L. Wainger. 1991. *Ecological Economics: The Science and Management of Sustainability*. New York: Columbia University Press.

de Laplante, K. 2004. "Toward a More Expansive Conception of Ecological Science". *Biology and Philosophy* 19: 263-281.

Diamond, J. 1997. *Guns, Germs and Steel: The Fates of Human Societies*. New York: W.W. Norton.

Fox, W. 1990. *Towards a Transpersonal Ecology: Developing New Foundations for Environmentalism*. Boston: Shambala.

Gibson, J.J. [1979] 1986. *The Ecological Approach to Visual Perception*. Boston: Houghton Mifflin.

Heft, H. 1989. "Affordances and the Body: An Intentional Analysis of Gibson's Ecological Approach to Visual Perception". *Journal for the Theory of Social Behaviour* 19: 1-30.

Johnson, L.E. 1991. *A Morally Deep World: An Essay on Moral Significance and Environmental Ethics*. New York: Cambridge University Press.

Kadar, E., and J. Effken. 1994. "Heideggerian Meditations on an Alternative Ontology for Ecological Psychology: A Response to Turvey's (1992) Proposal". *Ecological Psychology* 6(4): 297-341.

Light, A. and E. Katz (eds). 1996. *Environmental Pragmatism*. London: Routledge.

Light, A. and H. Rolston (eds). 2003. *Environmental Ethics: An Anthology*. Malden, MA: Blackwell Publishers.

Mathews, F. 1991. *The Ecological Self*. London: Routledge.

Myers, M., and J. Simon. 1994. *Scarcity or Abundance?: A Debate on the Environment*. New York: W.W. Norton.

Odling-Smee, F.J., Laland, K.N. and M.W. Feldman. 2003. *Niche Construction: The Neglected Process in Evolution*. Princeton, NJ: Princeton University Press.

Plumwood, V. 1991. "Nature, Self, and Gender: Feminism, Environmental Philosophy, and the Critique of Rationalism". *Hypatia* 6: 3-27.

Reed, E.S. 1996. *Encountering the World: Toward an Ecological Psychology.* New York: Oxford University Press.

Roszak, T., Gomes M.E. and A.D. Kanner. 1995. *Ecopsychology: Restoring the Earth, Healing the Mind.* San Francisco: Sierra Club Books.

Rowlands, M. 2004. *Externalism: Putting Mind and World Back Together Again.* Montreal: McGill-Queen's University Press.

Van De Veer, D. and C. Pierce. 1998. *The Environmental Ethics and Policy Book: Philosophy, Ecology, Economics.* 2nd edn. Belmont, CA: Wadsworth Publishing.

Zimmerman, M.E., J.B. Callicott, G. Sessions, K. Warren, and J. Clark (eds). 1998. *Environmental Philosophy: From Animal Rights to Radical Ecology.* 2nd edn. Upper Saddle River, NJ: Prentice Hall.

REDUCING PESSIMISM'S SWAY IN THE ENVIRONMENTAL ETHICS CLASSROOM[1]

Dr. James W. Sheppard, Ph.D.

Abstract

Increased awareness of the breadth and depth of existing environmental challenges is part of an environmental education. One effect of this increased awareness that can manifest itself in the environmental ethics classroom is pessimism. I outline two varieties of pessimism that have a tendency to hold sway in the environmental ethics classroom: 1) pessimism about the general state of the environment; and, 2) pessimism about being able to do anything about the general state of the environment. After outlining a few of the potential educational and vocational consequences of allowing pessimism to take root, I offer a pedagogical method for reducing the sway of pessimism in the classroom. I argue that William James' and John Dewey's writings on the subject of meliorism offer a framework that, when combined with some of the insights of incrementalism theory in environmental policy, can not only help students to reduce the sway of pessimism in the classroom, but also in their chosen career paths by, among other things, highlighting the "possibility of possibility".

Keywords: environmental ethics, environmental education, meliorism, pessimism, William James, John Dewey

Introduction

In this paper, I focus on the possible role environmental ethicists can play in the vocational training of students interested in environmentally-oriented career fields by considering the merit of including the subjects of pessimism and perceptions of change in environmental ethics courses. The type of vocational training environmental ethicists will be able to offer is unlikely to be of the variety students in environmentally-focused programs are used to receiving. While it is entirely possible, it is also probably unlikely that environmental ethicists will teach students how to take water samples, test paint for lead, carry out species counts, or lobby politicians for a certain piece of environmental legislation. The type of vocational training environmental ethicists can make part of their courses is of the intellectual or theoretical variety.

Stated as such, this is not a groundbreaking suggestion. After all, some environmental ethicists believe that the main practical role,

Clare Palmer (Ed.), *Teaching Environmental Ethics*, 63-76.
© *2006 Koninklijke Brill NV. Printed in the Netherlands.*

albeit indirect, of environmental ethics is to work toward the theoretical clarification of the back-story that informs policy (Callicott 1999: 27-43). Thus, one could imagine these same individuals arguing that environmental ethicists already participate in the vocational training of environmentally-oriented students by teaching them to appreciate the importance of aiming for greater theoretical precision in their arguments. While it is important that students in environmental ethics courses are made aware of the importance of aiming for greater theoretical precision in the arguments they advance, I want to suggest that environmental ethicists can make a more direct theoretical contribution to students' vocational training. This more direct theoretical contribution stems from the opportunity environmental ethicists have to teach students about change and to link those teachings about change with how environmental policy typically unfolds.

Pessimism in the Environmental Ethics Classroom

My motivation for outlining this role comes from my experiences with what I like to call the best kept dirty little secret of environmental ethics education—namely how pessimism has a tendency to creep into classroom debates and skew students' perceptions of change. At this point, one might argue that those who teach environmental ethics already have enough to worry about without having to deal with the extra burden of deciding how to include the subjects of pessimism and perceptions of change in their courses. For example: How much basic ecology does one teach? How much environmental politics and environmental policy does one include in a philosophy course? Should one characterize the current environmental situation as a crisis or should one characterize problems that exist as pressing, but not indicative of a crisis? Given these pedagogical questions, it is fair to ask why it is necessary to deal with a whole new set of questions relating to how students view change. There are compelling reasons for this inclusion.

Students are often pulled into pessimism's web in our classrooms and are often unprepared to deal with the skewed view of change it engenders. In and of itself this ought to be a concern for teachers. It becomes even more of a concern if we assume that some of these same students will be taking on the monumental task of addressing environmental challenges in their chosen career paths. I do not want to overstate the case here. I do not mean to suggest that all of my students are pessimistic. In fact, some of my students are downright full of cheer and optimism! I also do not mean to suggest that all of my students will go on to work in environmentally-oriented career fields. Not only will some of my students be advertising executives, stockbrokers, doctors, and computer programmers, some of them also will be environmentally insensitive to boot! With that said, and even though what I have to say here is written with a heightened sensitivity towards those students that will work in environmentally-oriented career fields, pessimism stands as a problem many people face or will have to face as they strive to understand how their work is or is not "making a difference."

   Over the last decade, I have noticed that some of my more "green" and activist-oriented students are indeed pessimistic about the state of the world.[2] There surely are many reasons for this. It is possible that the presence of pessimism in college students may be a by-product of the political and social culture and atmosphere of which the students are a part. Said differently, some of this pessimism may be context-driven.[3] Regardless of locale, pessimism also tends to be a by-product of increased student awareness of the depth and breadth of environmental challenges that exist now and that are apt to exist and increase in the future if current challenges are not dealt with effectively. Call this form of pessimism *pessimism about the general state of the environment*. Another reason for this pessimism derives from how students view the possibility of change. Call this form of pessimism *pessimism about the possibility of changing the general state of the environment*. Of the two types of pessimism, the latter presents itself as the more pressing of the two because it undermines the ability to even think about doing something about the set of challenges that engender the former. Given this, the question then becomes not how to make students view the world with naïve optimism, for doing this would be disingenuous and inaccurate. The question becomes how to encourage students to reconsider what it is they take change to be and why.

Pessimism and the Nature of Environmental Change

The rich environmental ethics literature that has developed over the past three decades is not short on radical philosophical proposals and philosophical justifications for revolutionary change. The radical and revolutionary edge that *some* social ecologists, deep ecologists, and advocates of ecotage, just to name a few likely candidates, bring to the field is a welcome component of the rich theoretical mixture that exists in the field. One thing that I find interesting about presenting these more radical and revolutionary types of environmental ethics in the classroom is that they tend to be the approaches to which students are most attracted. This may be the result of many factors, such as how I teach the material, the high levels of idealism students bring to the class, and the personality of the authors that often comes through in the their writing. I have a hunch, though, that it is also the result of students being attracted to the implicit message of these approaches—i.e., the range of problems that exist not only call for radical changes, but radical changes are the best method we have for dealing with these challenges. Put simply, these approaches tend to encourage students to adopt radical perceptions of change.

Students who view change as a product of bold, sweeping, radical and revolutionary proposals are often surprised to find out that change is difficult to engender. Faced with these difficulties and with the often slow rate and ineffectiveness of environmental proposals, it is to be expected that students become pessimistic. Let me be as clear as possible here. I have no problem with the fact that college campuses are breeding grounds for idealism. Student idealism should be encouraged, to an extent. But as an environmental educator, I do have a problem with highly-skilled young environmental practitioners that have not been prepared to deal with the reality that the process of change is a slow and extremely arduous one. Without this training, young, energetic, and skilled environmental practitioners are apt to be blindsided by this reality. Unequipped to deal with these realities, pessimism about one's role and effectiveness can creep into the picture causing, among other things, one to question the point of acting on behalf of the environment in the first place.

I partly wish I was making this scenario up for the sake of this discussion. Unfortunately the ideas I present here are the product of relationships I have with former students, one of whom I will refer to anonymously here as Mr. X. Mr. X recently officially chose to end his career in the environmental not-for-profit sector to pursue work in a non-environmentally oriented for-profit enterprise. While many considerations factored in his decision, he informed me that one reason he had to, in his words, "get out," was his increasing frustration over and inability to cope with slow rates of change.

If you are anything like me, you care about your students. Hearing my student's story frustrated and saddened me for a number of reasons, not the least of which was I felt partially responsible for not tempering some of the idealism often found in the environmental ethics proposals I teach with a frank discussion and consideration of how change typically unfolds in the United States and, for that matter, globally as well. I do not mean to suggest that had I taken one or two class periods to talk about change that Mr. X would still be working in an environmentally-oriented career field. I cannot be sure of this one way or the other. What I am sure of is that as an environmental educator I have an opportunity to talk about change and deal with pessimism in the classes I teach. Doing this will not be a cure-all for pessimism, but awareness of the slowness of change and frank discussion of the sway of pessimism may work to lessen the temptation of students in the future to "get out" if changes are not seen overnight. Talking about these subjects may be out of character for some environmental ethicists who may be more comfortable talking about intrinsic value, biospherical egalitarianism, and the socially constructed nature of nature than about what it takes to be an environmental professional. But as it turns out, environmental ethicists may be especially well-equipped to incorporate discussions of pessimism and change in their courses and become *de facto* vocational trainers simply by tapping into pedagogical resources that already exist. The first step to dealing with pessimism in the classroom is getting as clear as possible about the challenge it presents.

Given the breadth and depth of environmental challenges, it is tempting for students and teachers to adopt the view that small individual actions will be unlikely to impact on the overall situation in any significant manner. Efforts to address environmental challenges individually seem to present us with a hopeless situation wherein little gets done and the systemic problems are left unaddressed. If anything that falls short of systemic change is likely to fail, what would seem to be needed would be some type of radical and revolutionary change in thinking and behavior. Unfortunately, revolutionary change also is unlikely primarily because of the systemic nature of environmental challenges. Put differently, it is unlikely that any silver-bullet solution exists that would be able to permeate all parts of a system filled with so many problems on so many levels. In the absence of a silver-bullet solution, addressing challenges once and for all vis-à-vis some radical systemic reorientation of thinking and practice is unlikely. If revolution is unlikely and if small individual actions are viewed as unviable options, it is to be expected that the pessimistic mood will find a place to take root, especially when it comes to how students view the possibility of change. Under the sway of the pessimistic mood, apathy and aloofness is apt to set in and the problems that exist today are likely to remain unaddressed, potentially becoming more serious and numerous. As problems increase in severity and number, it is entirely possible that the very hopelessness and inaction that contributed to the initial situation that produced hopelessness and inaction will also increase—a vicious downward spiral if there ever was one. Put simply, pessimism has a tendency to reinforce itself.

I have witnessed the reinforcing tendency of pessimism in especially vivid ways in the classroom. It is no secret that students play off the ideas, moods, and general dispositions of others in the college classroom. Questions asked, answers provided, body gestures offered, and the overall worldview expressed by certain students can take root in a classroom in various ways, including—but not limited to—what happens in class presentations, class discussions, group work, and informal discussions. Classroom dynamics often evolve and change rapidly over the course of a term; these changes are often spurred on by the introduction of certain issues.

Dealing with Pessimism in the Environmental Ethics Classroom

In any course that deals with environmental issues, it is apt not to take too long before students realize that human beings have faced great difficulty arriving at and implementing solutions to environmental challenges. Different instructors include this set of realities in the classroom in different ways. I typically refer to what Zachary Smith (2000) has called the "environmental policy paradox" to illustrate this. In Smith's words, "The paradox of environmental policy is that we often understand what the best short- and long-term solutions to environmental problems are, yet the task of implementing these solutions is either left undone or is completed too late" (Ibid.: xi). That so many human beings tolerate this paradox year after year can be exasperating to students (I know it is to me!). Once the seed of this paradox is planted, a number of attitudes can be noticed in the classroom including apathy, outrage, anger, hopelessness, and of course, pessimism. These attitudes, following on what I said earlier about the tendency of classroom dynamics to take on a life of their own, can snowball throughout a class if one does not have a methodology in place to address them. One's immediate reaction to what I am recounting here might be: "Well, if you just don't talk about the paradox of environmental policy, you won't have to deal with the pessimism that follows about the possibility of change." My response to this is simple: making this choice cheats students of what they enter into a college classroom for in the first place—namely, frank, honest, and critical discussions of pressing issues. Is there then a better way to deal with the sway of pessimism in the classroom?

One suggestion might be to teach students about ethical systems and principles that call for radical changes. But these radical changes, because of the very fact that they are very unlikely, actually can reinforce the pessimism they are designed to address by contributing to a "what's the point of acting?" attitude. Despite the reinforcing tendency of pessimism, or perhaps in spite of the reinforcing tendency of pessimism, we can choose to think differently about change and in the process come up with new ways to address and reduce the sway of pessimism in the classroom. I, for one, tend to concur with late David Brower that "we can no longer afford the luxury of pessimism" (Brower 2000: ix). Besides, as Brower reminds us, "Hope is more fun" (Ibid.).

Despite the fact that the obvious alternative and answer to pessimism is optimism and hope, I am not so naïve as to think that it is as easy as just asking students to decide to adopt the attitude of optimism, even though the American philosopher William James seemed to suggest just such a move when he wrote the following:

> What can be more base and unworthy than the pining, puling, mumping mood, no matter by what outward ills it may have been engendered? What is more jurious to others? What less helpful as a way out of the difficulty? It but fastens and perpetuates the trouble which occasioned it, and increases the total evil of the situation. At all costs, then, we ought to reduce the sway of that mood; we ought to scout it in ourselves and others, and never show it tolerance. (James 1987: 87)

What I have always found interesting about this passage is that James stops just short of ruling out pessimism completely. True, he does say we should "scout it in ourselves and others," and "never show it tolerance." But he also uses the phrase "reduce the sway of that mood" to characterize what should be our proper plan of attack against pessimism. James knew that individuals were complex, that each individual's "interior is a battle-ground for what he [or she] feels to be two deadly hostile selves, one actual, the other ideal" (Ibid.: 159). In a sense, environmental challenges present concerned citizens, including students, with a similar situation. The actual: the challenges facing living systems globally, the myriad causes of those challenges, and also the difficulties involved in addressing those challenges. The ideal: environments that have been made to function better because of our efforts.

In view of this recognition, reducing the sway of pessimism in the classroom begins with deemphasizing the false dualism of optimism and pessimism and tapping into the pedagogical resource that is the idea of meliorism, first introduced by James and then further elaborated by John Dewey. For what it is worth, I have had success incorporating this pedagogical resource into my environmental ethics classes. Based on several classes I have taught, I have found that both William James' and John Dewey's writings on the subject of meliorism work nicely in the classroom, with the edge probably going to James due to his more accessible prose style. Whether in the writings of James or Dewey, teaching the doctrine of meliorism introduces students interested in confronting environmental challenges to the idea that the world is neither good nor bad in and of itself; it is only good or bad and only gets better or worse as a result of human intervention and action. Meliorism is not a cure-all for pessimism, but it does work against the sway of pessimism because it tends to undercut the defeatist, alarmist, and generally depressing appraisals of the future by encouraging us to invest in the possibility of possibility.

James invested in and was attracted to the doctrine of meliorism most likely because it encouraged a view of the world as containing multiple possibilities. One of these possibilities: things can get better. As the popular urbanist James Howard Kunstler poetically reminds us, however, ". . . There are no guaranteed rescues from the blunders of history" (Kunstler 2001: xiv). Meliorism takes this lack of guarantees seriously and offers itself as an alternative to the undesirable extreme positions of optimism and pessimism. To be excessively optimistic is to risk overlooking how ineffective human beings can be at changing undesirable circumstances. To be excessively pessimistic is to risk overlooking the possibility of change itself (McDermott 1986: 118). Meliorism, because it accounts for both ends of the spectrum, may not only offer itself as a foil to classroom pessimism, it also may be the psychological disposition best suited to dealing with environmental challenges. It allows us to remain grounded and realistically cognizant of the depth and breadth of challenges and at the same time keep an eye on the future with the hope that we will have the wherewithal to come up with effective solutions to make things not perfect, but better. Meliorism, then, abandons the false dream of a sudden systemic overnight change to a perfect future in favor of an emphasis on making things better step-by-step. It encourages us, in the words of the environmental activist William Shutkin (2003), to be careful to not "let the perfect be the enemy of the better" in our efforts. The melioristic posture thus requires that we abandon some of the human hubris that often prevents us from acting unless, that is, we feel as if we will be able to solve all problems once and for all through our actions. Echoing Brower once more, allowing our desire for perfection to override our responsibility to begin to make things better is a luxury that many living systems cannot afford.

The doctrine of meliorism links up nicely with the project of reconstructing how we view problematic situations and with how we view the possibility of coming up with solutions to those situations. John Dewey argued that a new understanding of progress and change was part of this with reconstruction when he wrote:

> Progress is not automatic, nor is it progress *en bloc*, it is cumulative, a step forward here, a bit of improvement there. It takes place day by day, and results from the ways in which individual persons deal with particular situations; it is step-by-step progress which comes by human efforts to repair here, to modify there, to make a minor replacement yonder. Progress is retail business, not wholesale. It is made piecemeal, not all at once. (Dewey 1973: 62)

If Dewey is on target, perhaps what was called *The Quiet Crisis* (1963) by Stuart Udall will be answered by a quiet revolution made up of a series of small reforms that are themselves made up of a series of small steps.

Admittedly, this amounts to a tacit endorsement of adopting an incremental understanding of change, which coincidentally runs counter to the methodology of some already working in environmentally-oriented career fields, such as landscape design and environmental planning, to name just two. Richard Forman (2002: 86 and 105), for example, has argued that environmental professionals, in order to reach a "new level" and to become "emergent leaders," should embrace the need to be bold as a professional norm; any-thing less than this norm ought to be viewed critically and as falling short of what is needed. In Forman's words, "boldness is an alter-native to tinkering or the status quo" (Ibid.: 86). One wonders, regard-less of the role such a view might have in the historical heritage of the professions of design and planning, whether this is the correct view or, better yet, the correct norm to teach students interested in environmentally-oriented careers? Should environmental ethicists decry incrementalism as mere "tinkering"?

I will be the first to agree that there is intellectual value to be derived from understanding what it requires to have bold visions for the future. In terms of curriculum content, students should be made aware of the bold visionaries of the past. These figures have much to teach us about having a theoretical vision, no matter how imprac-tical, against which actions can be judged. However, when it comes to understanding the public role students will play in the future as economists, politicians, social workers, designers, architects, planners, and citizens, a reconsideration of this unbridled boldness and ideal-ism is warranted.[4] As it turns out, there is merit for doing the exact opposite of what Forman recommends—students should be learning the importance of adopting incrementalism as a norm.

Conclusion: Teaching Incrementalism and Meliorism

I want to conclude this paper by explaining exactly how I teach incrementalism in my classes and how I think that it, combined with a treatment of the subject of meliorism, can work to reduce the sway of pessimism in the classroom and beyond. In the end, I think it is reasonable to suggest that pessimism might have a more difficult time taking root in a classroom that not only calls the false dualism of optimism and pessimism about change to task, but that also takes time to nurture a more moderate view of change.

Perhaps the best way to nurture this more moderate view of change is to rely on what tends to happen in the world of environmental policy. While some environmental ethicists may ignore environmen-tal policy in their courses, choosing instead to focus on a strictly philosophical approach to the subject, I typically complement my chosen texts in environmental ethics with at least one overview text of environmental policy so as to offer the students a view of environmental ethics that includes a consideration of how well philosophers do—or do not—account for developments on environmental policy. The text I have found to be the most accessible to a wide variety of students, some with an environmental background and some without any environmental background whatsoever, is *The Environmental Policy Paradox* by Zachary Smith (2000). It is undeniably United States centered; for this reason, similar texts would work just as well for this purpose in other parts of the world. Smith does two things well in this text that are especially useful for environmental ethicists looking to incorporate an element of policy into their courses. First, he does an excellent job explaining the basics of the policy-making process, the learning of which can be daunting for students more interested in philosophical arguments than layers of political bureaucracy (Smith 2000: 42-76). Second, he does an excellent job of explaining the incremental nature of policy-making (Ibid.: 51-56).

Borrowing from James E. Anderson (1984: 9), Smith outlines the four elements of policy incrementalism as:

1. Only some of the possible alternatives for dealing with a problem are considered by the decision maker. Either by virtue of limitations, ability, time, or because of the desire to achieve a consensus, a comprehensive evaluation of all alternatives is not undertaken.

2. The alternatives considered and the option ultimately selected will differ only slightly or incrementally from existing policy.

3. Only a limited number of consequences for each alternative are evaluated.

4. The problem being evaluated is continually redefined with adjustments being made to make the problem more manageable. (Smith 2000: 51)

The four elements of incrementalism theory—the limiting of possibilities, the reality that evolutions of/in policy are slight at best, the consideration of only a limited number of consequences, and strategies based on problem management—are easily incorporated into an environmental ethics course. This is especially so if that course contains not only attention to strictly theoretical disputes, but also to how philosophy might or might not be able to contribute to more effective environmental decision-making vis-à-vis improved methodologies and procedures. With this awareness of policy, students used to reading environmental ethicists who often call for radical changes are asked by me to analyze conceptions of change found in the environmental ethics literature alongside the reality of how changes in environmental policy tend to unfold. I do not want to restate all of the basic points Smith makes about incrementalism here. Important to note, though, is that by making students aware of the incremental nature of policy change, new avenues of discussion are opened. Furthermore, with this information, students begin to recognize that change is taking place, even when it seems as if nothing is being done. To be fair, one such avenue of discussion centers on critically assessing incrementalism; after all, incrementalism, strictly speaking, is a theory. It just happens to be a theory well supported by the "fact that many environmental policy decisions are made on an incremental basis" (Ibid.: 52).

The time sacrificed preparing these lectures and the readings left off the syllabus to make space for these subjects, not to mention the class periods needed to teach the subjects of meliorism and policy making incrementalism, may seem to be too high a price to pay for some environmental ethicists. The payoffs, however, are significant. For one, treating these subjects opens up new avenues of discussion. If policy is made on an incremental basis, and if change happens most often as a result of small changes to the system that compile over time, should our theoretical approaches be sensitive to this? Or do environmental ethicists still have an obligation to think about radical ideals and revolutionary absolutes? Can they do both? If it is recognized that radical and revolutionary approaches often contribute to feelings of hopelessness and helplessness due largely to the fact that such proposals rarely get off the ground, do environmental ethicists have an obligation to temper their teaching of such approaches with suggestions as to what philosophy might do to improve the procedural apparatuses within which policy unfolds? These and other meta-questions arise when meliorism and incrementalism are admitted as subjects in courses in environmental ethics. While these are valuable additions to any class in environmental ethics, the biggest payoff received for teaching students to adopt more moderate views of change and for reducing the sway of pessimism in the classroom may be related to something that happens outside of the classroom.

One of the interesting things about the subjects of meliorism and incrementalism is that they provide insights useful in a wide range of contexts. Students that want to end up working in some aspect of policy obviously stand to benefit from awareness of this subject matter. Not only will they be more effective at maneuvering the policy process, they also will hopefully be better equipped to deal with and reduce the sway of pessimism in their careers. Students that go on to work in non-governmental environmentally oriented enterprises may find themselves even more prone to the sway of pessimism because the change that they are working toward, and for, may not have the procedural and institutional support found in governmental enterprises. For this reason, the potential lessons learned about change and pessimism in a course on environmental ethics may be even more important for these future environmental professionals and activists. In the end, whether it is at the grassroots level or at the level of governmental policy-making, honing our views of change and encouraging our students to do likewise may contribute in some small manner to sustaining careers and efforts aimed at addressing environmental challenges by reducing the sway of pessimism and the tendency it has to undermine those very efforts. As I have argued elsewhere (Sheppard 2003), this will be the result of being able to appreciate the small successes enjoyed along the way toward larger longer-term goals. Valuing progress as such, no matter how small that progress might be, can steady and sustain our drive toward satisfying these longer-term goals.

Notes

1. The author wishes to thank his current and former students without which this paper would have been impossible to write, as well as Bob Mann, Carol Grimaldi, Dan Shapiro, and an anonymous reviewer for their helpful comments on earlier versions of this paper. An earlier version of this paper titled "Urban Environmentalism: Challenges and Opportunities" was presented as part of the Urban and Metropolitan Studies Forum Series: "Globalization—Localization and Cities" at Michigan State University; 20 February 2004.

2. Coincidentally, as I was working on a draft of this paper, I was visited by two students who wanted to discuss with me how to deal with the pessimism that they felt was creeping into their worldviews.

3. I have not conducted any surveys to determine if the prevalence of pessimism is a problem in places other than the United States, but I would be interested to hear of others' experiences and views on the subject.

4. To be fair, some designers and planners have argued that having an idealistic vision *is* that public role. I am reminded here of how Daniel Liebeskind stood by his winning plan for the WTC site in New York City, even in the face of criticism that has called his plan to task for its impracticality. For more on this discussion, see Hirschkorn 2003.

REFERENCES

Anderson, James E. 1984. *Public Policymaking*. 3rd edn. New York: Holt, Rinehart, and Winston.
Brower, David. 2000. "Foreword." in Willam Shutkin *The Land that Could Be: Environmentalism and Democracy in the Twenty-First Century*. Cambridge, Massachusetts and London: MIT Press.
Callicott, J. Baird. 1999. *Beyond the Land Ethic: More Essays in Environmental Philosophy*. Albany: State University of New York Press.
Dewey John. 1973. *John Dewey: Lectures in China, 1919-1920* in Robert W. Clopton and Tsuin-chen Ou (eds). Honolulu: University Press of Hawaii.
Forman, Richard T.T. 2002. "The Missing Catalyst: Design and Planning with Ecology Roots." in Bart R. Johnson and Kristina Hill (eds) *Ecology and Design: Frameworks for Learning*. Washington, DC: Island Press.
Hirschkorn, Phil. 2003. "World's Tallest Towers Proposed for WTC site." http://www.cnn.com/2003/US/Northeast/02/04/wtc.finalists/index.html. February 4th.
James, William. 1987. *The Varieties of Religious Experience* in Bruce Kuklick (ed.) *William James: Writings 1902-1910*. New York: Library of America.
Kunstler, James Howard. 2001. *The City in Mind: Notes on the Urban Condition*. New York: The Free Press.
McDermott, John. 1986. *Streams of Experience: Reflections on the History and Philosophy of American Culture*. Amherst: The University of Massachusetts Press.
Sheppard, James. 2003. "The Nectar is in the Journey: Pragmatism, Progress, and the Promise of Incrementalism." *Philosophy and Geography*. Volume 6, Number 2: 167-187.
Shutkin, William. 2003. "Building Communities of Place: From Ideals to Practices." Conference Presentation. *Designing for Civic Environmentalism* Conference. University of Texas—Austin; 12-15 November 2003.
Smith, Zachary. 2000 [1992]. *The Environmental Policy Paradox*. 3rd edn. Upper Saddle River, New Jersey: Prentice Hall.
Udall, Stewart. 1963. *The Quiet Crisis*. New York: Holt, Rinehart and Winston.

WHY TEACH ENVIRONMENTAL ETHICS? BECAUSE WE ALREADY DO

Raymond Benton, Jr. and
Christine S. Benton

Abstract
In this paper we argue for the importance of the formal teaching of environmental ethics. This is, we argue, both because environmental ethics is needed to respond to the environmental issues generated by the neoliberal movement in politics and economics, and because a form of environmental ethics is implicit, but unexamined, in that which is currently taught. We maintain that students need to become aware of the latent ethical dimension in what they are taught. To help them, we think that they need to understand how models and metaphors structure and impact their worldviews. We describe how a simple in-class exercise encourages students to experience the way metaphors organize feelings, courses of action, and cognitive understandings. This is then intellectualized by way of Clifford Geertz's concept of culture and his model for the analysis of sacred symbols. From there we present a brief interpretation of modern economics as the embodiment of the dominant modern ethos. This leads into a consideration of ecology as a science, and to the environmental ethic embodied in Aldo Leopold's "Land Ethic." We close with a personal experience that highlights how environmental teaching can make students aware of the presence of an implicit, but unexamined, environmental ethic.

Keywords: environmental ethics, environmental education, culture, neoliberal economics

Introduction

The question "*why* teach environmental ethics?" seems central to a collection of papers on the teaching of environmental ethics. We consider there to be two related reasons why environmental ethics should be taught. First, the last quarter century has witnessed the spread of neoliberal ideas and the concomitant increased reliance on market forces and the decreased reliance on non-market institutions, especially government. We suggest that Aldo Leopold, writing in the 1940s, well before environmental issues had entered the public consciousness, before the formation of the EPA, and before the passage of landmark environmental laws, foresaw the coming of this neoliberal turn. In his essay, "The Land Ethic," he wrote (1949: 213):

> There is a clear tendency in American conservation to relegate to government all necessary jobs that private landowners fail to perform.

Clare Palmer (Ed.), *Teaching Environmental Ethics*, 77-92.
© *2006 Koninklijke Brill NV. Printed in the Netherlands.*

Government ownership, operation, subsidy, or regulation is now widely prevalent in forestry, range management, soil and watershed manage- ment, park and wilderness conservation, fisheries management, and migratory bird management, with more to come. Most of this growth in governmental conservation is proper and logical, some of it is inevitable. That I imply no disapproval of it is implicitly in the fact that I have spent most of my life working for it. Nevertheless the ques- tion arises: what is the ultimate magnitude of the enterprise? Will the tax base carry its eventual ramifications? At what point will govern- mental conservation, like the mastodon, become handicapped by its own dimensions?

Leopold identified, in this passage, two issues that drive the neolib- eral project—taxes and the ultimate size of government. He also gave voice to the neoliberal solution—increased reliance on the indi- vidual. "The answer," Leopold continued in the passage just quoted, "if there is any, seems to be in a land ethic, or some other force which assigns more obligation to the private landowner." According to this argument we should teach environmental ethics because it is likely to be the only answer to the environmental problems generated in the context of the neoliberal movement in politics and economics.

The other, related answer to the "Why" question is that we should teach environmental ethics *because we already do*. This will be explained in some detail as we explore an answer to a second question, "How should we teach environmental ethics?" In addressing this second question, we focus primarily on teaching environmental ethics to a particular kind of student: those taking an MBA. Teaching MBA students requires, we feel, a different approach than would be required if teaching, say, philosophy majors. MBA students expect to learn something one day and apply it the next. Most are not accustomed to ideological and intellectual introspection, and most do not see the point in it.

When we write about teaching environmental "ethics" to MBA students, we have in mind a broader, less precise meaning to the term than we suspect is most often conjured. As Des Jardins points out (2001: 17-18), the word *ethics* is derived from the Greek word *ethos*, meaning "custom." In this sense, he writes, "ethics refers to the general beliefs, attitudes, or standards that guide customary behav- ior."[1] This is what we mean by ethics. Our meaning is more akin to what is meant by its use in the terms "the Puritan ethic" or "the work ethic." Our concern is not with explicating formal rules to be applied in decision-making contexts, but with explicating the beliefs, attitudes, values and standards that currently guide customary behavior. Our preferred term for what we are talking about is, in fact, *ethos* rather than *ethics*, and our jumping off point is not philosophy but anthropology, in particular the anthropology of Clifford Geertz.[2]

We do not view the teaching of ethics as an exercise in providing students with a new rulebook to follow. Instead, we view ethical responsibility as something that will come when students are given the critical thinking skills to self-reflect on their contemporary situation. Consequently, determining *what* or *which* environmental ethics should be taught falls outside the scope of this paper. Our main goal is to outline the initial steps that must be taken prior to tackling the "which environmental ethics" question. Suffice it to say, we would support an environmental ethics that respects different approaches to decision-making and different voices affected by those decisions. The environmental ethics that we would support would remain always contextually based, because to decide a course of action requires that the problem first be understood as situated and described as such.

Consequently, when we think about teaching environmental ethics we are thinking along the lines expressed, again, by Des Jardins who defined ethics as "a self-conscious stepping back from our lives to reflect on what we should do, how we should act, and what kind of people we should be" (2001: 6). To us this is what all education should be, and certainly should form the basis of a course in environmental ethics.

From our perspective, students first need to become aware of the latent ethical dimension in everything. But before that they need to understand how models and metaphors shape understanding, and then to become fully aware of which models and metaphors shape their own understanding. We begin with an in-class exercise that forces students to experience the way metaphors organize feelings, courses of action, and cognitive understanding. We then intellectualize this by way of Clifford Geertz's concept of culture and his model for the analysis of sacred symbols. We make reference to the dominant modern worldview before we briefly suggest an interpretation of modern economics as the embodiment of the dominant modern ethos. Then we venture into the realm of ecology as a science and take the road presented by Aldo Leopold's "The Land Ethic," tying it into the lineage of modern economics.

1. *Thinking, Conceptualizing, and Analyzing*

Des Jardins writes: "a primary role of descriptive ethics is to make explicit the models and metaphors that shape our understanding of the world" (Des Jardins 2001: 157). But most students (and many professors) do not really grasp how models and metaphors shape their interpretations, understandings, feelings, and courses of action. Demonstrating this is the first step in our approach to teaching environmental ethics. The following is a brief in-class exercise that makes the point.

We ask students to imagine that they have been on a trip, during which they bought something. On their return travels home, they strike up a conversation with somebody. This conversation turns to that which they have bought and, eventually, to the price paid. Upon learning the price paid, the other person indicates that they got a steal, a bargain. At this point, we stop and ask the students to describe how they *feel* about what they have just been told. Then we ask them what they might *do* given the information that it was a bargain, a really cheap price for what they bought. Finally, we ask them what they *know* about the situation at hand (including the original purchasing situation).

To the "how do you feel" question, in varying forms most students respond that they would be happy, elated, or proud. Some respond that they would be suspicious of the person giving them this information—how would they know whether it was a good deal or not? Both responses, pride and suspicion, are recognizable responses to everybody in the class. In the scores of times that this exercise has been executed in class, only once did a student indicate they would feel guilty. As a response, it was not recognized as realistic by the rest of the class; they could not understand how anybody would feel guilty in such a situation.

To the "what would you do" question, a variety of similar responses are offered: some would tell others, either out of pride of their ability to shop or so the others can get the item as well; some might try to sell it and realize a profit; some indicate they would return and buy more; others say they will just feel good about it. All are recognizable responses in that they make sense to others in the class.

The question regarding "what they know" about the situation generally brings puzzlement. They often do not understand what is asked. If a response is given, it is often simply, "Just because." They develop the ability to understand the question, and how to respond to it, in the second part of this exercise.

In order to change the circumstances of the thought experiment, we stop at this point and suggest they transport themselves to another place or to another time. This "other place" is seriously religious and relies on an organic analogy to think about, conceptualize, and analyze social and economic relations. Without identifying sources, we read a few passages from historical sources so they can grasp for themselves how these other people "see the world." For example, we read a passage from Wycliff:

> The Church is divided in these three parts, preachers, and defenders, and . . . laborers. . . . As she is our mother, so she is a body, and health of this body stands in this, that one part of her answers to another, after the same measure that Jesus Christ has ordained it. . . . Kindly man's hand helps his head, and his eye helps his foot, and his foot his body . . . and thus should it be in parts of the Church. . . . as diverse parts of man served unkindly to man if one took the service of another and left his own proper work, so diverse parts of the Church have proper works to serve God; and if one part leaves his work that God has limited him and take work of another part, sinful wonder is in the Church. . . . Surely the Church shall never be whole before proportions of her parts be brought again by this heavenly leech and by medicine of men (as quoted by Tawney 1926: 29).

During the discussion that follows, we emphasize that not only does each member occupy a defined role, members must receive the means suited to their stations in life so that they can carry out their functions. No more than this must be claimed, for, quoting Tawney this time (1926: 27), "if one takes into his hand the living of two, his neighbor will go short." If people run short, are deprived of necessary means, they will not be able to perform their functions.

A passage from John of Salisburg further makes the point:

> The health of the whole commonwealth will be assured and vigorous, if the higher members consider the lower and the lower answer in like manner the higher, so that each is in turn a member of every other (John of Salisburg, quoted by Tawney 1926: 29).

Finally, we quote a passage from an unpublished essay of John Locke:

> When any man snatches for himself as much as he can, he takes away from another man's heap the amount he adds to his own, and it is impossible for anyone to grow rich except at the expense of someone else (quoted in Spiegel 1971: 165).

This is generally enough. Now, after brief discussion, we revisit the initial scenario. We ask them how they would now *feel*, what they might now *do*, and what they might now reasonably *know* about the situation if they lived in this other time and conceptualized the world through this other conceptual scheme. This time most indicate they would now *feel* guilty. Some students insist that they would still feel good about their "steal."[3] We point out that they are thinking with our current conceptual model, not with the organic analogy introduced. Most students eventually see the difference. Admittedly, some never do. What would they now *do*? Generally they would return to the place of purchase and give the vendor his rightful due. What if it is too far and is not practical to return? With some discussion students usually come up with alternative courses of action: giving the excess to charity; going to church to pray for forgiveness.

To the question about what they might now reasonably *know*, they explain how, by not having given the vendor his or her "due," the vendor will go short, not be able to perform his or her social duties, and the community, as a whole, will suffer as a consequence. This is because they would be depriving somebody of the necessary means to perform their function in society. When asked to go back and explain why they originally felt good they are still, generally, without a response other than, "Just because it seems like a natural thing to do." But they grasp and understand that something is unconsciously guiding their reactions (how they feel and what they might do) even if they are unable to explain it. And they grasp the importance of understanding what this something is.

2. *Intellectualizing the Experience: the Concept of Culture*

At this point we can intellectualize the experience by introducing the anthropology of Clifford Geertz. Geertz's concept of culture, which he came to by way of the sociology of Talcott Parsons and the philosophies of Susan Langer and Gilbert Ryle, is defined as those "historically transmitted patterns of meanings embodied in symbols, systems of inherited conceptions expressed in symbolic forms," by and through which people "communicate, perpetuate, and develop their knowledge about and attitudes toward life" (1973: 89). It is by and through symbolic models, the imaginative universe within which social action takes place, that humans give form, order, point, and direction to their lives.

Behind the traditional concept of culture[4] is an image, referred to by Geertz as the Enlightenment image, of unembellished human beings lying somewhere below, or behind, the trappings of local custom and tradition. This image holds culture to be an addition to an otherwise biologically, neurologically, and anatomically completed animal. Conversely, archaeological evidence strongly suggests that culture, rather than being added on to an otherwise complete animal, was integral to its ultimate formation. Literally, people had a hand (or a mind) in making themselves. Consequently, the mind and the body evolved, at least during the final stages, within the framework of human culture and human symbolization. For this reason, human culture, in the Geertzian sense of systems of symbols and meanings, is not superfluous to human beings: it is defining, it is essential.

The argument can be put in terms of models. The term model has, however, a dual aspect to it: there are *models for* as well as *models of*. *Models for* exist in nature, as in the genetic code, which is a model—a blueprint—for reconstructing another of the same species. But *models of* are apparently uniquely human. Beavers build their houses, and birds fly south, according to genetic information contained intrinsically; humans build houses, and fly wherever it is they fly—in machines—according to symbolic and extrinsic sources of information, according to models of houses for house building, of aerodynamics for the construction and operation of airplanes.

To fully grasp Geertz's approach, the student must also grasp that human thought is largely a metaphorical process. Human thought consists of the construction and manipulation of symbol systems employed as *models of* other non-symbolic systems in such a way that the structure of these other systems, and how they may be expected to behave, is "understood."

When we think, conceptualize, formulate, comprehend, understand, or whatever, we match the states and processes of symbolic models against the states and processes of the wider world. "Imaginal thinking is neither more nor less than constructing an image . . . of the 'relevant features' of the environment and then manipulating it under various hypothetical conditions and constraints" (Galanter and Gerstenhabor 1956, quoted in Geertz 1973: 213).

Conscious perception is, then, a "seeing as" or an "interpreting as" phenomenon. People just don't *see* something, they are not just *conscious of* something, they see it and are conscious of it *as being something*. When they come upon an unfamiliar something they are seldom content to let it remain unfamiliar but immediately ask what that certain something is. "What is missing and what is being asked for are an applicable symbolic model under which to subsume the 'unfamiliar something' and so render it familiar" (1973: 215).

Anthropologists make models, too, and Geertz developed a model for the analysis of sacred symbols, a model of religion as a cultural system. It is with and through this model that we feel we can effectively approach the teaching of environmental ethics. We want to stress, again, that our concern is with the precursor to an explicit treatment of environmental ethics, rather than proposing an environmental ethics curriculum.

Sacred symbols function to synthesize a people's *worldview* and their *ethos*. Sacred symbols bring a metaphysical acceptance of the way things are, that is, the way they are thought to be (a worldview), together with a moral, aesthetic, or evaluative element (an ethos). The first, the worldview, is a sense of the really real, the concepts of nature, of self, of society, that provide the most comprehensive ideas of the general order of existence within which a people find themselves. The second, the ethos, is an underlying attitude toward life, a comprehensive moral and aesthetic attitude, a recommended style of life. The worldview is an accepted *model of* reality; the ethos, a *model for* living in that reality. The juxtaposition of the two gives to the recommended style of life what it needs most if it is to be coercive: the appearance of objectivity, an air of naturalness and simple factuality. Proper conduct is supported "by picturing a world in which such conduct is only common sense" (Geertz 1973: 129). Sacred symbols formulate a basic congruence between a particular style of life and a specific (if, most often, implicit) metaphysic and, in so doing, sustain each with the borrowed authority of the other (Geertz 1973: 90).

All sacred symbol systems assert that it is good for people to live realistically; they differ in the vision of reality that they construct. Those individuals that fail to go along with the moral-aesthetic norms formulated by the symbols, who follow an incongruent style of life (particularly in those societies where such formulations go uncriticized), are regarded not so much as evil but as stupid, insensitive, unlearned, or mad. For those who are committed to them—and, as anthropologist Edward T. Hall noted, we become very committed to them—"men have fought and died in the name of different models of nature" (1977: 14)—sacred symbols mediate genuine knowledge, knowledge of the essential conditions in terms of which life must, of necessity, be lived.

3. *The Dominant Modern Worldview and the Ethos that it Undergirds*

For many students, understanding that human thought is essentially metaphorical is illuminating; something they have never considered. Geertz's model of sacred symbols, of religion as a cultural system, permits a direct unpacking, a thick-description, of the worldview contained in traditional business courses and a reinterpretation of economic theory as an embodiment of the ethos that the worldview supports. To grasp the idea that there is a worldview lurking beneath, the ethos, and that this worldview is often implicitly held and unthinkingly accepted, is important in preparing the ground for whatever environmental ethics curriculum is to be taught.

This idea also lies behind our view that whenever we teach anything, we *already* teach an environmental ethic, a set of beliefs, attitudes, values and standards regarding the environment. It is difficult to recognize this ethic/ethos for what it is because it is unintentionally taught and not formally part of the curriculum (sometimes because instructors are not, themselves, aware of it). Consequently the unconscious teaching of this traditional environmental ethic/ethos is successful and has profound effects. For this reason, students should become consciously aware of their own ethos and of the worldview that underlies it. Geertz's model for the analysis of sacred symbols paves the way.

4. *The Dominant Modern Ethos: the Rules of the Game*

Most MBA students are taught that economics is a science. But economics can be recast as a cultural system and as a symbolic representation of the dominant modern ethos where humans and the rest of nature are seen as distinct, and the earth is seen as a resource and a sink for human wastes (Benton 1982, 1986, 1990).

It is not customary, at least not until recently (see Wight 2002), to ask why a moral philosopher such as Adam Smith was so concerned with increasing "the wealth of nations." After all, he did not place a high value on affluence, and in fact regarded the pursuit of riches as meretricious and its influence corrupting (Rotwein 1973, Wight 1999). So how is it that he was able to concern himself with its annual increase?

In part it was in deference to a matter of distribution: "No society," Smith stated, "can surely be flourishing or happy, of which the far greater part of the members are poor and miserable." While Smith was espousing the material well-being of the common people, luxury occupied most of the attention during the seventeenth and eighteenth centuries. Most men of luxury gained their fortunes by trading, transporting, or by lending. In *The Quintessence of Capitalism: A Study on the History and Psychology of the Modern Businessman* (1915: 34-35), Warner Sombart notes that a fifteenth century architect, musician, and courtier, Battista Alberti, listed wholesale trade, the seeking of treasure trove, the ingratiating oneself with a rich man to become his heir, usury, and the rental of pastures, horses, and the like as the best ways of getting rich. Sombart further cites an unnamed seventeenth century commentator as adding royal service, soldiering, and alchemy to the list.

If the medieval world was, as many have pointed out, a zero-sum game (and as implied in Locke's passage, above), how could Adam Smith advocate increasing the material well-being of the common folk without taking it from the rich? The answer lies in the lists provided by Sombart. Noticeably absent is "manufacturing." What Adam Smith was searching for, and what he bequeathed us, was an institutional order that would eliminate zero-sum games.

Although concentrating human effort on manufacturing, on producing more and more, might be a grand delusion if thought to enhance individual happiness (according to Smith), it would at least contribute to the social welfare. It would do this by contributing to the material well-being of the common people, relieving social tensions (at least those attributed to the inadequate provision for human wants) and contributing to a civil society.

This, of course, is the stance taken by Francis Bacon. The inspiration for true learning was, for Bacon, "not the pleasure of study and the excitement of discovery, but the needs of mankind" (Prior

1964: 47)—although not entirely with the welfare of the common man (Merchant 1983: 177, Mumford 1970).

Bacon's notion of a *species ambition* urged an enlargement of the power and dominion of the human race over the universe of things.[5] As a species ambition it was pure because it was not achieved at the expense of other persons or states. (The assumption was, of course, that nature has no interests, an assumption that is, itself, worthy of additional "thick description.") But by what rules, by what institution, should this be made effective? Social living requires some acceptance of and compliance with fixed, if generalized, rules of conduct. And these rules of conduct must be formulated in such a way that everybody understands them, accepts them, and acts accordingly. In order to grasp the real meaning and significance of economic laws, we must think of them as a specific set of rules appropriate for a specific mode of production and distribution found in a particular society.

The Law of Supply and Demand, rather than the symbolic expression of natural laws or natural processes, or even as the representation of statistical regularity,[6] is our most fundamental expression of a generalized guide for living. The Law of Supply and Demand is a social code. It should be formulated in terms somewhat like the following: "If commercial exchange is to be an effective instrument for want satisfaction, sellers should raise prices when buyers increase their demand," and so on, for its various propositions (Lowe 1942: 439-440). In this way the Law of Supply and Demand provides the beacon from which human action (in a market economy) takes its bearing. Only if people, in fact, act in accordance with the Law of Supply and Demand will the price system function to bring about the social world imagined by economists. The Law of Supply and Demand is a primary "rule of the game," perhaps *the* rule, of the Dominant Modern Ethos.[7]

5. *Ecology, an Emerging Worldview and Aldo Leopold*

At this point the door has been opened for a discussion of ecology as a science. Since so many environmentalists appeal to ecology, students should be familiar with at least some of the models that have guided ecological research. A brief discussion of ecology, especially the history of ecology,[8] leads to a direct consideration of Aldo Leopold and his essay, "The Land Ethic." The essay employs many of the concepts discussed in any historical overview of ecology (the community model and the energy flow model, for example); but because Leopold was an ecologist, and appealed to ecology to explain and justify his conclusions, it will have appeal to MBA students who already accept the intellectual hierarchy in which science and scientists occupy an elevated position.

As has been pointed out by Callicott (1987), and certainly by others, Leopold's ethics derive from the Scottish Enlightenment that extended from David Hume to and through Charles Darwin. This tradition placed moral sentiments at the center of ethics; significantly, Adam Smith, author of the *Theory of Moral Sentiments*, contributed to this tradition. Showing how Adam Smith, the "father" of economics and author of *The Wealth of Nations* is also the author of the *Theory of Moral Sentiments*, and in direct line of descent to Aldo Leopold can serve important rhetorical purposes in an environmental ethics class. It may also provide another way to "close the circle" between economics and ecology.[9]

Finally, Leopold's approach to ethics ties in with the general orientation of this paper: that we do not need ethical theories, rules, and principles to decide what is right, but detailed description of the relevant circumstances, including how it is we traditionally view things, in order to act ethically. As Des Jardins points out (2001: 198), "Leopold's ethics is focused less on rules that guide action and more on moral dispositions or virtues."

Any discussion of the science of ecology should make clear that all philosophers do not agree on the lessons to be drawn from ecology. Nor do they agree from which ecological model these lessons should be drawn. However, ecology might suggest new ways for approaching not only the management of environmental issues but the epistemological, metaphysical, and ontological questions that some argue underlie them (Devall and Sessions 1985). That is, we must recognize that many problems are traced to these kinds of deep philosophical questions and ecology may provide different models for thinking about them, models for treating the causes of environmental problems and not just the symptoms (Morowitz 1972, Everndon 1978, Callicott 1986, and Orr 2003).

Conclusion

To conclude, we offer the personal example that demonstrates a main theme of this paper, while introducing a further thought on the nature of environmental ethics education in general.

One of us regularly teaches an MBA course called *Business and the Environment*. It is billed as an environmental management class and students consider topics like ISO 14001, the Natural Step, full-cost pricing, and life-cycle analysis. Students always seem to consider the class an ethics class. This past summer, an undergraduate class was taught to a group of American students. All but one was a business major. The class, labeled *Global Marketing: Environmental Dimensions*, was taught in Rome, Italy.

The first week introduced students to environmental issues by reading J. Donald Hughes' *Pan's Travail: the Environmental Problems of the Ancient Greeks and Romans* (1994). Given the setting, this was chosen because it was an historian's account of the life and times of the ancient Romans—with an environmental focus. The second week they read and discussed an introduction to Karl-Henrik Robèrt's science based systems framework, *The Natural Step* (Nattrass and Altomare 1999). This is a managerial approach intended to help businesses understand and move toward sustainability.

On the last day of class the students were debriefed. Among the several questions asked of them was the following: "How many of you think this course was an ethics course?" All students in the class raised their hand. A course that has no ethics content in the traditional sense was, nevertheless, perceived by the students taking it to be an ethics class.[10] What we find particularly interesting here is that the books did not raise ethical issues in anything that would resemble what we believe would be the traditional way of raising them. The students saw the ethical issues on their own. This personal example makes clear that when the environment is considered in a course, it is unmistakable that an unconscious environmental ethic is being challenged—in this case the unconscious environmental ethic that has been part of all the students' other business courses.

This example also illustrates how teaching environmental ethics can be incorporated into almost any course in such a way that it challenges students to temporarily bracket the current modern worldview and ethos. Because the course dealt implicitly with environmental ethics, students were able to see connections and to think critically in ways that may never have been suggested before. This situation, first, allows students to "play" with the material and arrive at conclusions themselves. Second, it opens the door for students to pursue ethical concerns in ways relevant to themselves. These are what we consider to be the goals of education: students are guided and offered the freedom to think as well as inspired to take those thoughts in new directions.

Environmental ethics should be taught consciously because an environmental ethic is already being taught implicitly. But a conscious effort at teaching environmental ethics, if it is to be anything more than an exercise in repeating back that which has been learned, must be done in a way that encourages "a self-conscious stepping back" but without providing new rules for analysis and decision making. Students should be given the opportunity to wonder—and wander. The teaching of environmental ethics, therefore, is a prime vehicle of learner-centered teaching and values education.

Notes

1. Our dictionary defines *ethos* as "the disposition, character, or fundamental values peculiar to a specific person, people, culture, or movement."

2. Specifically, we draw on "The Impact of the Concept of Culture on the Concept of Man," "The Growth of Culture and the Evolution of Mind," "Religion As a Cultural System," and on "Ethos, World View, and the Analysis of Sacred Symbols," all in *The Interpretation of Cultures* (1973). Our general approach to the problem, is, we feel, akin to that of Iris Murdoch (*The Sovereignty of Good*, 1970), Stanley Hauerwas (*Vision and Virtue*, 1981) and Peter Levine (*Living Without Philosophy*, 1998), although none index *environment* or *ecology* in their books.

3. We do not know if, in fact, this is the origins of the expression "it was a steal," but when this exercise is complete, students can be asked to reflect on and consider from where this expression might have come.

4. E.B. Tylor first formulated the concept of culture in anthropology. On the first page of his book, *Primitive Culture* (1871), he defined culture as "that complex whole which includes knowledge, belief, art, law, morals, customs, and any other capabilities and habits acquired by man as a member of society." Culture was everything that man thinks and does that is transmitted extra-genetically.

5. There is an interesting parallel between Bacon's position and that of William James in the latter's essay, "The Moral Equivalent of War" (James 1970, originally 1910).

6. Economist Donald McCloskey has noted that empirical support, even for the most basic and fundamental of economic principles, the Law of Demand, is not too persuasive (1985: 57-62).

7. "We should not be surprised or disappointed," Alasdair MacIntyre wrote, "that the generalizations and maxims of the best social science share certain characteristics of their predecessors—the proverbs of folk societies, the generalizations of jurists, the maxims of Machiavelli (1984: 105)."

8. See, for example, Worster 1985 and Golley 1993.

9. We state at the outset and repeat throughout that we are not concerned with any particular environmental ethics curriculum. We do not hesitate to point out where the approach we adopt leads and how that integrates into what the students already bring (or should bring) with them to class.

10. After asking how many thought it was an ethics class, they were then asked what it was about the class that made it an ethics class. A variety of responses were received. Four student responses follow:

> "I thought the course in Rome could be considered an ethics course because each issue we addressed related to the morality of the situation . . . I think your class made us realize that environmental issues are moral issues."
>
> "The course was an ethics course because it made us think twice and gave us a choice. [W]e became aware of issues and choices that we may not have seen in the past, but we should realize because they will affect us in the future."
>
> In the context of a very anthropocentric response, a third student said, and later wrote out for me, this response: "Due to this class, I have come to understand [murder] in a stronger light. Everyday, we as people of this earth, are doing little things that are destroying our home . . . It was an ethical class because it led us to a crossroads where we have to make a decision to either continue killing or improve this world."
>
> "I thought that our class was an ethics class because it took into consideration the actions of humans on our environment and whether or not those actions were appropriate, morally. We looked at both the "inappropriate" actions as well as what is being done currently to correct our negative impact on our home."

REFERENCES

Benton, Raymond Jr. 1982. "Economics as a Cultural System", *Journal of Economic Issues* 16 (June): 461-469.

———. 1986. "Economics and the Loss of Meaning", *Review of Social Economy* 44 (December): 251-267.

———. 1990. "A Hermeneutic Approach to Economics: If Economics Is Not A Science, and If It Is Not Merely Mathematics, then What Is It?" in Warren J. Samuels (ed.) *Economics as Discourse*. New York: Kluwer Academic Publishing.

Callicott, J. Baird. 1986. "Metaphysical Implications of Ecology", *Environmental Ethics* 9 (Winter): 300-315.

———. 1987. "The Conceptual Foundations of the Land Ethic", in J. Baird Callicott (ed.) *Companion to A Sand County Almanac: Interpretive and Critical Essays*. Madison, Wisconsin: University of Wisconsin Press.

Des Jardins, Joseph R. 2001. *Environmental Ethics: An Introduction to Environmental Philosophy*. 3rd edn. Wadsworth.

Devall, Bill and George Sessions. 1985. *Deep Ecology*. Salt Lake City: Gibbs Smith, Publisher/Peregrine Smith Books.

Everndon, Neil. 1978. "Beyond Ecology", *North American Review* 263: 16-20.

Galanter E. and M. Gerstenhaber. 1956. "On Thought: the Extrinsic Theory", *Psychological Review* 63: 218-227.

Geertz, Clifford. 1973. *The Interpretation of Culture*. New York: Basic Books.

Golley, Frank. 1993. *A History of the Ecosystem Concept in Ecology*. New Haven, Conn.: Yale University Press.

Hall, Edward T. 1977. *Beyond Culture*. Garden City, New York: Anchor Press/ Doubleday.

Hargrove, Eugene C. 1980. "Anglo-American Land Use Attitudes," *Environmental Ethics* (2): 121-148.

Hauerwas, Stanley. 1981. *Vision and Virtue: Essays in Christian Ethical Reflection.* Notre Dame, Indiana: University of Notre Dame Press.

Hughes, J. Donald. 1994. *Pan's Travail: Environmental Problems of the Ancient Greeks and Romans.* Baltimore: The Johns Hopkins University Press.

James, William. 1970 [1910]. "The Moral Equivalent of War," in Richard A. Wasserstrom (ed.) *War and Morality.* Belmont, California: Wadsworth Publishing.

Leopold, Aldo. 1987 [1949]. "The Land Ethic," in *A Sand County Almanac, and sketches here and there.* New York: Oxford University Press.

Levine, Peter. 1998. *Living Without Philosophy: On Narrative, Rhetoric, and Morality.* Albany, NY: State University of New York Press.

Lowe, Adolf. 1942. "A Reconsideration of the Law of Supply and Demand," *Social Research* 9 (4): 431-457.

MacIntyre, Alasdair. 1984. *After Virtue.* 2nd edn. Notre Dame, Indiana: University of Notre Dame Press.

Merchant, Carolyn. 1983. *The Death of Nature: Women, Ecology and the Scientific Revolution.* New York: Harper & Row.

Morowitz, Harold. 1972. "Biology as a Cosmological Science," *Main Currents in Modern Thought* 28.

Mumford, Lewis. 1970. *The Pentagon of Power: the Myth of the Machine, Volume II.* New York: Harcourt Brace Jovanovich.

Murdoch, Iris. 1970. *The Sovereignty of Good.* London: Routledge & Kegan Paul.

Nattrass, Brian and Mary Altomare. 1999. *The Natural Step for Business: Wealth, Ecology and the Evolutionary Corporation.* Gabriola Island, British Columbia, Canada: New Society Publishers.

Orr, Matthew. 2003. "Environmental Decline and the Rise of Religion", *Zygon: Journal of Religion and Science* 38: pp. 895-910.

Prior, E. Moody. 1964. "Bacon's Man of Science," in Leonard M. Marsak (ed.) *The Rise of Science in Relation to Society.* New York: Macmillan.

Rotwein, Eugene. 1973. "The Ideology of Wealth and the Liberal Heritage: A Neglected View", *Social Research* 40 (Summer): 267-292.

Sombart, Warner. 1967 [1915]. *The Quintessence of Capitalism: A Study on the History and Psychology of the Modern Businessman.* New York: H. Fertig.

Smith, Adam. 1937 [1776]. *An Inquiry into the Nature and Causes of the Wealth of Nations.* New York: Modern Library.

Spiegel, Henry William. 1971. *The Growth of Economic Thought.* Englewood Cliffs, NJ: Prentice-Hall Publishers, Inc.

Tawney, R.H. 1954 [1926]. *Religion and the Rise of Capitalism.* New York: New American Library/Mentor Books.

Wight, Jonathan B. 1999. "Will the Real Adam Smith Please Stand Up: Teaching Social Economics in the Principles Course", in Edward J. O'Boyle (ed.), *Teaching the Social Economics Way of Thinking*, Mellen Studies in Economics, Vol. 4, Lewiston, NY: The Edwin Mellen Press: 117-139.

——. 2002. "The Rise of Adam Smith: Articles and Citations, 1970-1997", *History of Political Economy* 34 (1): 55-82.

Worster, Donald. 1985. *Nature's Economy.* Cambridge, England: Cambridge University Press.

A PRAGMATIC, CO-OPERATIVE APPROACH TO TEACHING ENVIRONMENTAL ETHICS[1]

Dr. Daniel F. Shapiro and Dr. David Takacs

Abstract
Our pragmatic, cooperative approach to teaching environmental ethics at California State University Monterey Bay nurtures students' moral development in both their public and private realms by putting into practice three principles. First, to propose what "we ought to do," students must first think deeply about what "*I* ought to do." Second, adequately justifying what "I ought to do" and what "we ought to do" requires that students acknowledge, understand, and respect differing perspectives. Third, a course that does not advocate for a particular environmental ethic enhances rather than inhibits students' moral development. This paper describes how—and why—we have designed our course in accordance to these three principles.

Keywords: environmental ethics, pragmatism, ethical pluralism, ethical relativism, pedagogy, environmental education

Introduction

"It's easy to ignore what you think you should be doing by simply not thinking about it; when you make yourself take a look at your ethics to this extent, it doesn't allow any room for avoiding a tricky topic. This course was important for my professional development as it taught me new things and reiterated older issues that I feel I should spend the rest of my professional and personal life working on."

"Throughout this course I learned a lot about myself. I had never taken the time before to think about how my actions affect the environment. Through writing [my] environmental ethic, I learned about how I would like to be."

Anonymous student comments from course evaluations for "Environmental Ethics and Environmental Policy" at California State University, Monterey Bay.

In his essay, "What is Education For?" David Orr claims that the "goal of education is not mastery of subject matter but mastery of one's person" (Orr 1994: 13). It is in this spirit that we have developed our course "Environmental Ethics and Environmental Policy" at California State University Monterey Bay. As the above statements by our students suggest, our course nurtures students' moral development in both their personal and professional lives. In developing our course,

Clare Palmer (Ed.), *Teaching Environmental Ethics*, 93-116.

we make a major assumption: that helping students make informed, reflective normative choices with their own lives while they also learn how to be ethical, effective members of their communities is the great work of higher education (e.g. see Colby *et al.* 2003); through our teaching, we hope to contribute to that great work.

Our constructivist, student-centered and student-driven formulation of environmental ethics follows a pragmatic approach to ethical inquiry (for discussions of pragmatism in environmental ethics, see Light and Katz 1996; Minteer and Manning 1999; McDonald 2004). In his analysis of Deweyan pragmatism, Fesmire (2003) could be describing our pedagogy when he writes "pragmatic ethics urges that moral reflection must begin where all genuine inquiry begins: *in medias res*, with the tangles of lived experience. [John] Dewey in particular argues that moral deliberation is not disembodied cerebration deciding which action is derivable from ultimate principles, but is a form of engaged inquiry touched off by an uncertain situation" (p. 28). As we will describe in this paper, our course uses constructivist pedagogy to actively engage with students' personal and professional decision-making.

Furthermore, our university's distinctive vision and our students' distinctive experiences have influenced the development of our pragmatic approach to teaching environmental ethics. California State University, Monterey Bay's (CSUMB) vision statement describes the university's explicitly applied approach to education, stating that the university will "value and cultivate creative and productive talents of students, faculty, and staff, and seek ways to contribute to the economy of the state, the wellbeing of our communities, and the quality of life and development of its students, faculty, and service areas." The vision statement goes on to state that, "Education programs at CSUMB will emphasize those topics most central to the local area's economy and ecology, and California's long-term needs." Additionally, we teach environmental ethics not within a context of a philosophy department (in fact, our university has no traditional philosophy department), but instead within the context of an environmental science program. In addition to environmental science majors, our course attracts students from majors across the campus.

A full theoretical justification for our approach to teaching environmental ethics falls beyond the scope and purpose of this paper. Rather, for those teachers of environmental ethics who share our assumptions about what education is for, and who would adapt a constructivist pedagogy, we hope to provide concrete approaches, concepts, and tools to be used in teaching. We hope that those teachers who do not share these assumptions and thus reject our approach to teaching environmental ethics gain a deeper understanding of their own approach to teaching environmental ethics that they can make clearer and more transparent to their students.

As a framework for presenting our course on environmental ethics, we describe three distinctive principles of our approach to teaching environmental ethics. First, to propose what "*we* ought to do," students must first think deeply about what "*I* ought to do." Second, adequately justifying what "I ought to do" and what "we ought to do" requires that students acknowledge, understand, and respect differing perspectives. Third, a course that does not advocate for a particular environmental ethic enhances rather than inhibits students' moral development. In the following sections, we describe how we put these three principles into practice so that students may live richer lives that sustain human and ecological communities.

Connecting "little-p" to "Big-P" Normative Claims

We believe that to propose what "*we* ought to do" students must first think deeply about what "*I* ought to do." We distinguish "Big-P"—what "*we* ought to do"—from "little-p"—what "*I* ought to do"—policy decisions. Big-P decisions are normative claims about how members of society ought to act: we ought not take more than "x" kilograms of rockfish per year; we ought to make more fuel-efficient cars; we ought not under any circumstances alter endangered species' habitat. In the real world, we usually make Big-P normative claims using a political process involving diverse groups of people with diverse perspectives. Big-P normative claims are typically written into law and enforced with negative consequences for individuals or groups who do not heed these normative prescriptions. In contrast, individuals make little-p decisions about how they ought to live their lives: I ought to walk to work; I ought not eat meat; I ought to use only public transportation; I ought to purchase only organic produce.

Many courses on environmental ethics focus primarily or exclusively on Big-P normative questions. Our course, in contrast, places a major emphasis on little-p normative questions before moving to Big-P questions. We believe focusing on little-p questions is an important end by itself. As we stated at the beginning of this paper, because we believe education is about helping students become ethical, reflective members of the civic lives of their chosen communities, we want our course to be more than a disinterested examination of environmental ethics and theory. Rather, we want to help students to think deeply about how their daily decisions affect human and ecological communities around them, to examine the ethical implications of these decisions, to articulate and justify a set of personal normative claims, and then to translate those claims into action as they live more ethical lives.

We also believe that examining little-p questions better prepares students to understand and evaluate Big-P questions. We have found that when discussion of environmental ethics is initiated in the context of a controversial policy question, many students do not feel directly connected to the issue. A handful of students may be deeply engaged because of prior experience or knowledge of the topic, but the majority of students—while often eager and willing to listen and learn—rarely reach the level of engagement needed for substantive discussion of embedded ethical issues. For example, one can examine the proposals and various arguments for and against removing dams on the Snake River or the arguments for and against listing a particular species of California rockfish as endangered. But even with the most effective classroom presentation of background information, knowledge is always limited, decision-makers are typically obscure, and the people who will be most affected by the decision are strangers. Often students have not seen the species or environments in question. As result, the majority of students tend to only superficially engage in readings, discussions and assignments.

In contrast, if we start with the ethical justification for vegetarianism or driving a car when public transportation is available, the situation changes. Students do not think about distant decisions others must make; they think about decisions they make every single day of their own lives. When students discuss the ethical justifications for and against purchasing organic food, ethical thinking doesn't end when they leave the classroom. Instead, ethical thinking begins to happen at every meal (much to the dismay of many students).

As they examine, and struggle to justify, their daily decisions, our students experience ethical theories as valuable tools that can help them live better, more examined lives. In these circumstances, students begin to closely examine, criticise and apply various ethical theories in remarkable depth. For example, a student asked to apply Paul Taylor's ethics of respect for nature (Taylor 1981) to the question of whether or not we should produce more fuel-efficient cars may do a fine job of summarizing Taylor's arguments, naming some major challenges to those arguments, and then using these ideas to justify a position. But we see more engagement, depth and sophistication of thought when we ask students more personal questions, such as how Paul Taylor's ethics of respect for nature informs their current struggle about whether or not to eat shrimp cocktail. In the latter case, we do not have to tell students the major challenges to Taylor's ethical theory; they discover them on their own and thus gain a deeper understanding not only of Taylor's ethic, but their own environmental ethic as well. Students who have applied theories of environmental ethics to their own lives tend to be better prepared and able to apply environmental ethics to real-world policy questions.

For these reasons, then, the first part of our course carefully walks students through the process of articulating and justifying their personal environment ethic: a description and justification of their personal moral beliefs about how they ought and ought not act towards the environment (see *Appendix I*). Students develop their environmental ethic in three stages. In the first stage, students—who have not yet been exposed to ethical theory and environmental philosophy—name and define in detail the general normative claims that guide their actions towards the environment. For example, a student may claim that she ought not waste natural resources. She would then go on to define what she means by "natural resources" and then provide examples of specific actions she feels are consistent with this claim, specific actions that are not consistent with this claim, as well as specific actions that she perceives as ethically ambiguous (i.e. it is not clear whether or not they are consistent with the general normative claim). In other words, we first ask students to describe only *what* they believe they ought and ought not do, but not *why* they ought and ought not do these things.

In the second stage, students justify their normative claims. During this part of the course students study various theories of environmental ethics and begin to relate them to their normative claims. For example, in justifying her environmental ethic, a student who believes she ought not eat meat might discuss how her personal justification for not eating meat relates to Peter Singer's arguments for not eating meat. During this second stage we ask students to think deeply about their personal normative claims. While doing this, students often begin questioning and sometimes even no longer believing the normative claims they set out during the first stage. When this happens, students go back and revise what they previously wrote during the first stage of developing their environmental ethic.

In the third and final stage, students choose a personal ethical dilemma from their own lives. This might be a decision they have made in the past, a decision with which they are currently struggling, or a decision they will need to make some time in the future. We ask students to describe their dilemma, explain why it is a dilemma, and list possible solutions to the dilemma. Students then use their knowledge of theories of environmental ethics to evaluate the various options available to them, and if they have come to a decision, to justify that decision. If they have not come to a decision, they must name the reasons why they have not yet been able to reach a decision and explain what will help them determine the most ethical action to take.

For example, in the second stage of her essay, Aimee Kerr, one of our students, defines herself as an anthropocentric non-consequentialist who acts in accordance with God's principles. She also explains that while she believes only humans have moral standing, she also believes non-human life has intrinsic value and that it is her duty to act in ways that promote sound stewardship of "God's creations." For Aimee, this duty compels her to purchase only organic food. Aimee then goes on to explain her ethical dilemma:

> My ethical dilemma occurs when I am purchasing the food [for my church]. In the position that I am given I am representing my church and therefore must make decisions that reflect the wishes of this church body; it is their money that I am spending. Good stewardship of the money is an issue that often conflicts with my own environmental ethic, which is to buy strictly [more expensive] organic food.

In the end, she presents a compromise:

> I have bought as much organic produce at the Farmer's Market as possible for the meals because I receive an added on discount for being a fellow vendor, therefore I am also saving the church money. And I have bought organic produce at the supermarkets when the price difference has not been very great. For the items where there is a marked price difference I bought the least expensive [conventionally grown] item.

But she also decides that she should do more: "Perhaps through educating my pastors about what I know of the agricultural practices and what I have read and interpreted God to be asking of us I may be given a greater allowance [as well as] influence their personal shopping choices."

In illustrating her environmental ethic in the context of a personal ethical dilemma, Aimee uses many theoretical frameworks for ethical analysis including consequentialism, divine command theory, value theory, holism, anthropocentrism, and deontology, among others. While she clearly uses a pragmatic, pluralistic approach to ethical problem-solving, we do have other students who attempt to formulate more monistic environmental ethics in a search for unifying principles they can use to guide their personal actions. Either approach is fine with us. What have found, as in Aimee's case, is that regardless of the approach individual students take to justifying their environmental ethic, the process leads students to more carefully examine their individual behaviors as they relate to the environment, which in turn leads them to act in ways that most of us would agree promote environmental health and sustainability.

Completing these three stages takes up the first nine weeks of this fifteen-week course. During the final six weeks students select a specific environmental (Big-P) policy issue, research that issue, and complete an ethical analysis of alternative policy options (see *Appendix II*). We ask students to attempt an objective analysis of the various policy options before advocating for a particular policy recommendation. That is to say, we ask them to name the various normative prescriptions various stakeholders might offer, and we ask them to explain why each stakeholder might consider their prescription to be an ethically acceptable choice. Having done all this in depth for little-p decisions they face in their own lives, students are now much better prepared to engage in ethical analyses of Big-P policy questions. In an anonymous course evaluation, one student captures our philosophy nicely: "I think it is beneficial to study yourself and find out what really makes you tick. After all, if you don't know yourself, who can you know?"

Making connections between environmental ethics in the little-p realm and the Big-P realm raises many interesting meta-questions for discussion. To what extent are the actions of individuals similar to and different from the actions of corporations or governments? Can the actions of corporations be reduced to the actions of individuals?

Can one determine the moral beliefs of a government or corporation, and if so, how? What are the similarities and differences between Big-P and little-p normative claims? Can ethical theories be applied to government or corporate behavior (for example, does it make sense to analyze a corporation's virtues)? Questions such as these promote rich discussion at the point the class transitions from the little-p realm to the Big-P realm.

Respectful Listening and Cooperative Argumentation

This brings us to our second principle: justifying what "I ought to do" *and* what "we ought to do" requires that students acknowledge, understand, and respect differing perspectives. Here we rely heavily on the work of Josina Makau and Debian Marty (2001) who describe their cooperative approach to argumentation in their book, *Cooperative Argumentation: A Model for Deliberative Communities.* This form of argumentation—which Makau and Marty (2001) contrast to traditional, competitive argumentation and debate—proposes that we "view those who disagree with us as resources rather than as rivals" (2001: 88) and that demonstrating an understanding of differing viewpoints "demonstrates respect for other members of the deliberative community and helps sustain cooperative relationships" (2001: 258). By "respect," we do not mean students should agree with all their classmates, nor do we mean students should condone or otherwise validate values and value hierarchies that differ from their own. Rather, by respect, we mean students should listen to and try to understand on a deep level perspectives and arguments that differ from their own.

Starting from a position of respect for differing viewpoints opens up students to better understand and more deeply examine those differing viewpoints. This, in turn, helps students better understand their own viewpoints by helping students discover—and question—deeply held assumptions about the world. For example, a student, Alicia Vieira, analyzed a proposal to require fishers in the Northwestern Atlantic to attach electronic pingers to reduce porpoise by-catch in gillnets; in a personal reflection about her analysis, she offers: "I had an undeniable urge to protect the harbor porpoises. I did not consume myself too much with the worries of fishers, as they have been the ones degrading the oceanic environment for years with their fishing gear. As I dove into the literature more carefully,

I found that fishers were not these horrible monsters I had once thought they were. Many of them are for saving the marine mammals."

In class, we help students strengthen their sometimes weak listening skills. We emphasize at the beginning of the class that their success depends on their ability to relate their own ethic to the ethics held by their classmates. Respectful listening can have several possible good outcomes: 1) students deepen their justification for the choices they make; 2) students come to respect other ethical choices, even if they do not make those choices; 3) students are so impressed that they actually switch their practices. An open mind, and ethical flexibility are key to this approach. Only I have lived my life and only you have lived yours. It is possible that your experiences will lead me to alter my approach to solving my ethical dilemma. This requires a difficult—and often liberating—shift for some students: "listening to understand" as opposed to "listening to win." As students learn how to listen to understand, their inner voice shifts from "I think I can refute that point" to "I want to know more about why this person thinks that way." When students do not listen to understand, class discussions can digress into raucous debates among a few opinionated students. In contrast, when all students strive to understand each other, class discussions engage all students in curiosity-driven searches for differing opinions so that each of us understands the world more fully.

We help students adopt this attitude through various means. Early in the semester students engage in structured small-group, active listening exercises that teach them how to listen to learn as opposed to listen to win (see *Appendix III*). Then students identify classmates who can offer them differing perspectives. In one exercise students write one or more normative claims of their environmental ethic on a piece of paper and post that paper on the wall. Students then circulate around the room and write their names on those pieces of paper containing normative claims that differ from their own. When done, each student has a list of classmates who hold different perspectives. Students then discuss their normative claims with those classmates who can offer different viewpoints. In their formal essays, students relate their normative claims and justifications for those claims to differing claims made by one or more of their classmates. We assess students on their ability to present these differing viewpoints in a respectful, thorough, and substantive manner as well as on their ability to explain how understanding those differing viewpoints affected their own positions. Students appreciate this approach. One student wrote in an anonymous course evaluation, "On the last day [we were] asked . . . which student(s) influenced [us] the most. I loved this because the students in the class really influenced how I thought about my own ethics and eventually my final policy piece. Having a chance to listen to other students' views and feedback just helps so much."

Students motivated by curiosity to understand those who think differently promote rich classroom discussions that can't help but include students' religious/spiritual worldviews. Christians, Buddhists, atheists and agnostics alike can share personal connections between deeply held values and how they believe they ought and ought not treat the environment. One student wrote in an anonymous class evaluation, "After the last class I went out with [another student in the class] who happens to be very religious and I am not at all. We had a really pleasant talk about our differences and beliefs and in the end it made me realize a part of me that I had set aside when my grandfather died." Creating opportunities for bringing religious and spiritual beliefs into the classroom serves two purposes. When religious and spiritual beliefs are admissible in a classroom, it legitimizes those beliefs. This is important because religion often does play a strong role in students' lives, depending on students' previous commitments. Yet students have been trained at secular universities not to discuss how their religious beliefs influence their ethics and actions. Furthermore, this pedagogy allows students with no traditional religious/spiritual worldviews to formulate frameworks for making normative decisions, an endeavor which has traditionally been the role of religion.

We believe having students focus on personal behavior is a justifiable end in itself, but we also believe that the better a student understands her own and others' frameworks for ethical decision making the better she will be able to function in the policy realm with divergent view points. If Susan can understand why she does things differently than Marcia does, the better she will understand why the Sierra Club wants to immediately ban the use of methyl bromide while various agricultural advocacy groups want to continue to use this highly effective but toxic fungicide. This, in turn, avoids the black and white, "both sides," adversarial policy making and instead fosters the more cooperative and respectful dialogue necessary for the resolution of environmental problems. This approach to cooperative environmental problem solving is emerging in various public policy forums (e.g. see Masor 1996; Wondolleck and Yaffee 2000), and our course helps prepare students to contribute to dialogue, not diatribe on environmental problems. Even in cases where irreconcilable differences emerge, the ability to clearly and respectfully name those irreconcilable differences can help foster meaningful discussion, progress and change.

In helping students respect diverse viewpoints, we do not mean to imply that students ought to respect and give equal consideration to positions based on poor, fallacious, or invalid reasoning. In developing their positions, we expect students to be highly critical not only of their own reasoning but their classmates' reasoning as well. We help students distinguish differences among empirical claims, value claims and policy claims (Makau and Marty 2001; Takacs, Shapiro, and Head, in review), make clear and logical connections among those claims, and evaluate the strength of those connections— both for their own positions and positions articulated by others.

Respectful listening, however, raises a particularly troublesome issue: how does one engage in cooperative argumentation and respectful listening with others who hold positions we deem clearly wrong or even evil? Should one have to listen respectfully to a racist's rationale for discrimination or a hunter's desire to kill the last member of a species? We admit to struggling with this issue on nearly a daily basis and regret that we do not have an answer. Nevertheless, we continue to use this pedagogy for three reasons. First, we believe that the benefits of a pedagogy that actively engages a greater number of students outweigh the costs of potentially having to listen to offensive positions. In understanding why others hold different opinions—whether or not we see those views as bad or even evil—we come to understand ourselves and our arguments on a deeper, more fundamental level.

Second, we believe that the ability to listen respectfully to others— even those who espouse views we may find offensive—is an important skill, even if one plans to enter a more adversarial policy realm. Again, we agree with Makua and Marty (2001) who claim that, "the most comprehensive arguments are those that acknowledge dissenting viewpoints and engage the reasoning behind the disagreement" (2001: 258). Our experience of teaching respectful listening has been that it helps students become more critical of their own reasoning and the reasoning of others precisely because students are actively engaged in class discussions, readings and writing. When placed in a more adversarial, real-world policy environment, we believe our students can better articulate their own positions as well as better evaluate other positions. Anecdotal feedback we have received from our graduates confirms this. But, we strongly agree with an anonymous reviewer of this paper that if one adopts the pedagogy we describe here, one ought to discuss with students the differences they will likely experience between the cooperative methods of discourse they use in our classrooms and the more adversarial methods of discourse that currently dominate real-world policy arenas. A more cooperative real-world policy process is a worthy long-term goal, and we believe that in providing our students with the skills to engage in a more cooperative policy process, we can begin to move towards that goal.

Finally, having worked with hundreds of students, we find that our approach more often than not leads students to beliefs (and, we assume, actions) that are more beneficial to the planet and its human and nonhuman inhabitants. That is to say, they tend not to choose beliefs or actions that a reader of this journal might find objectionable or repulsive. Instead, by not imposing our beliefs or professing the superiority of one type of ethic over another, students engage in deep and respectful inquiry and discussion, and nearly always students end up finding their ways to ethics of great environmental sophistication, depth, and sensitivity.

Benefits of Respectful, Non-advocacy Driven Discussion

This brings us to our third principle: a course that does not advocate for a particular environmental ethic may enhance rather than inhibit students' moral development. In our course, we facilitate respectful listening and discussion that have as their goal not a search for the right argument but instead a search for better understanding of diverse viewpoints (note that this does not preclude a search for sound arguments). In promoting respectful listening and discussion, however, we are not promoting ethical relativism. Our course explicitly assumes that there are better and worse, more ethical and less ethical ways of being and acting. We make this assumption explicit to students early in the semester when we discuss ethical relativism and its negative implications for collaborative ethical inquiry. But we also believe that minimizing or eliminating classroom advocacy for specific ethical positions promotes critical thinking and discussions— particularly among students who have had little or no experience with moral reasoning. Advocacy for a particular environmental ethic can occur in two forms: instructors advocating—either explicitly or implicitly—for their personal environmental ethic and students advocating for their personal environmental ethic. Each of these forms of advocacy raises a different set of issues.

As teachers of ethics, we believe our role is to help students discover and clearly articulate what they believe and why they believe it; we do not believe we ought to tell them what they should believe or why they should believe it. Why not advocate for a particular environmental ethic? Due to the power difference between student and teacher, we believe that advocating for a particular environmental ethic shuts down transformational class discussions that foster the moral development of *all* students. Once students see that the professor has an agenda, different types of students react in different ways, all of which tend to shut down the open sharing and development of ideas. Students with no agenda of their own (or those who believe thinking like their teacher will get them a better grade) simply go along with what the professor tells them without being challenged to form their own views. Students with agendas that agree with the professor quietly nod in agreement. Quiet students who disagree with the professor protest silently in class and sometimes not so silently outside of class. Outspoken students who disagree with the professor, depending on the classroom environment, either engage in frequent public—albeit friendly, but sometimes not—debates with the professor, or are silenced. Such classrooms tend to be dominated by the professor and one or a few outspoken students and tend not to foster the thoughtful, ethical reflection in which we want *all* our students to engage.

We also believe expecting students to advocate for their own environment ethic inhibits open discussion. To promote effective learning and personal moral development we tell students that the classroom is a place not for advocacy, but for peer-aided self-examination and exploration. Removing student advocacy from class discussions serves three purposes. First, it frees students from the fear of possible "attacks" while exploring normative claims with which others might disagree. Removing this fear particularly helps thoughtful students in the early stages of defining their environmental ethic because it creates the space for them to comfortably struggle with still-developing opinions during class discussions. Second, it creates space for discussion input from students who do not want to be seen as preaching what is and is not ethical. Third, it pushes students who tend to focus only on "you ought" statements to be more self-reflective and think more about their own actions. For those students who feel compelled to advocate or otherwise influence the behavior of others, we offer this question for discussion towards the end of the semester: does your personal environmental ethic compel you to influence the behavior of others? This excellent mid-semester question leads to rich discussions among students who have the confidence that comes from having collectively and cooperatively engaged in the challenging work of defining their personal environmental ethic.

To better understand our pedagogical approach here, it is helpful now to distinguish ethical means from ethical ends. We think of ethical means as the arguments one uses to justify particular ethical ends. For example, one might use Tom Regan's (1985) arguments for animal rights as an ethical means for justifying vegetarianism, an ethical end. In and out of the classroom, we are pluralists with respect to ethical means: we believe that there are many morally equivalent pathways to "better" ethical ends (for discussions of pluralism in environmental ethics, see Stone 1987, 1988; Callicot 1990; Norton 1991; Wenz 1993). We believe that multiple pathways exist to ethical behavior, and those pathways may grow from each student's "positionality" or unique life experiences and identities (Takacs 2003). For example, a student may decide she ought not eat meat because she does not want to inflict pain upon sentient beings; because God made humans stewards, not dominators of living creatures; or because she believes eating cattle is ecologically inefficient.

Outside the classroom we are not relativists with respect to ethical ends: we believe that actions and beliefs that promote environmental health and sustainability are better than ones that do not. During classroom discussions, however, we and our students operate as functional relativists, at least during the period when students are developing their personal environmental ethic: we treat all means and all ends as morally equivalent, *for the sake of discussion*. In other words, we temporarily adopt relativism for the purpose of creating the space and classroom atmosphere students need to name and justify their moral beliefs. We also share with students that we are doing this as well as explain why we are doing this.

But what if students hold ethical positions that do not assume—either explicitly or implicitly—that it is better to promote environmental health and sustainability? Commonly students enroll in our course whom we might characterize as having an environmentally unfriendly ethic. These are students who, for example, see all non-human life and entities solely as material for unquestioned human consumption. Still, we believe such students deserve to have their views heard without being attacked or judged. While some might find such behavior on our part unethical (e.g. see Bowers 1995) we disagree for two reasons. First, we believe that effective learning occurs in a classroom that nurtures respectful listening, genuine dialogue, and respect for diverse viewpoints. When we allow such views to emerge, we actively create the kind of open classroom essential for effective and productive dialogue and learning among *all* students. Second, we believe that allowing such views to emerge leads to more ethical behavior, or at least does not lead to less ethical behavior. Shutting down or otherwise discrediting an environmentally unfriendly ethic serves only to alienate students holding those views, possibly entrenching them further in their attitudes and behaviors. In contrast, we have found that when these students engage in mutually respectful dialogue, they are more open to consider environmentally friendly views and are more likely to desire environmentally respectful ends for their own lives. Even if this doesn't happen, creating space for environmentally unfriendly views in the classroom exposes environmentally friendly students to perspectives that differ from their own, requiring that they search for a deeper understanding of why they believe what they believe as well as develop the skills needed to dialogue more productively outside the classroom with others who think differently.

Paradoxically, promoting functionally relativistic discussion in which all present listen respectfully to all views in the classroom eliminates the typical negative influences relativism has on ethical discussion. Teachers of ethics often lament that a majority of their students claim to be ethical relativists, reluctant to take and explore positions on what they believe is or is not ethical behavior; this view tends to prevail early in the semester in our classrooms, as well. Such students may end discussion and inquiry by simply stating, "who am I to say what is and is not ethical?" or, "I don't want to impose my values on anyone else." But if students have the freedom to share and get feedback on their own internal dialogue about what they consider is and is not ethical for themselves and *only* themselves, discussion flourishes. At the end of this process students will often admit that they do believe some behaviors are morally superior to others, *for other people*. That is to say, in many cases students new to ethical discourse are not really ethical relativists. Rather, they just have not gone through the challenging process of defining their personal environmental ethic and they have not yet gained the ability and confidence to engage in substantive, *respectful* conversations about what others ought and ought not to do.

Respectful listening and discussion also helps students better evaluate Big-P policy questions. All Big-P policy discussions are about what "we ought to do." Once students have respectfully discussed with their peers what "I ought to do," they are much less likely to describe Big-P policy issues in black and white terms. Even if they hold strong opinions about a particular policy outcome, they are much more likely to keep the open mind needed to fully understand differing perspectives. For example, Amy Vigallon, a first-year student in one of our courses, wrote a policy report on Australia's regulation of kangaroo hunting which legalizes the shooting of female kangaroos and their babies, or "joeys." This student began her research appalled that such actions were sanctioned by law and believed that the relevant laws should be repealed. In her cover letter to the paper she wrote "I had so much bias before I started this paper that it could fill a whole room!!!" But as she prepared her thoughtful and respectful presentation of the arguments for allowing hunters to shoot female kangaroos and joeys, she began to see the complexities of the debate. In the end she wrote, "I think of myself as an environmentalist and animal rights activist and usually agree with that side of an issue. But with the issue of whether the kangaroo industry should continue, I found myself on the other side of the picket line. I believe that [the industry] should still continue, although I disagree with how they handle the joeys." Had she not done the earlier work on relating her own environmental ethic to the environmental ethics of those who thought differently, we doubt she would have presented the nuanced argument she did. Our experience has been that teaching respectful listening and discussion does not make students relativists or immoral. On the contrary, our experience has been that teaching respectful listening and discussion makes students careful, considerate thinkers capable of ethical decision-making and behavior.

Here we want to highlight a distinction between classroom advocacy and real-world advocacy. We hope our students become effective real world advocates for what they believe in. Our desire to reduce or eliminate advocacy in the classroom should not imply a desire to reduce or eliminate real-world advocacy. On the contrary, we believe reducing or eliminating advocacy in the classroom creates the space students need to develop a depth of understanding of their own views and the views held by others needed to become effective, engaged, real-world advocates for ethical behavior and policy. In other words, we believe that suspending advocacy in the classroom allows students to develop the critical thinking skill and confidence to be effectives advocates in the real world.

Our approach raises two very important questions. First, when guiding any discussion, can a teacher of environmental ethics create a course that does not begin with the instructor's preferred ethical approach? Our answer to this question is no. Our personal values and ethics influence everything about our course: how we structure class discussions, choose readings, respond to students, design assignment, etc. But we try to minimize those influences as much as humanly possible. For instance, we try to find readings that present different viewpoints. We try to question all viewpoints equally and identify fundamental assumptions and values that define and differentiate different viewpoints. In class discussions and through feedback on written work, we make a conscious and explicit effort to challenge those students with views similar to our own to the same degree that we challenge those students with views divergent from our own. It is not always easy, and sometimes we fail, but as we become more practiced in this pedagogy, we do get better at it.

This raises the second question: when an ethics course does not begin with the instructor's preferred ethical approach, does this create distinctive challenges? For students who have not been exposed to this pedagogy, there are significant challenges, particularly at the beginning of the semester. Commonly students feel frustrated and adrift in moral uncertainty when left to determine for themselves what is most ethical, particularly students enrolled in their first course in moral reasoning. Generally students are much more comfortable when they only need to understand what and how the teacher thinks, or what and how a particular philosopher thinks. For us, this creates tension between creating space for student to explore different perspectives and avoiding situations where students become so frustrated that they disengage from the course. We use several strategies to keep students engaged. In the first week of class—followed by constant reminders throughout the semester—we carefully explain to students what we mean by respectful listening and discussion and why we believe it promotes student learning. Additionally, we try to ground students by helping them understand what and how various scholars of environmental ethics think. Finally, we try to structure assignments and discussions so that students do not have to deal with too much at one time and can develop their perspectives one small step at a time. In the end, students typically feel a great sense of satisfaction, confidence, and power having developed their own moral perspectives.

Once our students have developed their own environmental ethics and presented and justified their environmental ethics to the class, we present our own environmental ethic to our students. By this time, students have gained the skills and confidence to examine and question our environmental ethics without automatically assuming ours are superior or that they must mimic them. The depth and sophistication of their questioning and genuine interest in what we believe and why we believe it always impresses us. Furthermore, the extent to which our students' ethics have influenced our own environmental ethics always surprises us. This is an exciting moment because it becomes clear to our students and to us that, to a certain extent, we are peers.

Conclusion

In allowing students to struggle through formulating a personal environmental ethic, we have found that they end up more committed to living by that ethic than they would if we promoted a particular environmental ethical means and/or ends, or if we treated ethical inquiry as a theoretical project that may or may not have anything to do with their personal lives and daily decisions. Furthermore, we believe—because we have seen it repeatedly—that such an approach contributes towards ethics and subsequent behaviors that in fact, and in general, promote environmental health and sustainability. Nevertheless, we do not intend to negate the importance of courses in environmental ethics that focus more substantially or exclusively on the disinterested study of environmental philosophy. Our course exemplifies the importance of such work. The theories and ideas generated by environmental philosophers form a crucial component of our course: our students read, study, and discuss seminal works by environmental philosophers and then our students apply these ideas to their own lives and public policy. We must continue to provide the kind of education students need to make future contributions to the many important philosophical debates that preoccupy modern academicians and policy makers. But, very few, if any of the students we encounter at CSUMB will make formal contributions to the philosophical debates that preoccupy modern academicians or policy makers. The majority of our students at CSUMB will use "environmental ethics" to make decisions in their personal and professional lives. Consequently, we have chosen to offer a course that provides students with a sound, pragmatic, personal understanding of environmental ethics that will guide their daily decision making at home, in their communities, and in their work places. The future well-being of our environment and human communities requires citizens who can analyze and understand their own ethical choices with respect to the environment around them.

NOTE

1. Acknowledgement: We would like to acknowledge all our students, who have taught us more than we have taught them, and we appreciate the continuous support of Hester Parker and Larry Carbone. We also thank two anonymous reviewers for their thoughtful comments on this paper.

REFERENCES

Bowers, C.A. 1995. *Educating for an Ecologically Sustainable Culture: Rethinking Moral Education, Creativity, Intelligence, and Other Modern Orthodoxies*. Albany, NY: State University of New York Press.

Callicott, J.B. 1990. "The Case Against Moral Pluralism". *Environmental Ethics* 12:99-112.

Colby, C., Ehrlich, T., Beaumont, E. and J. Stephens. 2003. *Educating Citizens: Preparing America's Undergraduates for Lives of Moral and Civic Responsibility*. San Francisco: Jossey-Bass.

Fesmire, S. 2003. *John Dewey & Moral Imagination: Pragmatism in Ethics*. Bloomington & Indianapolis: Indiana University Press.

Hinman, L.M. 1998. *Ethics: A Pluralistic Approach to Moral Theory*. Fort Worth: Harcourt Brace & Co.

Light, A. and E. Katz (eds). 1996. *Environmental Pragmatism*. London: Routledge.

Makau, J. and D. Marty. 2001. *Cooperative Argumentation: A Model for Deliberative Community*. Long Grove, IL: Waveland Press.

Maser, C. 1996. *Resolving Environmental Conflict: Towards Sustainable Community Development*. Florida: St. Lucie Press.

McDonald, H.P. 2004. *John Dewey and Environmental Philosophy*. Albany, NY: State University of New York Press.

Minteer, B.A. and R.E. Manning. 1999. "Pragmatism in Environmental Ethics: Democracy, Pluralism, and the Management of Nature". *Environmental Ethics* 21(2):191-207.

Norton, B. 1991. *Toward Unity Among Environmentalists*. New York: Oxford.

Orr, D. 1994. *Earth in Mind: On Education, Environment, and the Human Prospect*. Washington D.C.: Island Press.

Regan, T. 1985. "The Case for Animal Rights", in P. Singer (ed.) *In Defense of Animals*, Oxford: Basil Blackwell, Inc.

Stone, C. 1987. *Earth and Other Ethics: The Case for Moral Pluralism*. New York: Harper and Row.

———. 1988. "Moral Pluralism and the Course of Environmental Ethics". *Environmental Ethics* 10:139-154.

Takacs, D. 2003. "Positionality & Social Justice in the Classroom". *Social Justice* 29(4):168-181.

Takacs, D., Shapiro, D.F., and W. Head. In review. "From *Is* to *Should*: Helping Students Translate Conservation Biology into Conservation Policy". *Conservation Biology*.

Taylor, P. 1981. "The Ethics of Respect for Nature". *Environmental Ethics* 3:197-218.

Wenz, P. 1993. "Minimal, Moderate, and Extreme Pluralism". *Environmental Ethics* 15:61-74.

Wondolleck, J.M. and S.L. Yaffee. 2000. *Making Collaboration Work: Lessons from Innovation in Natural Resource Management*. Washington, D.C.: Island Press.

Appendix I: Student guidelines for preparing a personal environmental ethic

We will assess your essay based on your ability to 1) describe your personal environmental ethic in the context of the ideas and theories we have been studying, 2) demonstrate respectful listening skills by relating your personal ethic to different environmental ethics followed by one or more of the authors we have read *and* one or more of your classmates, and 3) present your ethic in a clear, focused and organized manner. Below we list what we expect to see in your essay:

Part I: What You Believe

1. Your essay provides your personal definition of an environmental ethic: including what you mean by "environmental."
2. Your essay presents the primary normative claim(s) and/or question(s) your personal EE makes and/or asks, with detailed examples to illustrate each of them.

Part II: Why You Believe What You Believe

1. Your essay justifies all the normative claims you discuss in your essay.
2. Your essay explains what has moral standing, and whether for you there is a hierarchy of moral standing.
3. Your essay explains whether what you consider to have moral standing has intrinsic value, instrumental value, or some combination.
4. Your essay explains whether your environmental ethic is primarily or completely anthropocentric, biocentric, or ecocentric.
5. Your essay explains whether your environmental ethic is utilitarian.
6. Your essay explains whether your environmental ethic is consequentialist or anti-consequentialist.
7. Your essay explains to whom or what you grant "rights," and on what basis.
8. You relate your own environmental ethic to Deep Ecology, Social Ecology and/or Ecofeminism.
9. Your essay explains how your environmental ethic can be used to resolve conflicts or make priorities when our actions may cause harm.

Part III: Personal Ethical Dilemma

1. Your essay describes a complex environmental issue that you have encountered or do encounter in your personal, educational, social or professional life.

2. Your essay provides a statement of the ethical issues embedded in this problem: you explain what choices confront(ed) you and why it was difficult to decide between alternative courses of action.

3. Your essay explains how the choices you made (or make, or might make) reflect the tenets of your own environmental ethic that you have been developing).

4. For this personal ethical dilemma, you compare your framework for ethical decision making to a different framework for ethical decision making that would result in a different decision. You can do this in one of three ways: 1) If this is a past decision that you would make differently today, explain how your framework for decision making has changed, and why. 2) If there is someone in the class who would make a different decision than you, explain how your framework for ethical decision making differs from her or his, and why. Note that do to this well, you will have a substantive conversation with that person; it will not be sufficient to guess what they would do and why. 3) If you believe one of the authors we have read this semester would make a different decision than you, explain how your framework for ethical decision making differs from his or hers, and why.

*Appendix II: Student Guidelines for preparing an ethical
analysis of a policy issue*

Part I: Objective Policy Analysis

1. *Introduction*: Identify the problem/issue you are analyzing, identify the major stakeholder groups affected by this problem/issue (stakeholders can include non-human elements like otters, rockfish, invasive plant species, native plants, rivers, kelp, although there may be human organization that claim to speak for those groups); identify the primary normative question you analysis addresses; and identify the major alternative normative claims for how we should respond to the problem (note: "we should do nothing while we gather more information" is a policy recommendation).

2. *Decision-making Process*: Identify who will decide what will happen in the future, explain how that decision will be made, and identify differences in each stakeholder's ability influence the decision-making process.

3. *Policy Alternatives*: Identify at least two policy alternatives, and for each: name the stakeholders who support that policy recommendation, the most important empirical claims used to support that policy recommendation, and the most important value claims made by stakeholders supporting that policy recommendation (these value claims may either be explicitly stated in the article or inferred by you).

4. *Ethical Analysis*: Identify major differences in a) frameworks for ethical decisions making (e.g. utilitarian vs. rights-based ethic), b) value claims, and/or c) fundamental assumptions that you believe lead the stakeholder groups to support different policy recommendations.

Part II: Policy Recommendation

1. Identify which of the policy recommendations identified in Part I you support.

2. Explain why you support this policy recommendation. Your explanation should be based solely on your previous analysis; you should not be introducing new information here. (Note: If your policy recommendation is that we should do nothing until we obtain additional empirical information, you will need to justify the decision to do nothing and explain how the additional empirical information you propose we collect will help you determine the best course of action.)

3. Explain why you rejected the alternative policy recommendations.

Part III: Personal Reflection

1. Identify your personal interest in this problem/issue.

2. Identify your position on this issue before you started your research and explain why you held that position.

3. Explain the extent to which you feel your personal values and biases affected your ability to present all perspectives in a fair and non-judgmental manner.

4. Explain how consideration of alternative perspectives affected your position.

5. Explain how your personal environmental ethic influenced your final decision.

Appendix III: Example of a respectful listening exercise
(derived from Makau and Marty 2001)

In small groups of 4-5 students:

1. Each person writes her or his answer to the following question: Do you believe it is ethical for you to eat meat? Why or why not?

2. Each person takes 2.5 minutes to explain his or her answer to this question to the rest of the group. Nobody else can talk during these 2.5 minutes.

3. Each listener writes down at least one question for the speaker for later discussion.

4. The next person takes 2.5 minutes to explain his or her answer to this question to the rest of the group.

5. When everybody is done, everybody asks the first speaker at least one question.

6. After all group members have had a chance to address questions, the group identifies points they all agree on as well as points that distinguish differing perspectives.

7. Small groups share results of exercise with entire class.

A BEING OF VALUE:
EDUCATING FOR ENVIRONMENTAL ADVOCACY

Lisa Newton

Abstract
This paper explores the conceptual links between the intellectual mastery of the content of a course on the ecological and economic aspects of environmental preservation, and the felt commitment to environmental preservation. I discuss the sense in which a practical ethics course is necessarily oriented to the adoption of a normative agenda, in this case to making recognition of environmental value part of the requirements of the course, and present some experience from my own university's seminar on environmental studies.

Keywords: environmental education, environmental value, environmental ethics

> "In the end we will conserve only what we love; we will love only what we understand; and we will understand only what we are taught."
>
> Senegalese ecologist Baba Dioum, 1968. (Norse 2003: 240)

Introduction

The purpose of this paper is to clarify, essentially for myself but possibly also for my colleagues, a curious aspect of my own experience in the teaching of environmental ethics: I get annoyed at students when they make presentations, or give answers on tests, that fall below my standards of environmental consciousness, that is, consciousness of the value of the natural environment. I of course get annoyed at students who do lazy or incompetent work in any of my courses, including that on environmental ethics; and in all my classes I am troubled by students who do not seem to grasp the central concepts (about what Plato is doing in that Cave, for instance). But in environmental ethics I seem to think that students have not grasped the subject matter until they see the natural environment as a being of value, something to be cherished and protected, whether or not they intend to go out there and protect it. It is not that I expect them to adopt one policy or position rather than another with regard to environmental protection, and reward and punish accordingly—a student who makes a cogent case for de-regulation in the environmental

Clare Palmer (Ed.), *Teaching Environmental Ethics*, 117-129.
© *2006 Koninklijke Brill NV. Printed in the Netherlands.*

118 LISA NEWTON

field will get a better grade than a student who makes a sloppy case for saving every tree—but I look for an understanding that is one step beyond the outlines of the subject matter: the stuff they memorize for the test. I expect them to care about the subject, not just about the fascinating arguments adduced, not just about the grade they will receive, but about the natural world itself. Whatever policy conclusions they adopt for the nation, or whichever activist agenda for themselves, I expect them to appreciate the value of the natural heritage.

It is certainly possible to teach about natural objects without any normative fragments adhering to the presentations: the biology department does it all the time. What would environmental ethics look like if the assumptions governing it were entirely neutral as to the value of the natural environment? And what is added to the course if its assumptions have a strong normative content, such that the course cannot be said to be "understood" if the student leaves the class without finding any value whatsoever in the natural world? If we teach environmental ethics under strong normative assumptions, does that mean we are educating for advocacy? Do we teach students that they should have deep-seated convictions about the value of the environment, should adopt a public position favorable to measures designed to protect the natural environment, and show a willingness to act on that position to achieve positive results in environmental protection? Would that be right?

In the first part of what follows I will set up the problem as it troubles me; in the second I will look for guidance from such predecessors as Rachel Carson and Aldo Leopold; in the third part I will talk about the practical implications for our seminar; and in the last part reach some very tentative conclusions.

1. *Is Environmental Ethics Essentially Normative?*

When we teach anything, what do we affirm, or advocate, simply by the act of professing to teach? The answer to that question would certainly include certain habits of mind, or virtues: integrity, we hope; honesty, patience, curiosity; tendencies to seek out information and reflect upon it. So of course we are advocates. After that, what? Certainly we advocate the value of the subject matter at least to this point: that it is worth studying. We stand before the class as professionals who have dedicated their lives to this endeavor, so we

certainly believe there is something worthwhile in what we are doing.
We also would maintain that the requirements of the course are not
imposed simply to implement our natural sadism; if there are facts
to be learned, they are learned for a purpose; they are important.
If there are methods of dealing with the subject matter, they are
learned because we judge that someday our students may need to
know how to deal with this or similar subjects. All of this we teach in
any course, even in those courses that contain, we might insist, nothing of the "practical" or the "vocational."

The nature of this level of advocacy in teaching can best be
summed up in the notion of "respect". Whatever else we teach, we
teach respect for the subject matter—the beauty of language and the
visual arts, the majesty of history, the precision of science, and the
intriguing puzzles of philosophy. Could we say that the subject matter of a Fine Arts course has not been understood by the student
until the student sees the subject matter as "beautiful," or at least
understands why others think it so? Is this a good parallel for the
expectation that a student of the natural environment will see the
natural world as valuable? This advocacy is limited according to
what we may call the rule of "academic forbearance": the authority
of the instructor in the academic setting does not extend to authority
outside, and the respect demanded for the subject in the classroom
does not command anyone to perform or do anything outside the
classroom.

Courses in ethics, of any kind, used to be cited as exceptions to the
rule of academic forbearance. In the nineteenth century, when philosophical ethics was generally referred to as "moral philosophy," the
object of teaching was to show students how they *ought* to live their
lives, with no apologetic waves in the direction of pluralism, objectivity, or professorial humility. In the twentieth, that expectation was
reversed. The ethics professor might be the world expert on the logical connections and implications of non-cognitivism, prescriptivism,
and emotivism, and well-versed on the historical thought of utilitarianism and natural law theory, but when it came to deciding the
right thing to do, academic "opinion" was no better than anyone
else's. The learned doctor, newly humble, became an ordinary man.
The teaching of "ethics," then, became like the teaching of every
other course in analytic philosophy: it was to be respected for its
historical interest and its fascinating puzzles, but not expected to
have any effect on the students' lives beyond the sharpening of their

analytic skills. By the twenty-first century, we have divided the ancient discipline of "ethics" into three parts: (1) "descriptive ethics," (now safely ensconced within the departments of anthropology and sociology), which surveys the actual beliefs, past and present, that cultures have espoused on matters of human life and conduct; (2) "metaethics" (analytic or theoretical ethics), the product of the twentieth century analytic turn in philosophy, which examines the terminology and forms of reasoning appropriate to this academic discipline; and (3) "normative ethics," which intentionally feeds certain normative assumptions about right conduct into the premises, and proceeds to draw out implications. (Only in normative ethics can we reach a conclusion, "this is the right thing to do in this situation," because only in normative ethics do we have normative, or "ought," premises in the reasoning. It is not that these premises are ignored, or beyond question; but that the reasoning takes place in a framework that permits evaluations of conduct.) All the forms of practical and professional ethics that have assumed their places in the college curriculum of the last quarter century—medical ethics, business ethics, ethics for engineers—are branches of normative ethics.

When we teach normative ethics, then, we are "advocates" for right conduct in the field under consideration, because the normative assumptions that ground the subject are not questioned within the subject. In this respect, normative ethics joins the majority of non-philosophical disciplines, such as physics or economics, for which the grounding assumptions, while questionable, are not questioned within the discipline itself. ("Is there really such a thing as scarcity?" is a valid question, but it is not an *economic* question, just as "Is time real?" is not a question in the discipline of physics.) The student is not committed to believing anything new at the end of the class, nor to having different opinions or moral convictions. But if the student accepts the assumptions of the course to begin with, the course should provide him or her with the skills to live a life that more closely conforms to those assumptions. That is all that is claimed. A normative alignment is expected, but not in the sense that it would be *wrong* for the student to claim at the end of the general course in normative ethics that "moral conduct is undesirable." (Or as Plato's character Thrasymachus would put it, "a just life will make you unhappy.") But it would be a bit puzzling. Consider: it would not be illogical for the medical student to claim at the end of the medical school's ethics course that "the welfare of the patient is of no concern to me," but the statement would be misaligned with the assumptions of the course and with the covenant the student assumed when undertaking the study of medicine. (It might also be bad for the student's future to maintain that as a public position.) The student who claims at the end of the physics course that the entire subject is claptrap because the physical world really doesn't exist is not misaligned in the same way, for the discipline of physics does not assume that the material world *exists*—just that certain laws govern its appearances.

Is environmental ethics necessarily normative? On this analysis, certainly not. It is possible to teach the ecology course in the biology department without being an advocate for the preservation of the natural environment. It is also possible to teach environmental ethics as an "Attitudes Cultures Have Adopted Towards Nature" course in the anthropology department—a descriptive ethics of the infinitely various human orientations to the natural world in which we live. It is possible to teach an analytic "Ethics of the Natural Environment," Environmental Metaethics, course in the philosophy department, in which the contested terminology in environmental ethics—stewardship, holism, integrity (of ecosystems), rights (of species, for instance), are dissected and examined. The course might—probably would, in departments familiar to me—conclude that there really is no substance at all to claims that the natural environment is "valuable," or "deserves" our protection. The environmental ethics course that is taught, as is mine, in the "practical ethics" division of the curriculum—which states in its learning objectives that the students will acquire a deeper appreciation of the complexities and value of the natural environment—must be quick to present the assumptions of the course and distinguish it from others.

It should be noted that there would be a good deal of overlap among such courses. Normative environmental ethics cannot accomplish its ends without pointing out the analytic controversies. Action on behalf of compassion, justice, or environmental protection cannot be effective (at least not toward its intended objective) if it is not ecologically informed, or if it is acting on confused metaethics, or confused understandings of the central terms of engagement. Additionally, if only to orient the students, we need to do a quick survey of the actual views of nature that have been held, even if constraints of time limit the survey to the orientations that appear in the political history of our own country. But the distinctiveness of the subject matter makes normative environmental ethics a separate course, with assumptions of value built in (and waiting to be specified), and part of the student's growth in understanding the subject will be an increased appreciation of that value. Demonstrating this appreciation—a protective response to the problems of the natural environment, or at least an understanding of what that response would be—is part of the course objectives. Conduct demonstrating, or failing to demonstrate, that response is therefore as subject to classroom evaluation as any other classroom conduct. That is why I get annoyed when students do not manifest that appreciation in their presentations.

2. *Theorizing the Pedagogy of Environmental Appreciation*

If "appreciation" is on the agenda of learning, the usual pedagogical techniques of teaching philosophy that are the stock in trade of my profession will not be sufficient for the task. We will have to move explicitly to an agenda of cultivating feelings and reactions that are at least in part emotional, and these are tasks with which philosophers rarely deal. For guidance in this enterprise, we turn to two of the most revered pioneers of the field, Rachel Carson and Aldo Leopold.

Rachel Carson's last book, the one on which she was working when she died, was on environmental education, *Help Your Child to Wonder*. (Lear 1997: 280 ff.) Following an article of the same title that had appeared in *Women's Home Companion*, the book was to be an essay, profusely illustrated with pictures of children interacting directly with tide pools, forest creatures, and wild plants, on the irreducible value of exposing children directly to Nature, and allowing them to form their own questions about what they saw. Linda Lear, Carson's biographer, describes what this enterprise meant to Carson (and shows why philosophers tread gently on this turf):

> As in no previous piece of writing, this article reflected Carson's passion to help others to *feel* rather than to know nature. Wonder and awe were, for her, the highest emotions. In her outline she had written almost as a simple credo, "Once you are *aware* of the wonder and beauty of earth, you will want to learn about it." In the published version Carson elaborated on the significance of an emotional response to nature. "Once the emotions have been aroused—a sense of the beautiful, the excitement of the new and the unknown, a feeling of sympathy, pity, admiration or love—then we wish for knowledge about the object of our emotional response. Once found, it has lasting meaning." (Lear 1997: 284, citing Carson 1956)

Adults, she believed, had often lost the capacity to wonder about the new and strange, but even adults, in their attempts to present Nature to a child, could learn to see through the child's eyes and become more aware of the beauties of the natural world.

> A child's world is fresh and new and beautiful, full of wonder and excitement. It is our misfortune that for most of us that clear-eyed vision, that true instinct for what is beautiful and awe-inspiring, is dimmed and even lost before we reach adulthood. If I had influence with the good fairy who is supposed to preside over the christening of all children I should ask that her gift to each child in the world be a sense of wonder so indestructible that it would last through life, as an unfailing antidote against the boredom and disenchantments of later years, the sterile preoccupation with things that are artificial, the alienation from the sources of our strength. (Lear 1997: 46)

The essence of environmental education was not new with that book; all her books (until *Silent Spring*) were designed to bring their readers into the environmental enterprise, immediately accessible for the beginner, and were all about what you can see in the sea, and on her beloved shores of the sea, with lots of pictures. (Carson 1941, Carson 1955). Rachel Carson's life demonstrates at least the temporal priority of perception, experience, and love over intellectual conviction. She was a scientist, but the science served the cause of appreciation and advocacy. "The Wonder book," as she called it, was her last project, and focus of her last enthusiasm: "I want very much to do the Wonder book," she wrote to Dorothy Freeman near the end of her life, "That would be Heaven to achieve." (Lear 1997: 466) She did not finish it; the *Women's Home Companion* article was issued as a short book, *The Sense of Wonder*, after her death. (Lear 1997: 483) It is clear enough: realization of the agenda must be based in experience—sometimes in one signal experience.

The second guide for our course is Aldo Leopold's *A Sand County Almanac*, and the question we ask the students to answer is very simple: What did Leopold *see*, that made him so sure that the natural world was worth preserving? It takes a half hour lecture on the assignment to convince students that we are not interested in how Leopold "saw" the deforestation of the West, the destruction of the natural environment, or the future of the world. We are interested in what he saw with his eyes. When debriefing on the assignment, it is equally important to point out that this is not a question of logic. Leopold's "seeing," after all, had started in the South West, where he worked in the Forest Service as a hunter, a dubious environmental occupation if ever there was one. He was attempting to exterminate the predators that were threatening sheep and decimating the deer population. He describes the experience that changed his mind, following the appearance of a wolf and her cubs in range of his and his partner's rifles:

> In those days we had never heard of passing up a chance to kill a wolf. In a second we were pumping lead into the pack . . . When our rifles were empty, the old wolf was down, and a pup was dragging a leg into impassable slide-rocks.
>   We reached the old wolf in time to watch a fierce green fire dying in her eyes. I realized then, and have known ever since, that there was something new to me in those eyes—something known only to her and to the mountain. I was young then, and full of trigger-itch; I thought that because fewer wolves meant more deer, that no wolves would mean hunters' paradise. But after seeing the green fire die, I sensed that neither the wolf nor the mountain agreed with such a view. (Leopold 1966: 130)

There is not much pure logic in the move from the fierce green fire to the recognition that it was not a good idea to shoot the wolf. At first glance there seems to be more logic in his first idea: wolves are killing the deer, so if there are no wolves, there will be more deer. Over the next part of this autobiographical essay, he moves from that very personal description of a single observation—the fierce green fire, dying in a wolf's eye—to a good naturalist's description of what happens when you cull the predators at the top of the food chain (Leopold 1966: 130-132). In this personal description, Leopold leads the reader along the path of environmental education, and that is the path we want our students to follow. If we see, really see, what is going on, we will see past the simple logic of the Corps of Engineers—any change we induce in the landscape will have one and only one predictable effect—to a much deeper understanding of the complex symbiotic interactions of millions of living things.

3. Applying the Theory in the Seminar

Bringing Carson's agenda and Leopold's insight into the classroom poses a new challenge for the philosophers among us, and we meet it by a type of assignment—"journaling"—that has not traditionally been part of the philosophy curriculum. We begin by teaching the framework of philosophical normative ethics, which supplies the language for all debates about policy and justice. We continue with a survey of orientations that have played a part in the environmental debates. But at this point, if Carson is right and Leopold's experience is valid, we can go no further without including in the curriculum some direct observation, and participation, in the natural world. How do we do this? In the last few years, my colleagues and I supervising our capstone Seminar on the Environment have tried requiring the students to keep a journal—a notebook, if they like, or its electronic equivalent—in which they make daily entries on some natural forms that they have observed. The assignment is simple: 1. Go outdoors. 2. Look. 3. See. 4. Describe what you see. 5. Then begin to try to understand what you see. Start writing at the third step and don't stop.

My experience with this assignment has been mixed. Some students are simply incapable of step 1, and turn in unreflective responses to newspaper articles. That won't suffice. Others are incapable of going beyond 3, and come back with mixed bags of impressions demonstrating only their desire to get through the assignment. Others pick a topic they really enjoy, like automobiles, and manage to make all observations of the great outdoors through the windshield of their SUV, squeezing their analyses into the automotive box in their minds. At the other end of the seminar, some of the students are senior biology majors with minor concentrations in environmental studies, and include complete ecosystem analyses of everything in sight. But the ones I really like, the ones that keep me reading these journals, are the ones that change. Entry number one may boil down to "There's a *skunk* under our porch! Ew!" Entry number two wonders how to get rid of it and reluctantly decides against trying to kill it. By entry number four, we may have a description of the skunk, a realization that no one's going to get sprayed as long as everyone is polite, and a tacit recognition that the world is large enough for skunks and people too. Entry number seven has begun to wonder what the skunk eats and whether it has a family. By entry number twelve, we have an understanding of what the skunk eats (and why it lives under the porch), and a broader understanding of the whole food web that surrounds students, townhouse dormitories of wood construction, skunks, squirrels, feral cats, and termites. (For the last, we tell them to call the Housing Department.)

The students are not encouraged to go to the books (or the Web) to learn more about skunks; that's not the point of the assignment. They studied skunks in second grade in primary school. But since primary school, they have not been outdoors, except to walk to the car or to play sports, neither activity yielding much in the way of opportunity to interact with nature. Our first job is to remind them that there is, indeed, an outdoors, and that if they look at it, they will see and learn.

4. *The Recognition of Community and the Directions of Education*

For Carson and for Leopold, the fundamental insight was not that nature has economic worth that we are just too benighted to see (although they both believed that), nor yet that the creatures and locales with which and within which they spent so many joyful hours should enjoy rights at law (although they may have believed that, too), but that in the natural world they, and all of us by extension, are at home, among our relatives, in the village that nurtured us, in the community where we belong.

Why are we so at home in the natural world? Edward O. Wilson nicely describes the relationship:

> The life-sustaining matrix (for human life) is built of green plants with legions of microorganisms and mostly small, obscure animals—in other words, weeds and bugs. Such organisms support the world with efficiency because they are so diverse, allowing them to divide labor and swarm over every square meter of the earth's surface. *They run the world precisely as we would wish it to be run, because humanity evolved within living communities and our bodily functions are finely adjusted to the idiosyncratic environment already created.* Mother Earth, lately called Gaia, is no more than the commonality of organisms and the physical environment they maintain with each passing moment . . . (Wilson 1992: 345)

Holmes Rolston III also cites the million-year intimacy of co-evolution as the source of the value that nature has for us. In the course of considering, and rejecting, a radical subjectivism as the basis for the value we place on nature, he concludes:

> But the valuing subject in any otherwise valueless world is an insufficient premise for the experienced conclusions of those who respect all life. Conversion to a biological view seems truer to world experience and more logically compelling. Something from a world beyond the human

> mind, beyond human experience, is received into our mind, our expe-
> rience, and the value of that something does not always arise with our
> evaluation of it. Here the order of knowing reverses, and also enhances,
> the order of being. (Rolston 1991: 93)

Again, the reference to "conversion" lies at the heart of the description.

Wilson and Rolston, among the other environmental philosophers
who inherited the mantle of Carson and Leopold, are saying the
same thing: there is a real and valuable community, to which we
belong as part of our birthright, and we can call it nature or Gaia
or Mother Earth or just the world of living things, and when we
really see it, we will feel at home in it and value it, and no more
philosophical justification will be needed for that feeling than would
be needed for feeling at home in our own house. What tore Carson
and Leopold apart was that people would just not look, would just
not engage in the simple seeing. There seemed to be a sort of wall
around people—a sort of transparent cube in which they lived, an
SUV with windows closed—through the windows of which all nature
appeared silent, flat, two-dimensional, just a collection of resources
to be monetized. How can that wall be broken through?

Rachel Carson was convinced that the answer lay in the children.
The passage cited at the beginning of this essay is typical; children
have a fresh, natural approach to the world, while adult perception
is distorted by too much attention to artificial things. Here, I think,
is where environmental education meets its greatest challenge. The
world in which Rachel Carson grew up—like the world for the thousand generations before her—held no instruments systematically dedicated to training the pre-school mind in indelible artificial images.
All but the poorest inner-city children had regular access to the out
of doors, and the sights and sounds to be found there were the most
immediately interesting to their senses. (The alternative was badly
lit silent rooms.) But now all but the oddest children in our affluent
society are bombarded from six months of age and earlier with the
flickering colors of the TV set, and the socially approved characters,
teletubbies and purple dinosaurs, that they soon recognize as part
of their world, their family. It is no wonder the world out of doors,
with its dirt and crawling things, is initially experienced as repulsive.
The television has conditioned the child to passive reception of stim-
uli; no wonder the act of exploration in the natural world seems
distastefully burdensome. The innocent, unformed, child, eager to
interact with the world and curious to find out how it works, is gone,

at least from the technologically advanced portion of this world, along with the fresh and unspoiled outlook he or she was supposed to bring to it.

Deprived of the innocent eyes of the child, where will we get the vision to see the world as alive and valuable, familiar and supportive? We may recall that even Aldo Leopold first became aware of the value of natural processes only after many years of doing what he could to exterminate it (one recalls the vision of St Paul on the road to Damascus.) Holmes Rolston also speaks of "conversion": one needs no conversion if one is simply following out an initial innocent perception of the world. Possibly the quintessential environmental experience, conversion to what Rolston calls the biological perspective, is often a grace of maturity. There can be no doubt that filling the child's world with artificial bright colors and cartoon substitutes for real mice, cats and frogs will make it harder for children to form relationships to and in the natural world. But if Rolston is right, and I think he is, then the ultimate foundational value of the natural world will assert itself if we look for it, no matter what our age.

Where does this leave environmental education? First, with a firm foundation in environmental value: the objective of the education is not to imprint an arbitrary ideology, but to bring the student to a face to face acquaintance and critical understanding of all that has been valuable in the history of the species, and the appeal is immediate. Second, with two major tasks to accomplish: teaching the children and teaching the adults. In children, we have little hope of capturing the freshness of the child, for children are not fresh any more. Instead, we must retrain the children, even those who have been routinely dropped off at "nature" classes to acquire a veneer of environmental consciousness in between television shows. First, the children will have to stop expecting the rapid unforced procession of bright images, and slow down to the pace of the bugs and the worms. Then they will have to be taught to use their eyes, to find objects that do not leap up in bright colors and black outlines with no effort of looking on their part. Third and most importantly, after years of watching cats thrown through stone walls and dogs catapulted over trees (not to mention coyotes falling over cliffs, run down by trucks, and plastered to trains) only to reconstitute themselves unhurt in the next frame, children will have to be taught gentleness with the fragility of the real living things of their world.

There will be a lot of catching up to do, and it may not be the children's favorite thing, because watching television is easier.

For adults, we need to develop a program for reverse engineering. If we cannot slowly enrich the appreciation of the unspoiled child with the fully adult consciousness needed for environmental work, we will have to work backwards, from the learning to the response. Ultimately, Baba Dioum was right: if we cannot love intuitively, we will only love what we have come to understand. The only way we will understand the environment is to study it. If the study begins somewhat unsympathetically, this need be of little concern; in the field of ecology, we have a long history of sending out scientists and receiving back advocates—the better scientists for fully understanding their subject matter, to the point of knowing its value.

REFERENCES

Carson, Rachel. 1941. *Under the Sea Wind: a Naturalist's Picture of Ocean Life.* New York: Oxford University Press.
——. 1951. *The Sea Around Us.* New York: Oxford University Press.
——. 1955. *Edge of the Sea.* Boston: Houghton Mifflin.
——. 1956. "Help Your Child to Wonder," in *Women's Home Companion* 83 (July 1956): 25-27, 46-48.
Lear, Linda. 1997. *Rachel Carson: Witness for Nature.* New York: Henry Holt & Co.
Leopold, Aldo. 1966. *A Sand County Almanac with Other Essays on Conservation from Round River.* New York: Oxford University Press.
Norse, Elliot. 2003. "Marine Environmental Ethics," in Dorinda G. Dallmeyer (ed.) *Values at Sea: Ethics for the Marine Environment.* Atlanta. Excerpted in (eds) Donald VanDeVeer and Christine Pierce *The Environmental Ethics and Policy Book.* 3rd edn. 2003. Wadsworth.
Plato. 1954. "Euthyphro" in Tredennick and Tarrant (eds): *Plato: The Last Days of Socrates.* London: Penguin.
Rolston, Holmes III. 1991. "Environmental Ethics: Values in and Duties to the Natural World," in F. Herbert Bormann and Stephen R. Kellert (eds) *Ecology, Economics, Ethics: The Broken Circle.* New Haven: Yale University Press.
Wilson, Edward O. 1992. *The Diversity of Life.* Cambridge, MA: Harvard University Press.

WALKING THE TALK:
PHILOSOPHY OF CONSERVATION ON
THE ISLE OF RUM

Emily Brady, Alan Holland and Kate Rawles

Abstract
This paper describes our experience of teaching environmental ethics as part of a Philosophy of Conservation field trip to Rum, off the West coast of Scotland. The field trip was formalised into an M.A. Module in 1999. After outlining the educational aims of the module, and how these are implemented in this setting, we indicate some of the key issues in ethics and aesthetics that emerge as we explore two specific conservation sites. We close with a reflection on the value of experiential education in this area, and the importance of combining experiential, emotional and intellectual engagement in any exploration of normative issues.

Keywords: Environmental ethics, environmental aesthetics, environmental education, nature conservation, environmental values, wilderness

Introduction

Rum is an island off the west coast of Scotland. For some years philosophy lecturers from Lancaster University have been visiting the island with a small party of postgraduate students and we have constructed a module on the Philosophy of Conservation around our visit. We tell our students that the text for the module is the island itself. It is not such a large text, being approximately lozenge-shaped and measuring some fourteen kilometres across at its wider points. But since it is rough and rugged terrain, the idea takes some getting used to, and our foot-sore students do on occasion hanker for more conventional texts. It is an excellent site for studying the philosophy of conservation since it challenges almost every pre-conceived idea one might have on the subject. More generally it is an excellent site for doing (the ill-named) "applied philosophy", when this is properly understood not as the application *of* philosophical ideas to particular situations but as an engagement with the challenge posed *to* philosophical ideas by particular situations.

We stay in simple hostel accommodation on the island, sharing all the chores between us, and eating our meals under the baleful

Clare Palmer (Ed.), *Teaching Environmental Ethics*, 130-147.
© 2006 *Koninklijke Brill NV. Printed in the Netherlands.*

gaze of some long dead deer. The fact that this "simple hostel accom-modation" occupies the former servants' quarters of a nineteenth century castle built for the recreation of a wealthy Lancashire mill-owner spices our meal. Already we are divided. The castle, which along with the whole island passed into the ownership of Scottish Natural Heritage (SNH) in 1957, is in a sorry state of repair. Some of us would have it restored. Some of us would happily see it fall into ruin.

In the mornings or evenings we hold semi-structured discussions, huddled for warmth around a log-fire in the old game-keepers' room. For the rest of the day we walk and talk, whatever the weather. The hills reach heights of 800 metres and ring to the names once given them by passing Viking sailors: Barkeval, Askival, Hallival, Ainshval and Trollaval—so named because the Manx shearwaters mewing in their burrows on its slopes at night were mistaken for trolls. Our only concession to comfort is that we time our visit before the arrival of the Scottish midge.

Beginnings

The Rum trip started, as so many things do, with a chance convergence of people. These people happened to share a penchant for wild places. Some had experience of Rum. Others still thought of it as a magical, dark and off-limits place.[1] In conversations snatched between more regular teaching commitments we sketched out what a trip to Rum might usefully include. The idea was, roughly, to use the island—owned and managed entirely as a conservation site by SNH—as a springboard and context for exploring issues in the phi-losophy of conservation. What is conservation trying to achieve? Why and for whose benefit? Whose voices and interests shape current conservation policies and whose should, perhaps, have more of a say? And, in a site such as Rum, should conservation be primarily "nature" oriented, or should it also be concerned with social and cultural heritage? We decided from the start that a contrast would be helpful, and so we included a short visit to Scottish Wildlife Trust's "Falls of Clyde" site at New Lanark on the Scottish main-land—some four or five hours south of the Rum Ferry—on the way. The Falls of Clyde site is a completely different, and much more industrial, setting; and we anticipated that the contrast would throw up a host of issues. The Philosophy Department Field Trip was beginning to take shape.

The trip was at that point optional and not-for-credit, and we ran the whole thing at cost—accommodation, petrol, food, donations for the conservation sites and whisky for the people who gave up their time to speak to us. We kept the price as low as possible. The Philosophy Department joined the Youth Hostel Association, and we negotiated a mini-bus deal with the campus garage.

Those who made the trip invariably caught the sense of magic. Runrig playing on the tape deck, and the way the skies get bigger as you cross the border. A bus full of interesting, keyed up people, conversations ranging through environmental activism to arcane philosophers to sandwiches. And the absolute joy of the last part of the drive, edging round the shores of Loch Lomond, up through Crianlarich, hills crowding the road and then opening out into the huge spaces of Rannoch Moor and the spectacular line-up of volcano-shaped peaks dropping down to Glencoe. On through Fort William and then swinging West until suddenly the ocean is there, and, yes! the unmistakable silhouette of Rum on the far horizon. Then the clutter of Mallaig, fishing boats, seagulls, the excitement of loading our gear onto the ferry and of leaving the land; the sense of a crossing, of passing over to somewhere normally out of reach.

Objectives of the module

The success and popularity of the trip prompted us to formalise it into a one week, optional, intensive MA module. This has meant the introduction of coursework and more formal teaching sessions but, despite worries to the contrary, this has not fundamentally changed the character of the experience. Changes in staff and their particular interests have, however, inevitably had some influence on the course content—just as particular conservation managers influence the way conservation is practised on their sites—with Kate Rawles leaving (after several years of Rum trips) and Emily Brady becoming a key figure, leading the trip with Alan Holland, and introducing a more prominent role for environmental aesthetics.

The immediate aims of the module (as it has developed) are twofold:

1. to establish what the objectives of nature conservation are, or should be, through an examination of the practices, policies and problems of particular conservation organisations and sites;
2. to subject these aims and objectives, and the rationale behind conservation, to critical examination and debate.

In a fairly obvious way, therefore, the module points students towards the idea of an environmental ethic. Whatever nature conservation is, it is clearly intended to uphold or maintain something of value. So in pursuing the question of its rationale, we are inevitably pursuing the question of what value or values nature possesses that merit this degree of attention.

A critic might observe that this could encourage a somewhat narrow view of environmental ethics, since it encourages the idea that nature is only to be found in nature reserves, and that an environmental ethic only has relevance in this context rather than to matters that are nearer to home. But as we shall later explain, one of the surprises awaiting those who first visit the island is to discover how much humans have contributed to shaping its ecology. Thus an environmental ethic that might emerge from Rum would have relevance across a wide range of human-influenced as well as "wilder" ecologies. Moreover, there are clear links between the values that underpin nature conservation and wider environmental issues. These links can be readily drawn out, for example, through considering how climate change might impact on conventional forms of nature conservation, and what this might imply for the effective conservation of "nature", wherever it occurs.

There are three further, over-arching, aims that we believe to be of key importance. The first, (and often most relevant when the course is taken by people with a largely scientific rather than humanities background) is simply to reveal the ways in which conservation practice, fundamentally and inevitably, is underpinned by sets of values and involves making value judgments. These judgments are unavoidable, but are often obscured, for example, by presenting conservation aims in scientific language and as if they could be derived from, say, biology, without the intervention of values at all.

The second aim is to show how an environmental ethic might be constructed, but without assuming that there is only one such way and without assuming that there is any predetermined result. This aim runs counter to some common approaches to environmental ethics. One such approach starts with a tale of environmental woe, and infers that we should "change our values" if we are to make things better. The Rum trip, while it might connect at a number of points with wider tales of woe, largely moves along different routes from practice to values. But it is passionately concerned with values, and part of this includes challenging three (at least) commonly held assumptions about values and what they are like:

- One is the assumption that we can simply "change our values", as if this were a process somewhat akin to changing a suit of clothes. Instead, we believe that, if values change is called for, this in turn will require a lot of hard and sustained critical, emotional and experiential engagement with a range of issues.
- Another assumption is that values precede and determine actions. Whilst the interplay between values and actions is complicated, we believe it is often more accurate to picture values as what we reason towards, rather than what we reason from.
- A third is the tendency to regard values as "subjective"—a matter of opinion and beyond the reach of critical reflection. But in our view, values are pre-eminently a subject for critical examination, debate and reflection, as well as being importantly connected to emotions and experience. We start, then, not from tales of environmental woe coupled with recipes for their solution, but from the practical problems faced on the ground by those charged with conserving nature on our behalf. And, if we reach the tales of woe at any point in our journey, we work hard to take a robust, critical understanding of values into this particular fray with us.

The third over-arching aim is to point up the fact that environmental policy-making, much like our field trip itself, has to be conducted in all weathers. From the sudden storms of political upheaval to the icy blasts of EU regulation, all must somehow be accommodated in the current management plan, alongside the possibly gentler demands of local councils, boards of managers and local residents. Again, this works to debunk any myths about the detached, scientific and "objective" nature of conservation practice. The manager of the Falls of Clyde, for example, has to meet exacting conservation standards, but he also has to fell a swathe of trees that are at risk of interfering with the overhead power lines that run across his site. He makes the most he can of the situation by letting the trees lie where they are felled, choosing to face out the criticism that "they look a mess". The contributions from the site-managers, who can provide graphic descriptions of the pressures, complexities and conflicting interests they have to deal with, are therefore a valued and indeed crucial component of the module.

Implementing the module objectives

The character of Rum and the Falls of Clyde

Both of the sites that we visit are rich with ethical conundrums, which readily shape the module syllabus and influence the way the module objectives are achieved.

In the first place both sites are undertaking restoration projects, involving trees especially. The over-riding objective in each case appears to be a return to "the natural vegetation"; but when pressed, it turns out that both site managers approach the project with mixed feelings. For one thing it involves unsightly fencing; but they are also reluctant to drive out newcomers, whether flora or fauna, who have shown an ability to thrive in their new home.

In the second place, both are hosting rehabilitation schemes involving birds of prey. But they show an interesting contrast. The peregrine falcon came back to the Falls of Clyde of its own volition, but requires round the clock monitoring to ensure its protection. The white-tailed sea eagle required assistance from the Royal Air Force to find its way back to Rum (from Scandinavia), but has since been left to its own devices. So far it has chosen to nest elsewhere but condescends to do some of its hunting around Rum.

In the third place, both sites have a considerable historical and archaeological interest that is not always easy to reconcile with nature conservation objectives. Some important archaeological sites on Rum, for example, have been seriously disturbed by the tree-planting scheme. But so far, much of its history that is still extant to view, such as the lazy-bed agricultural system, the deer traps, the black houses and the summer houses or "shielings", is, and probably should continue to be, protected from the nature conservationists! What the Falls of Clyde provides, in addition to its history, is some insight into how such sites were viewed by earlier generations. It hosts a small hydro-electric power station that reduces the River Clyde at this point to a fraction of its former glory. But long before the power station was

built, visitors were so overcome by the sight of the falls of Corra
Linn in full flow that it was thought desirable to construct, at a key
viewing point, a building within which mirrors were placed so that
the falls could be viewed indirectly as well as directly. The building
remains and there are plans afoot to restore it.

In addition, both sites face the problem of how to accommodate
the human community, though the problem is different in each case.
The Falls of Clyde must live alongside the New Lanark World
Heritage site, and always be aware of the need for public access.
The problem for Rum, on the other hand, is whether and how to
build a human community on the island that might be sustainable
in the long term. There is always the alternative, of course, of simply tip-toeing quietly away.

Finally, both are sites of considerable aesthetic appeal, raising the
issue of the role of aesthetics in an environmental ethic. We shall
return to this issue below.

Testing philosophical concepts

Both the Falls and Rum are experimental sites. On Rum, the deer
have been studied for some decades by a team from Cambridge
University, interested among other things in the effects of different
management regimes. But conditions that make Rum a good laboratory for the study of deer do not necessarily serve the aims of
nature conservation, if these include, for example, the planting of
trees. Hence there is conflict, uneasily solved in this case by erect-
ing a three-metre high deer fence that cordons off a section of the
island and has permitted the planting of over one million trees. The
quieter experiment undertaken by the manager at the Falls of Clyde
involves investigating the effects of different tree management schemes.
Some of this serves a clear educational purpose, as with the reten-
tion of a stand of more recently planted conifers, to demonstrate the
very different ecology that they permit.

But both are excellent sites for a different kind of testing—the
testing of cherished concepts of environmental philosophers such as
biodiversity, ecological integrity, wilderness, wildness, ecosystem health,
nature and sustainability.

Take the example of wilderness. Rum is a relatively wild and
inhospitable place (so far as humans are concerned), and we might
come to it, either expecting to find wilderness, or, if we fail to find

it, resolved to advocate its restoration. Intimate contact with the island can nevertheless dash our expectation, and weaken our resolve. We encounter desolation indeed, but much of it wrought by the early human inhabitants striving to eke a living from its unyielding soil and climate. The island was stripped bare of trees long before the sheep and—currently—the deer had their say. The latter simply prevent regeneration.

So if wilderness is not to be found, perhaps it should be restored? We tramp the path to the old village of Kilmory, annihilated by the clearances of the 1820s. We encounter the ribbed fields, witness to the old lazy-bed system of agriculture, adopted where soil is too thin to dig. Instead seaweed is piled in strips to provide cover for potatoes, and other root vegetables. The foundations of the houses are clear to see, and most poignant of all, the little cemetery, with headstones that tell of hard lives and early deaths. We fall to wondering whether it is not just as important to conserve the (hi)story of the human struggle with the land. On a number of our visits our debates on this topic especially have been greatly enriched by Andy Samuel (currently teaching at the University of Abertay), whose knowledge of the island, especially the social and cultural aspects of the island's history, is second to none. Andy passionately defends the importance of the island's social history and its future human community (Samuel 2000). Is this a position that conflicts with a commitment to wilderness? Or can people be part of wild places? Testing the concept of wilderness, we unearth previously unseen complexities and are drawn deeper into philosophical debate.

Discussing ethics and values on Rum

As already indicated, we believe that drawing attention to the way in which values and value judgments inevitably underpin all conservation practice is central to the module. Raising the question, "what are we conserving, why and for whom?" can be a powerful and effective way of beginning this process, and one that leads naturally into considering the sources of particular sets of values (in, for example, tradition, different scientific communities, political interests, personal interests, and so on) and opening these values out for critical scrutiny, debate and reassessment. How appropriate is their genesis? And, are these the values that, after careful, engaged reflection, we believe conservation policies should be based on? (Holland and Rawles 1993).

In this way, a philosophical approach to conservation can be seen as mirroring philosophical work that, we believe, is extremely useful in the wider environmental agenda. Here too, environmental problems such as climate change or biodiversity loss can be presented in a way that obscures the value issues that inevitably underpin them (as soon as a phenomenon is described as "a problem", value judgments are involved). Values and value judgments also underpin our responses to environmental issues and the way they are prioritised and framed. Drawing attention to these values, and opening them out for critical debate is, arguably, a key component of the kinds of changes that many of us believe will be part of a transition to more sustainable ways of living (Rawles 1998).

On a number of occasions we have encountered conservation organisations and individual practitioners who, while arguably sharing very similar values and objectives, nevertheless have strikingly different styles or attitudes. Sometimes these differences can be discerned within the same practitioner as, for example, when a former warden of Rum told us both that he saw Rum as an "outdoor laboratory" and that he believed that the trees "should be allowed to go where they choose". Clearly, one suggests a much more interventionist and controlling approach than the other. Here too, parallels can be explored between different conservation attitudes and more general ways in which humans understand their relations with the non-human world. Do we see ourselves as part of the environment or immersed in it? Is our attitude towards the environment largely one of co-operation, or management or domination? Does it make any sense to ask these questions about "human attitudes to non-humans", or do they need to be located in specific practices, such as agriculture? And so on. Again, once underlying attitudes have been identified, they can be critically considered and appraised (Rawles 1995).

A range of more specific ethical dilemmas and challenges emerge from these encounters with conservation practices and underlying values and attitudes. One that has not already been mentioned is the tension between an ethical concern for sentient animals as individuals, and a focus on entities and concepts such as habitat, species or biodiversity. By no means all of the young Sea Eagles flown in jets from Norway survived the journey, and the survivors experienced significant levels of stress. Conservation practice often rests on the assumption that compromising the welfare of individual creatures is justified in the interests of goals such as protecting biodiversity through reintroduction. This may or may not be the case. But an exploration of these kinds of issues—in the UK, killing introduced grey squirrels to try to protect native red squirrels would be an another one—sometimes reveals interesting black holes where argument falls without trace into passionately held convictions. And a certain amount of double-thinking when it comes to the impact of the human species on the environment, and what this does or does not justify, might also be detected. A range of other ethical issues that emerge have already been indicated above (Rawles 1997).

Discussing aesthetics on Rum

As an island, Rum is the ideal nature reserve. Its wild, bare mountains, rugged coastal areas, sheltered bays, green valleys, small forest, and various creatures are protected by the convenient boundary of the sea. It would appear that changes to this remote environment occur mainly through the natural forces of growth, decay, weather, erosion, geological change and so on. But, as we have seen, human culture has influenced both Rum's past and its present, and may well have a significant role in shaping its future. The earliest human communities were probably on Rum nine thousand years ago but, more recently, among the desolate moors and sublime mountains we find the ruins of black-houses and the moss and lichen covered shielings. Many of the old forests, which may have covered about forty per cent of the island, have disappeared as the result of human use and deer and sheep grazing. In Kinloch, on the other side of the island, the most blatant reminder of human history is found in the red sandstone castle that has been maintained and preserved for heritage and tourism. Here, also, we find newer houses and even a purpose built community hall and post office to serve the present day inhabitants, conservation workers and their families.

What kinds of aesthetic problems are thrown up by such a place, an environment dominated by its coastline and treeless mountains up to 800 metres high, but punctuated by the remains of human settlements and the living community in Kinloch? In terms of a formal conservation designation, Rum is recognised as having great aesthetic value by Scottish Natural Heritage. Besides being a UNESCO Biosphere Reserve, a Special Protection Area, a Site of Special Scientific Interest and a candidate Special Area of Conservation, Rum is recognised as part of the Small Isles National Scenic Area

(NSA). The forty NSAs in Scotland are defined as areas of special protection that represent the most prized of Scotland's scenery.

But on our field trip, the experience of Rum is only occasionally one of scenery. During our 2003 trip we had fine weather on the day of our departure. From the ferry, the magnificent peaks of the island form a dark outline against the blue green sea and clear sky. On another fine day (there are not very many of these), standing on top of one of these peaks one can take in much of the island's textures, from a creamy, sandy beach to the bushy tops of the forest by the castle, to the dark, distant peaks of the Cuillin range on the neighbouring island of Skye. During our May trips, the reality of our day to day aesthetic experience of Rum is its dramatic weather patterns: low clouds and mist obscuring higher ground, usually windy, changing rapidly from sun to driving rain, maybe to hail and back again to a sunny spell. Besides the sounds of the weather, it is a relatively quiet place, especially inland, away from the sounds of coastal birds, except at night when the huge population of Manx shearwaters return to their burrows, and in the morning when a dawn chorus is heard in the woodlands around Kinloch.

Along these lines, one issue raised with students is the need to move beyond Rum's scenic value to discuss and grasp the aesthetic features of the island as an environment all around us, through all the senses, perhaps also through our imaginative and emotional responses. That is, we attempt to capture the dominant aesthetic character of Rum. The field trip setting is ideal for teaching environmental aesthetics, primarily because our discussion is based on first hand experience of a case study. Not only is it first hand experience of the island environment, but the same environment is experienced by all of us, at our own leisure or at the same time while out together taking a walk across the island or up one of its peaks. Such first hand experience is especially relevant to studying philosophical aesthetics, because many would argue that the aesthetic response is by definition based on first hand experience. The opportunity to discuss a shared experience is invaluable to the process of understanding the relevance of aesthetics to conservation strategy on Rum.

On the third day of our five days on Rum, we have a classroom seminar session on landscape designations and the concept of the aesthetic character of environments. This lecture and discussion gives students knowledge of a range of concepts and strategies used for understanding the aesthetic value of environments, and how that value is protected in conservation policy in the UK. The course material for this session is drawn mainly from Emily Brady's work on environmental aesthetics (see Brady 2003) and supplemented by Frank Sibley's analysis of aesthetic concepts (see Sibley 1959); some students on the trip will have taken a Masters in Values and the Environment module earlier in the year in which they learn about a range of theories of environmental aesthetics, including work by Allen Carlson (2000), Ronald Hepburn (1984), and others.

The session begins with a discussion of the role of aesthetic value in UK environmental conservation. We take a critical look at the various landscape conservation designations used and their tendency to overlook aesthetic qualities beyond the scenic. Using an "integrated aesthetic" approach, we then work toward developing a richer concept of aesthetic value, which takes in multi-sensuous experience, emotion, imagination and knowledge. Students are asked to reflect on and try to identify aesthetic and non-aesthetic qualities of Rum and to feed this into an overall description of its aesthetic character. This classroom knowledge is importantly combined with their actual ambulatory touching, hearing, smelling, tasting, seeing, reflective and emotional responses to different environments of Rum. Based on these experiences, words used by students to describe its character have ranged from: "austere", "sad", "bleak", "lonely", "melancholy", like a "grumpy old man", "rugged" to "humbling", "magnificent", "majestic", "wet", "alive", "mossy", "stimulating", "inspiring", "exhilarating", "magical" and, simply, "bonkers" (see Aslet 2003). Certainly many of us agree that the island could be described as a sublime, austere landscape. These responses are not just impressionistic. Importantly, most are highlighted after spending a few days exploring different parts of the island in different weather conditions, in different moods or energy levels (the latter depending on the day's walking), at different times of day and in light of discussion with others.

Two more specific questions posed to students relate to the relationship between aesthetics and other environmental problems on Rum. One issue concerns an early conservation aim of re-establishing woodlands on Rum. The successes of this, in the woodlands found near Kinloch, arguably add aesthetic value through the increased diversity and richness of aesthetic qualities to be found in the variety of bird activity and birdsong, changing colours, new forms and shapes of trees and leaves, as well as the sheltered atmosphere of the forest.

Students are asked to consider this in light of their first hand experience of the forest and despite their opposition to reforestation—would this alternative add to or detract from the aesthetic value of the Rum environment? And, how should aesthetic values be prioritised in relation to other values of concern to conservationists?

We also ask what role aesthetics plays in the Kinloch castle controversy. Is it an excellent example of Edwardian architecture that ought to be restored or should it be left to natural forces, or in fact removed piece by piece so that the island may be in left in a more natural state (a recent bid for lottery money to restore the castle failed)? Although we stay in the hostel accommodation of the castle and explore some of it in this way, we are also able to reflect on this issue by taking an optional tour of the interior of the castle with all its decadent finery. Some students and staff opt out of the tour, usually those who find the castle jars too strongly with the deeply natural character of Rum.

All in all you cannot really hope for a better learning context than Rum for thinking about issues in environmental aesthetics and also, of course, ethics. Rum has it all: varied environments, the grand to the small in scale, mixed environments with both natural and human history, and current/future problems that stimulate debate about the relationship between aesthetic and other environmental concerns.

Teaching sessions and assessment

Implementing the module's objectives involves a set of talks, seminar sessions and two forms of assessment. A couple of weeks before the trip, we hold a pre-trip meeting to go over logistics and to receive course materials (module handbook and readings, including background reading on Rum, for instance Countryside Commission for Scotland (1978) and the SNH website). Besides walks and talks by nature reserve managers at the Falls of Clyde and Rum, on the first day on Rum there is a seminar session with an introduction to the philosophy of nature conservation. This is followed on the second day by a discussion of conservation problems on Rum. The aesthetic dimension of Rum and related topics in environmental aesthetics are explored on the third day. On the fourth day we discuss Rum as a site for the practice of a "land ethic". The module concludes with a general roundtable discussion, giving everyone a chance to reflect on their experience of the island and the issues and problem raised during the trip. None of these sessions is set in stone, and we try to be flexible in order to allow room for raising new topics that emerge as we explore the island. A week or so after the trip there is a debriefing session back in Lancaster.

A field diary and essay form the basis of assessment for the module. The field diary is designed to prompt students to take notes along the way, serving as a record of their reactions and engagement with the environment. It enables immediate reflection on and interrogation of their experience, and highlights thoughts and questions about the issues raised. We encourage students to be creative with their diaries, for example, using illustrations such as photographs or sketches. The essay topic is chosen by students based upon some of the main topics and problems raised during the course.

Finally, in addition to the arranged learning contexts described above, there is a significant amount of informal learning going on which is vital to the success of the course. As well as the studying time that students have before and during the trip to digest the literature in the course packs and in the castle library, one free day is scheduled for students to spend time reading, exploring the island, catching up with their field diaries, resting, etc. People spend this day in different ways. Often a keen group will take a walk additional to the scheduled walk and talks. Some like to stay at the castle and relax, taking time out from group activity. Others take short walks nearby, or explore the community around the castle, taking a seashore walk or visiting the post office and shop. One student described how much she learned about the day-to-day lives of the families living on the island by just speaking to people in Kinloch village—how long they had been there, what they do for fun, schooling arrangements for the children, and so on.

Other informal settings for discussion include conversation over a well-deserved cup of tea after a long day's walk, conversation over dinner or, perhaps mainly, gathering together for a glass of wine in front of the fire in the old gamekeepers' room. Sometimes staff stay for these evenings in, but this is also a time for students to explore their thoughts without staff around, enabling more freedom in some ways, and in any case, a different, very relaxed setting for discussion.

In organising the course, we find that this free time and more informal learning context complements the more formal sessions by giving important space for reflection. It gives students the time to explore various issues at greater length and in a more leisurely manner. Inevitably, with such a small group spending lots of time together, tensions arise, but over the years, this "down time" has helped to enable everyone to resolve problems or concerns that emerge.

Conclusion: Learning from Rum

The Rum trip has always been popular with students, with some returning several years running, and taking over aspects of the planning and organising. Almost invariably, those taking part have a great time. They get to know each other a little better and they spend time in a magical place that they might well not otherwise ever have gone to. The shared experiences contribute to co-operation and a feeling of being part of something when they return. None of this surprises us at all. What is really striking and perhaps initially a little more unexpected is the way it works from a more academic, intellectual perspective. The "walk and talk" conversations on the island are typically fruitful—engaged, open-minded and critical in the most constructive sense. And we always come back genuinely fired up by the debates and issues. Our experience has been that the discussions continue long after the trip is over, with students arranging their own follow-up discussion groups and the experience informing high quality essays.

Why does the course work so well? Obviously the island of Rum is not only magical but also relevant. It raises a huge range of issues pertinent to any kind of critical engaged exploration of conservation and wider environmental issues and problems.

Beyond this, a key component to the course's success has to be its experiential nature. In one sense, this is not especially remarkable. Experiential approaches to teaching and to learning are widely held to be effective across a range of subject areas; appealing to different learning styles, aiding the understanding and application of new knowledge, and so on (Boud, Cohen and Walker 1993). In this sense, the philosophy of conservation is just one subject amongst many that can benefit if there is an experiential dimension to the way it is taught (Dewey 1938; Warren, Sakofs and Hunt 1995).

But there are particular reasons for thinking that a values-focussed exploration of conservation issues, and of environmental issues more generally, can be greatly enhanced by an experiential approach.

First, we would argue that a critical approach to values and ethics in any context requires emotional as well as intellectual engagement, and that this emotional engagement is often best achieved through relevant experience. Moreover, experience contributes to robust critical reflection about normative issues in other ways, for example, by militating against any tendency towards over-abstract or over-general conclusions, and by keeping the real, concrete, messy details of particular issues in focus. This of course challenges a key assumption still dominant in much Western thinking about ethics and values— that the process of forming and reflecting on ethics and values is a largely rational one. Hence it can be carried out perfectly effectively in, for example, a lecture theatre. On Rum, we certainly engage intellectually and rationally with a range of values-related issues. But we engage emotionally and experientially as well, and we think all these dimensions are important.

Second, we think that in the case of taking a critical approach to values and ethics in the specific context of conservation and environmental issues, there are reasons for believing that spending time in certain kinds of outdoor environments is important and useful. Hence an experiential approach is suggested almost by default.

What are these reasons? In brief, there is the obvious point that critical reflection on conservation is bound to be enriched in a range of ways by spending time on conservation sites, talking with managers, observing the impacts of different practices and commitments and so on. In feedback from the most recent trip a student wrote that "no amount of time in a class room could develop a 'feel' for conservation in the way observation on Rum/Falls of Clyde did".[2] Observation in this context clearly involves being outdoors.

Beyond this, certain kinds of outdoor experience, perhaps especially those of relatively wild places, can give us humans a chance to see ourselves in a different light and can act as a catalyst for rethinking assumptions and values that previously may not even have been visible. Of course we all know, intellectually, that humans are one species amongst many, and that we depend on the ecological systems of which we are a part. But there is a vast difference between exploring this in a classroom, where humans control the light and the heat, the colours, shapes and sounds—and curled on the cliffs of Hallival at midnight. Here, listening to the eerie, wailing cries of the Manx Shearwaters as they fly to their burrows on the hill-side, knowing that these small birds have flown to Scotland for the summer from Brazil, we are offered the rare chance to suddenly glimpse our own culture's values as options, and the reality of being a tiny part of an immense system—and what this might mean for our environmental ethics—truly comes home.

Above all, the re-energising of respect and awe for other forms of life, that can happen so vividly when we actually spend time with them, and more on their terms than ours, reminds us powerfully why conservation, in the broadest sense, *matters*; and why the values of a culture that has sustained overwhelming losses in biodiversity are worth challenging. The philosophy of conservation re-emerges from Rum with an urgency and significance vastly beyond that of an interesting intellectual exercise. It deserves its time in the hills.

ACKNOWLEDGEMENTS

Highly valued contributions from site-managers include, among others, John Darbyshire and Ian Cornforth from The Falls of Clyde, Scottish Wildlife Trust, and over the years, Martin Curry and Mick Blunt of Scottish Natural Heritage.

Kate Rawles would like to acknowledge NESTA (National Endowment for Science, Technology and the Arts). She is currently working on a fellowship to develop "Outdoor Environmental Philosophy", a critical and motivational approach to education for sustainable development that has its origins in the Rum Trip.

NOTES

1. In earlier days, the island had been closed to the public. Access was granted only to a favoured few, who had to apply for permission from SNH to obtain it.

2. Dan Firth, Philosophy of Conservation discussion on MAVE discussion site, IEPPP website (restricted access).

REFERENCES

Aslet, Margaret. 2003. "Field Diary: Rum". Lancaster University, unpublished manuscript.

Boud, D., Cohen, R. and D. Walker. 1993. *Using experience for learning*. Bristol: Open University Press.

Brady, Emily. 2003. *Aesthetics of the Natural Environment*. Edinburgh: Edinburgh University Press.

Carlson, Allen. 2000. *Aesthetics and the Environment: The Appreciation of Nature, Art and Architecture*. London and New York: Routledge (esp. chapter 8).

Dewey, J. 1938. *Experience and education*. New York: The Free Press.

Countryside Commission for Scotland. 1978. "Scotland's Scenic Heritage".

Hepburn, Ronald. 1984. "Contemporary Aesthetics and the Neglect of Natural Beauty" in *Wonder and Other Essays*. Edinburgh: Edinburgh University Press: 9-35. First published in Bernard Williams and Alan Montefiore (eds) *British Analytical Philosophy*. London: Routledge and Kegan Paul, 1966.

Holland, Alan and Kate Rawles. 1993. "Values in Conservation". *ECOS* 14(1): 14-19.

Rawles, Kate. 1995. "The Missing Shade of Green" in Don Marietta and Lester Embree (eds) *Environmental Philosophy and Environmental Activism*. Lanham: Rowman and Littlefield. pp. 149-167.

———. 1998. "Philosophy and the Environmental Movement" in David Cooper and Joy Palmer (eds) *Spirit of the Environment*. London: Routledge. pp. 131-145.

———. 1997. "Conservation and Animal Welfare" in T. Chappell, (ed.) *The Philosophy of the Environment*. Edinburgh: Edinburgh University Press. pp. 135-155.

Samuel, Andy. 2000. "Rum: nature and community in harmony?". *ECOS*, Vol. 22, Issue no 1; 36-45.

Scottish Natural Heritage. Website, "http://www.snh.org.uk" www.snh.org.uk

———. 1997. Scotland's Natural Heritage, No. 11 "Rum—The First Forty Years" Perth: Scottish Natural Heritage.

Sibley, Frank. 1959. "Aesthetic Concepts". *Philosophical Review* 68:4: 421-450.

Warren, K., Sakofs, M. and J. Hunt (eds). 1995. *The theory of experiential education*. Kendall: Hunt Publishing.

FROM DELIGHT TO WISDOM:
THIRTY YEARS OF TEACHING
ENVIRONMENTAL ETHICS AT CORNELL

Richard A. Baer, Jr., James A. Tantillo, Gregory E.
Hitzhusen, Karl E. Johnson, and James R. Skillen

Abstract
In this paper, the authors retrace the philosophy and method of Natural Resources
407, "Religion, Ethics, and the Environment," which has been continuously taught
at Cornell University by the lead author since 1974. The works of Iris Murdoch,
Stanley Hauerwas, Reinhold Niebuhr, Joseph Sax, and Thomas Merton are discussed,
culminating in an aesthetic vision of environmental ethics as "praise for all things."
The course aims more to foster a general moral maturity rather than to instill any
any particular set of environmental behaviors in students, and the authors believe
that such an aim makes a lasting contribution to environmental ethics.

Keywords: environmental ethics, environmental education, environmental philosophy,
Iris Murdoch

Introduction

In the fall of 1974 Richard A. Baer, Jr. came to Cornell University
from Earlham College in Indiana to start an environmental ethics
program in the College of Agriculture and Life Sciences. The program was housed in the Department of Natural Resources, and during its early years was funded by the Lilly Endowment, the Rockefeller
Brothers Fund, and several other foundations. The core undergraduate course in the program, designed for juniors and seniors but also
open to graduate students, has been Natural Resources 407: *Religion,
Ethics, and the Environment* (NR407).

Richard Baer retired in August 2004, and it is time to look back
over these thirty years and ask: What have we accomplished? "We,"
because from the very beginning, this has been a collaborative effort
with some incredibly talented teaching assistants, mostly graduate
students of Baer's, but also including the occasional visitor or Ithaca
resident, sometimes with Ph.D. in hand, whom Baer was able to
persuade to give a helping hand. Since 1974, close to twenty-five

Clare Palmer (Ed.), *Teaching Environmental Ethics*, 148-159.
© 2006 *Koninklijke Brill NV. Printed in the Netherlands.*

individuals have been involved in teaching the course, including the co-authors of this article.

Granting that there are severe limits to what normally can be achieved in a college level environmental ethics course, courses such as NR 407 nonetheless can play an important role in a student's overall journey to maturity, and even may at times provide a crucial element in their ethical formation. Several fundamental points have been critical to our approach, which notably is not mainly about preparing students to do further study in ethics in a philosophy graduate program or in a theological seminary, but rather about what is effective, appropriate, challenging, and fulfilling for students who will likely take only one ethics course during their college/graduate school years.

From the very beginning, our goal has been not to focus on giving students specific answers to particular problems in environmental ethics—e.g., the ethics of white-tailed deer management, whether or not wolves should have been re-introduced to Yellowstone National Park, tradeoffs between concern for individual animals and for ecosystems—but rather to help students learn how to think about ethical issues, in particular to learn what kind of understanding is necessary even to begin to think clearly about such matters. To be sure, we have looked at a range of specific policy issues, occasionally in considerable detail. But the main focus of the course has been more theoretical than applied. An examination of the syllabus of *Religion, Ethics, and the Environment* makes clear what we mean by this approach.[1]

The Influence of Iris Murdoch

Our thinking and practice with regards to how to do ethics has drawn heavily on the work of British novelist and philosopher Iris Murdoch.[2] Murdoch argues that the fundamental questions to address in ethics concern who we are and what the world is like, and that once we gain clarity on these fundamental questions many moral dilemmas resolve themselves rather quickly. Thus we spend a good deal of time in the course discussing issues like the meaning of nature, the nature of animals and human beings, what constitutes knowledge, whether or not moral claims can rightly be considered knowledge claims (closely related to the issue of moral relativism), and whether there is such a thing as the public interest as something other than the summing of private interests.

This approach is in marked contrast to more traditional approaches to ethics that focus more narrowly on what ethical theories such as utilitarianism or Kantian deontology have to say about ethical dilemmas, or on ethical teaching that is loosely based on existentialist philosophy. A generation ago, "situation ethics" enjoyed a brief heyday as a popular means of teaching ethics. Ethicists who favored situation ethics or dilemma-based scenarios in their teaching of the subject emphasized personal choice, individual moral freedom, and the idea of a rationally autonomous self that was free to select a "personal" approach to ethics in various moral dilemmas/situations. This approach to teaching ethics soon fell out of favor, but not before spawning problematic approaches like "values clarification."[3] Although this approach ostensibly guards against indoctrinating students in a particular value system, in many ways it merely accomplishes moral indoctrination in a different meta-ethical system, and an apparently relativistic one at that! The important point to note is that the near-exclusive emphasis on the autonomous self and on free choice in such relativistic approaches is dramatically different from the perspective of Murdoch and of traditional modes of religious and casuistical thinking.

Murdoch, for example, argues that we probably are far less free when it comes to making moral decisions than most people think. This point really is quite obvious the moment we begin to reflect on the combination of genetic endowment, self-interest, peer pressure, social conditioning, and all the other realities that shape our identity. She believes that to focus too exclusively on particular decisions tends only to mire us more deeply in our self-preoccupation, and that what we need is to be "unselfed" through our encounter with great art and literature, music, nature, and perhaps quintessentially through the experience of falling deeply in love with another human being.[4]

Murdoch claims that we live out much of our lives under the spell of our illusions and fantasies, especially our neurotic preoccupation with ourselves. "When clear vision has been achieved," she writes, "self is a correspondingly smaller and less interesting object" (Murdoch 1970: 66).[5] With respect to both ethics and the academic life, she holds that perhaps the greatest virtue is humility, which is not a putting down of self but instead a deep and abiding respect for the way the world really is. Seeing the world clearly, however, is no simple task, for our constant self-preoccupation always threatens to prejudice and distort our thinking.

Nearly all of the great naturalists in our own American tradition understood this point, as did the great Taoist sages such as Chuang Tzu. For example, treating nature rightly is not just a matter of rules and ideas (although correct scientific understanding is absolutely essential), but rather a matter of discovering the incredible beauty, mystery, diversity, and wonder of this reality we call nature. It is a matter of the heart as well as of the head.

The Teaching of Religion and Ethics in a Secular Setting

With Murdoch setting the stage for an open inquiry into our vision of reality and what it means to be human, students begin to grapple with ethics at a deeper level. It is at this point in the semester that we introduce some of the foundational insights of Christianity, and to a lesser extent of Judaism. For the questions that Murdoch raises are ones that theologians wrestle with as well, and indeed religion provides the framework in terms of which many Americans do ethics.

Although Murdoch was not a theist, her position is similar to that of many religious traditions in her view that an understanding of the nature of reality precedes and grounds the doing of ethics. Actually, the same is true of virtually all ethical traditions, whether religious or secular,[6] although theologians are perhaps more likely than secular philosophers to acknowledge this fact. What we judge to be the nature of reality overall is dispositive for how we construe moral reality. "Knowledge informs the moral quality of the world," she writes. "The selfish self-interestedly casual or callous man *sees* a different world from that which the careful scrupulous benevolent man sees" (Murdoch 1992: 177, emph. original). In common with many theological traditions, Murdoch argues that human freedom is dependent both on a clear vision of reality and on the humility born of knowing that we are not the center of things. "Freedom is knowing and understanding and respecting things quite other than ourselves," she insists. "Virtue is in this sense to be construed as knowledge, and connects us so with reality" (Murdoch 1998: 284).

Stanley Hauerwas summarizes Murdoch's understanding of freedom in these words: "Contrary to Sartre, freedom is not in the self but in the other. Without love, without recognition and respect for the other, freedom is but an illusion of our neurotic self-preoccupation" (Hauerwas 1981: 41). What pulls us out of the cocoon of self-preoccupation and makes it possible to live generously and justly is not just right thinking but falling in love—with art, music, literature, people, animals, nature, or, on a more transcendent level, with the Good, the Tao, or with God. "Love," as Hauerwas reads Murdoch, "is any relationship through which we are called from our own self-involvement to appreciate the self-reality that transcends us. That is why it may be a profound moral experience to take self-forgetful pleasure in the sheer alien pointless independent existence of animals, birds, stones, and trees" (Hauerwas 1981: 39).[7]

This point is illustrated further when students read sections from Reinhold Niebuhr's *The Nature and Destiny of Man*. Understood theologically within the Christian tradition, our self-absorption begins with our own fear and anxiety. As we confront our fear, we either fall into sin or we open ourselves to God's grace. In sin we seek to control our lives and the world around, in grace we begin to accept life as a gift and a promise. In other words, in grace God draws us out of our self-absorption and fear.[8]

We have long faced the issue in our course of how best to explain such theological concepts as grace to an audience of undergraduates that typically includes many "non-believers." We have found that students can sometimes be led to a better understanding of grace, for example, through the use of parallel or analogous concepts from nature writers and other sources. A saying that has been attributed to Nathaniel Hawthorne serves well to suggest the psychological dynamics of grace: "Love is like a butterfly: If you pursue it, it flies away. But if you sit quietly, it may alight upon you." Theologically, God's grace is not at our beck and call, but we can open ourselves to its possibility.

These larger frames of reference for the course (vision, unselfing, falling in love) then take specific shape as we employ guiding examples from religious traditions (especially Christianity and Judaism) and show how these influence our understanding of our natural environment. When we see the world rightly, we recognize life as the gift that it is, which in turn opens up new perspectives on particular moral issues.

Hauerwas and Murdoch label such a perspective an "aesthetic vision" of ethics. In contrast to such an aesthetic vision approach, moral issues like land preservation and pollution control are too often packaged almost entirely as technical concerns. As Joseph Sax suggests in his book *Mountains Without Handrails*, society's concern for preservation is fundamentally moral, but we often argue exclusively in terms of ecological impact statements and hide our moral views behind scientific claims (Sax 1980: 14-15, 59, 103-104). In truth we want to preserve wilderness because we think doing so is a morally better path than letting utilitarian use hold sway, but we argue the case mainly in terms of the science of ecology, not on the basis of a higher moral ground. Politically we assume that moral views can make for undue controversy, so we "stick to the facts," but both sides then endlessly throw conflicting facts at each other as the real moral ground at issue goes unnamed. If we want to be more honest about who we are and what we want (and what we believe is a good way to live), we may need to become more comfortable with responsible moral language. We ignore the need to integrate the motivation of our hearts and our minds to our own confusion.

On Teaching Ethics: some practical lessons learned

There are a few practical lessons we've found indispensable in helping to revive students' engagement with moral claims. For example, in various class sessions we facilitate a kind of Socratic dialogue on terms like "nature," "value," "fact," and "religion." A consistent pattern that emerges is that students tend to say they can "know" facts, but can't really "know" whether particular value claims are true or false. Yet when they honestly examine their views in respectful dialogue, they find, for instance, that while they may not "know" that $E = mc2$, they do "know" that what Hitler did to Jews, Polish Christians, gypsies, and gays was wrong.

Such dialogues allow us to look at the nature of fact claims versus value claims, and also to criticise the relativism that most students profess. As in any ethics course in any college or university today, a large percentage of our students claim to be moral relativists, even though few hold to relativism consistently. As a course in normative ethics, NR 407 examines the nature of moral judgments from an epistemological standpoint. Specifically, such meta-ethical study helps students understand why moral relativism is an incoherent position to hold.

When helping students wrestle with the issue of moral relativism, we have found it helpful to discuss the epistemological status of scientific claims.[9] In doing this we provide students (mainly from the

College of Agriculture and Life Sciences at Cornell) with a basic introduction to the philosophy of science. It is important for students to understand that scientific claims are not as absolute as they tend to think but are part of a tradition with its own assumptions, initiation rites, operating procedures, etc. Knowledge in science, as in other human practices, is what might be called justifiable belief or warrantable assertion. Once students begin to understand that scientific claims are not as absolute as they once thought, it is easier for them to be open to moral truth claims. They come to understand that factual claims and moral claims are not as radically different from each other as most of them have been led to believe, even though available and acceptable means for justifying scientific claims and moral claims typically differ substantially.

We also tell stories, both in lectures and in discussion sections, including stories from personal experience, that tend to help draw the students into more personal dialogue.[10] Sometimes we draw upon rabbinic literature, using it as an example of moral commentary and teaching from a Jewish perspective. On occasion, Baer tells the story of a former student who scolded him in seminar by saying, "You use your mind just like a weapon!" This humbling/self-deprecating anecdote allows us to expand upon a theme of how violent our language is in the academy—how we admire "incisive critiques," "sharp minds," and "hard facts." We become overly dependent on such control-based modes of knowing and living and tend to ignore the need to balance such an approach with softer modes of knowing such as empathy, love, intuition, and wisdom. Baer and teaching assistants alike will sometimes share stories of when we've come to a moment of realization or growth in our lives—a transformative "Aha!" moment. Also, we frequently use poetry to get at ideas that are hard to voice persuasively by rational argument alone. Examples would be the Taoist poems "The Woodcarver" and "The Useless Tree," from Thomas Merton's *The Way of Chuang Tzu* (Merton 1965: 110-111, 35-36). As Robert Frost once remarked, a poem "begins in delight, and ends in wisdom" (Frost 1949: vi).

Towards the end of the course we devote a few lectures to themes such as playfulness, as a gift, and praise for all things (see Baer 1979). We find that these are interesting and strong ideas that in the end suggest that humans are able to join in what Thomas Merton refers to as "the cosmic dance." We make ethics an invitation to a way of life that is joyful and fulfilling in itself rather than simply a series of obligations or duties, or, even worse, endless rules and regulations that we must follow in order to avoid killing ourselves and our children. In theological terms, one could say that gospel precedes law, the indicative the imperative. The celebration of the world around us in all of its rich complexity and mystery is not unrelated to the right treatment of nature.

Little evidence exists, that taking the average college ethics course leads to students actually living more moral lives, and at the end of the semester we would be hard pressed to give quantitative evidence that taking NR407 has resulted in better behavior by most of our students. It seems to us that over the past thirty years, much of environmental education and occasionally environmental ethics as an academic discipline has aimed at a reductive list of desired environmental behaviors or even environmental advocacy as its end.[11] Yet part of the reason that improved environmental behavior is hard to demonstrate over the course of students' and citizens' lives is that "environmental behavior" is not a fixed entity. Nor do we believe that environmental ethics *necessarily* entails the endorsement of any particular *foundational summmum bonum*—e.g., the belief in the intrinsic value of nature, in Aldo Leopold's land ethic, or in anti-anthropocentrism—in apparent contrast to some environmental philosophers.[12]

We believe that environmental ethics ultimately must follow from a larger ethical vision rather than from the narrowly analytic frameworks of utilitarian or Kantian ethics. And so rather than aiming to induce particular environmental behaviors or beliefs as the primary goal, we aim in NR407 to nurture a capacity for moral thinking and moral vision that can then empower any number of positive environmental actions. The course is pragmatic, then, in the sense that we believe honest people of good will who differ in their foundational commitments may still converge upon shared ethical and political objectives that are good for the environment.[13]

Nonetheless, we have ample anecdotal evidence that this course has made at least some difference for students in their living as well as in their thinking. In anonymous evaluations students commonly claim that no other course has made them "think like this," and students often rank NR407 as one of the most important courses they've ever taken.[14] Occasionally we receive letters from past students telling us how NR407 has impacted their lives for the better. Their responses reflect, we believe, the fact that this course does not simply convey

new information to the students; rather it awakens ideas that the
students already hold fiercely and passionately, stretches them to
think beyond their assumptions, and provides space for respectful
debate about larger questions.

Conclusion

All of us, professor and teaching assistants, share the view that students
have responded so positively to the course not mainly because it has
been well taught but because the approach and the content deeply
engage students as total persons, not just as disembodied minds. Most
of the students have found it difficult to remain disengaged observers;
rather they encountered ideas and a kind of teaching that addressed
them as total persons, constantly challenging them to live differently
and not just to think differently.

For thirty years, Richard Baer has concluded his semester's final
lecture with the following quotation from Thomas Merton. In *New
Seeds of Contemplation*, Merton writes this:

> What is serious to men is often trivial in the eyes of God. What in
> God might appear to us as "play" is perhaps what he himself takes
> most seriously. At any rate the Lord plays and diverts himself in the
> garden of his creation, and if we could let go of our own obsession
> with what we think is the meaning of it all, we might be able to hear
> His call and follow Him in His mysterious, cosmic dance. We do not
> have to go very far to catch echoes of that game, and of that dancing.
> When we are alone on a starlit night; when by chance we see the
> migrating birds in autumn descending on a grove of junipers to rest and
> eat; when we see children in a moment when they are really children;
> when we know love in our own hearts; or when, like the Japanese
> poet Bashō we hear an old frog land in a quiet pond with a solitary
> splash—at such times the awakening, the turning inside out of all val-
> ues, the "newness," the emptiness and purity of vision that make them-
> selves evident, provide a glimpse of the cosmic dance.
>   For the world and time are the dance of the Lord in emptiness.
> The silence of the spheres is the music of a wedding feast. The more
> we persist in misunderstanding the phenomena of life, the more we
> analyze them out into strange finalities and complex purposes of our
> own, the more we involve ourselves in sadness, absurdity, and despair.
> But it does not matter much, because no despair of ours can alter the
> reality of things, or stain the joy of the cosmic dance which is always
> there. Indeed, we are in the midst of it, and it is in the midst of us,
> for it beats in our very blood, whether we want it to or not.

Yet the fact remains that we are invited to forget ourselves on purpose, cast our awful solemnity to the winds, and join in the general
dance (Merton 1961: 296-297).

Our initial conclusion to this paper included the following sentence:
"*Religion, Ethics, and the Environment* is a course that has asked students
the question, 'How should I live?' Students today (as always) crave
an answer to that most important of human questions—and we have
aimed to provide, if not the answer, at least a sensitive discussion
of the question."

On the final editing, however, we found this conclusion not quite
right, for countless students over the past 30 years have told us that,
even though we have left them with more questions than they had
when they began the course, they nonetheless found answers—at
least tentative, beginning answers—to some of their deepest questions.
To be sure, they did not always arrive at the same answer, but we
helped them understand that this outcome did not in itself entail the
conclusion that all answers to moral questions are inevitably relative.

Plato writes in the *Republic*: "For we are discussing here no trivial subject but how one ought to live." Had he been able to eaves-
drop on our classes and discussions in Religion, Ethics, and the
Environment, it is our conviction that he would not have been altogether displeased.

NOTES

1. Baer's most recent syllabus is included here as an appendix, and a similar
version taught by Tantillo in 1996 is available on the ISEE syllabus project web
site, currently at http://appliedphilosophy.mtsu.edu/ISEE/JimTantillo/TantilloReligion
EthicsEnvironment.htm.
2. See, for example, Murdoch 1970. Our reading of Murdoch in turn has been
deeply influenced by Stanley Hauerwas. See especially "The Significance of Vision:
Toward an Aesthetic Ethic," chapter 2 in Hauerwas 1981: 30-47.
3. See Baer 1977, 1980, 1982.
4. Hauerwas writes (1981: 39, n. 30): "Like so many of Miss Murdoch's themes
this understanding of love is derived from Simone Weil." See, for example, Weil's
work *La pesanteur et la grace* [*Gravity and Grace*] (1952).
5. For discussion, see Hauerwas 1981: 34.
6. See "Ethics of Inarticulacy," in Taylor 1989: 53-90.
7. Hauerwas 1981: 39. See Murdoch 1970: 85-85.
8. Niebuhr 1955. Students read Vol. I, pp. 178-207 and 228-240, and Vol. II,
pp. 98-126.
9. Barbour 1966, although dated, has been particularly useful. See, especially,
chapter 6, pp. 137-174, "The Methods of Science."
10. See Coles 1989.
11. See generally the essays in Marietta and Embree 1995, for discussion of this
point.

12. Cf. John O'Neill's claim: "To hold an environmental ethic is to hold that non-human beings and states of affairs in the natural world have intrinsic value" (O'Neill 1992: 119).

13. See also Norton 1991.

14. Here are just a few of hundreds of similar comments from thirty years of students:

> "As a student somewhat disenchanted with the university, I would not regret my decision to attend Cornell based on this course alone."
>
> "I would consider this the best class I have had in my career at Cornell simply because it has caused me to think and to engage more than any other class I have taken."
>
> "Natural Resources 407 is probably the most important course I will take in college, because it has allowed me to form a basic world view from which I will conduct the rest of my education and future career."
>
> "You have empowered more people than you know with this course and I thank you for your service."
>
> "Without a doubt, it is the class that I have found the most valuable in my four years at Cornell."
>
> "I was totally unprepared for the radically different kind of learning that was found in this class. . . . [It] asks more of its students. It says, there is more to the human experience than a sum of simple, separable and discrete parts."
>
> "This course is inherently valuable. . . . It is one of those key experiences in a student's career that will greatly affect the way they continue to live once they have left the course and the university."
>
> "Although frustrating at times, [NR 407] will prove to be incredibly rewarding in the future."
>
> "I wished that schools would tape the mantra 'life is a gift' on top of every blackboard, because I believe acceptance of that fact goes a long way toward making us better people."
>
> "The material in this class isn't just for a grade, but for a lifetime of application and that is why I value this class so much."
>
> "I come away from this course with some answers, some tools towards finding new answers, and a lot of questions."

REFERENCES

Baer, Richard A., Jr. 1977. "Values Clarification as Indoctrination." *The Educational Forum* 56 (2) January, 155-165.
———. 1979. "Praise for All Things." *Princeton Seminary Bulletin*, 11 (2) (New Series): 124-133.
———. 1980. "A Critique of the Use of Values Clarification in Environmental Education," *The Journal of Environmental Education*, 12 (1) Fall: 13-16.
———. 1982. "Teaching Values in the Schools: Clarification or Indoctrination?" *Principal*, 61 (3) January: 17-21, 36.
Barbour, Ian G. 1966. *Issues in Science and Religion*. Englewood Cliffs, NJ: Prentice-Hall.
Coles, Robert. 1989. *The Call of Stories: Teaching and the Moral Imagination*. Boston: Houghton.
Hauerwas, Stanley. 1981. "The Significance of Vision: Toward an Aesthetic Ethic," *in Vision and Virtue: Essays in Critical Ethical Reflection*. Notre Dame, IN: University of Notre Dame Press, pp. 30-47.

Marietta, Don E., Jr., and Lester Embree. 1995. *Environmental Philosophy and Environmental Activism*, Lanham, MD: Rowman and Littlefield.

Murdoch, Iris. 1970. *The Sovereignty of Good*. London: Routledge.

——. 1992. *Metaphysics as a Guide to Morals*. NY: Penguin Books.

——. 1998. *Existentialists and Mystics: Writings on Philosophy and Literature*, ed. Peter Conradi. NY: Penguin Books.

Niebuhr, Reinhold. 1955. *The Nature and Destiny of Man: A Christian Interpretation*, II Volumes. New York: Charles Scribner's Sons.

Norton, Bryan G. 1991. *Toward Unity Among Environmentalists*. New York: Oxford University Press.

O'Neill, John. 1992. "The Varieties of Intrinsic Value." *The Monist* 75(2): 119-137.

Taylor, Charles. 1989. *Sources of the Self: The Making of the Modern Identity*. Cambridge: Harvard University Press.

Weil, Simone 1952 [1948]. *Gravity and Grace* [*La pesanteur et la grace*], ed. Gustave Thibon, trans. Arthur Wills. NY: Putnam.

TEACHING ENVIRONMENTAL ETHICS: NON-INDIGENOUS INVASIVE SPECIES AS A STUDY OF HUMAN RELATIONSHIPS TO NATURE[1]

Dorothy Boorse

Abstract

This paper uses the question, "what ethical issues inform our response to non-indigenous invasive species?" as a basis to explore human relationships to nature in the context of teaching environmental ethics. While ecologists express increasing concern about the introduction of non-indigenous invasive species (NIS), the public is sometimes unaware of, or ambivalent about, the problems they cause. I argue that this ambivalence stems from conceptual problems—about human-nature relationships, about ethical conflict and about human behavior—that can be addressed in a course on environmental ethics. Such a course can look at NIS in the context of different ethical traditions, and the different bases for action (or not) with regard to NIS that such ethical traditions imply. I suggest ways to use NIS as case studies in either a science course or an environmental ethics course, to introduce fundamental questions and to explore basic worldviews with respect to humans and nature.

Keywords: environmental ethics, exotic species, invasive species, environmental education

Introduction: The Field Course

I am an ecologist who teaches environmental ethics in a number of courses. On the first day of a fall field class, I walk with my students to a portion of our campus between a highway and dorms. There we find a thicket of a bamboo-like plant with large plate-like leaves, each plant over two meters tall. Long inflorescences lean from the tops. The students collect a long stalk and return to the lab. They have 1.5 hours to identify it in teams. Eventually, I find them looking in *Trees and Shrubs of Northern New England* (Steele and Hodgdon 1968).

After some time, we discuss their efforts, which appear to be futile.

Me:	"Have you ever seen this plant before?"
Class:	"No."
Me:	"It is a huge plant that forms thickets and shades everything around. How could you have lived in this area 20 years and never have seen it before?"
Class:	"We have no idea."
Me:	"Does it look like other trees and shrubs? What does it remind you of?"
Class:	"No. Bamboo, grass. It is not woody."
Me:	"Aha, are you looking in the right place? Is this a tree? A shrub?"

Clare Palmer (Ed.), *Teaching Environmental Ethics*, 160-172.

Class: "No."
Me: "Does it look like anything else around? Where might it be from?"
Class: "No. Someplace else?"

With that brief exchange, the students are plunged into the world of invasive exotic species. These are exotic ("non-native" or "non-indigenous") organisms transported by humans that burgeon uncontrollably in a new area, becoming a pest. Sometimes they are called non-indigenous invasive species (NIS).

Thirty minutes later, after an intense search on the internet, the students have found four sites that tell them the plant is Japanese knotweed (*Fallopia japonica* or *Polygonum cuspidatum*), a member of the buckwheat family that is native to Asia and was brought to the United States as an ornamental shrub. Here it has escaped cultivation and forms dense stands that crowd out native plants (Remaley 1997). Armed with that information, students begin a seven week project mapping and identifying NIS on campus and in the county. In the course of the project, the students are exposed to the enormity of problems with NIS introductions, particularly plant examples. They discover that while our campus has many established exotic species, Japanese knotweed only occurs in the one patch and could be eradicated. Armed with that information, we request removal and are gratified when our advice is heeded.

Throughout the course, the students are exposed to science, management, and politics surrounding non-indigenous invasive species. For conservation biologists and ecologists, this background is essential. But why was it so obvious to my students and myself that the Japanese knotweed patch *ought to* be removed to avoid a larger infestation on campus? We agreed because we began with certain basic assumptions—that biodiversity is good, that invasive species should be slowed if possible to maintain native diversity, and that natural processes, including the pace of invasions by new species, should be maintained.

From the Field to the Ethic

These beliefs come from, and help to form, an environmental ethic. However, they should not be assumed, and not everyone would agree with them. It is essential, therefore, that students think about the ethical bases and assumptions they have that pertain to NIS both in classes about environmental ethics, and in classes about environmental science or ecology where ethics plays a role in subsequent decision-making. Suppose, that instead of the plant, Japanese knotweed, the species we had first investigated had been brown-headed cowbird (*Molothrus ater*), a brood parasite native to North America that has expanded its range and parasitizes the nests of 100 other native songbird species including the endangered Kirtland's warbler (Cornell Laboratory of Ornithology 1999). Would students have been comfortable with the killing of cowbirds to protect the warbler? Does it matter whether the cowbird is an indigenous or non-indigenous species? Suppose an exotic species promotes economic gain for some humans and causes economic harm to others. Would it matter who was harmed or benefited? Suppose the exotic species had been a feral pig (Rosenberger 1994). Would the pig have individual rights that might allow it protection not afforded a rare native orchid?

These are all real questions that are being addressed (or avoided) currently. Students benefit from looking at them in an environmental ethics curriculum. Thus, NIS offer case studies that allow us to look at the framework of environmental ethics, including the fundamental questions about relationships of humans and nature, what is "natural", and what "ought to be".

The Problem

Non-indigenous invasive species are a subset of the species introduced by humans to new environments. Not all introduced species become uncontrolled (Pimetel et al. 2000, Sagoff 2000). Those that do, often have a suite of characteristics such as high reproductive capacity, high dispersal capacity and few biological controls in the new environment. Some remain at very low levels and suddenly become uncontrolled later (Allendorf 2003, Simberloff and Strong 2000). On the other hand, not all species considered to be pests are exotic. Some native species, such as the white-tailed deer (Kenney 1990), have lost their native predators (e.g. mountain lions and wolves) and are well adapted to the environments around human activities such as fields, forest edges, and suburban lawns (Curtis and Richmond 1992). Finally, some non-native species could be rare or endangered (Dunn et al. 2001) and may warrant protection. While exceptions such as non-invasive exotics and native pests exist, most of the discussion in this area is about species that humans have transported from an environment in which they may have evolved to a new environment and which subsequently show uncontrolled growth.

Invasive species are costly. The U.S. spends an estimated $138 million to control invasive species annually (Pimentel et al. 2000). For example, the Formosan termite costs an estimated $300 million annually in property damage in New Orleans alone (NISC 2001). An estimated 10,000 species are transported daily around the globe in ship ballast water (EPA 2004). Invasive species introduction is second only to loss of habitat and landscape fragmentation as a cause of biodiversity loss (Allendorf 2003). IUCN, the World Conservation Union, estimates the cost of the worldwide damage from invasive species at $400 billion a year (Kirby 2003).

More than ten years have passed since the Office of Technology Assessment (OTA) produced the first comprehensive report on invasive species in the United States (OTA 1993). Presidential Executive Order 13112 of February 3, 1999 established a federal Invasive Species Council. This order triggered a debate about whether the concern about species invasions was alarmist (Sagoff 2000, Simberloff 2000). Since then, concern has only increased. In December 2003, the National Environmental Coalition on Invasive Species (NECIS) issued a "Call to Action on Invasive Species" signed by over 750 scientists and experts and over 100 citizens groups (Union of Concerned Scientists 2004). A special section of the journal *Conservation Biology* was recently dedicated to invasive species (Allendorf 2003). In January 2003, the Director of the U.S. Fish and Wildlife Service called invasive species "the biggest environmental threat to this country" (EPA 2004). Thus, concern about invasive species is high in the ecological and conservation communities, and government agencies are taking steps to control NIS.

If NIS are such a big economic and ecological *disvalue*, does the public respond as might be expected? Surprisingly, people seem less knowledgeable, concerned or willing to intervene than the problem seems to warrant and than government agencies and scientists propose (Ehrlich 2002, Lodge and Shrader-Frechette 2003). Anecdotally, I have found my non-ecologist friends and many students to be completely unaware of the size and impact of the problem, unable to recognize NIS common in our area, and unfamiliar with the terms "exotic" and "invasive". Part of this lack of response is due to ignorance of the situation. This may be because the problem is growing so rapidly (ten years is not enough time to have found its way into most text books), the general public has a low understanding of ecology, the science is unclear (Shrader-Frechette 2001), educational materials are lacking (Brewer 2001), or peoples' attention is diverted by other issues such as domestic and foreign policy or global warming. The issue of species invasions may not have "trickled down" to the public (Brewer 2001). To counter these problems, educational initiatives are beginning to promote information about invasive species (Krasny and Lee 2002).

Mixed Messages

Ignorance is not the only issue however. The public receives mixed messages about the ecological dangers of invasive species (Lodge and Shrader-Frechette 2003, Sagoff 1999, 2000, Simberloff and Strong 2000). In part these mixed messages stem from issues that relate to environmental ethics. First is a fundamental question about the relationship of humans to the non-human parts of nature that underlies many of the questions asked in environmental ethics (Botkin 2001, Callicott 1991, 1993, Humphrey 2000, Rolston 1993). After all, if humans are a part of nature, then surely their actions are natural. In any case, species invasions and extinctions happen even in the absence of humans. Why then would we consider NIS invasions a problem? Indeed, might one not argue that labelling introduced species "exotic", "alien" or "non-native" could be interpreted as a type of xenophobia (Sagoff 2000), perhaps similar to a distrust of immigrants by people who have been established in a region for some time? Yet this is certainly not the only interpretation.

There are two main ways of responding to these points. One is to say that humans are not part of nature. However, that comes with the cost of dualism and potentially with either furthering human misuse of nature, or misanthropic promotion of human-less wilderness (Humphrey 2000). Claiming that humans are not part of nature means that we can define species introduced by humans as different in some way from native species. However, this does not clarify what we should do about them. Second, we could view all human activities as "natural" and nature as good. But nature does not define what ought to be, only what is. Deriving the "ought" from the "is" is the "normative fallacy" (Callicott 1990). Indeed, if human actions are all "natural" and nature is good, then the basis for civil and criminal law would be undermined. If we reject the normative fallacy, it could be that human actions, such as introducing non-indigenous species are "natural" but still unethical.[2]

There is a middle ground. Some conservationists suggest that human introduction of species is natural and could be benign. It is not the fact of some introduction of species that is the problem; it is the pace at which those introductions occur. This pace is so rapid that it does not maintain the processes that allow biodiversity, even in a world where flux is the norm (Lodge 2003, Lodge and Shrader-Frechette 2003). This argument, that the action itself may be ethically neutral but the *cumulative impact* is unnatural, harmful to ecosystem health and therefore unethical might be represented by Leopold's land ethic (Callicott 1990, 1992; Leopold 1977).

Another problem concerns conflicts between different kinds of rights involved. There may be conflicts between the rights of invasive and native species (assuming that it makes sense to talk of species as having rights); conflicts between the rights of individuals of one species and individuals of another; conflicts between individual rights and species rights; not to mention conflicts of individuals and species with the rights of individual humans. Many people can easily imagine that the removal of kuzu, gorse, Asian longhorned beetle, gypsy moths, or zebra mussels from areas where they are non-native pests would be a good thing. These species are seen as invasive, harming native species and composed of nonsentient individual members, lacking in individual rights. But those same people might blanch at efforts to kill sentient feral pigs in Hawaii or rabbits in Australia. They might wince over the control of cowbirds, or feral cats. Yet cats, pigs, cowbirds and rabbits cause tremendous damage (Dougherty 2002, Rosenberger 1994, NISC 2003, OTA 1993, Pimentel 2000).

Animal rights supporters, for whom the value and moral status of an individual are dependent primarily on its sentience, do not differentiate between indigenous and non-indigenous species (Regan 1983). In this view, if an animal is aware and can feel pain and suffering, it will always have moral standing; but a plant or lower animal lacks such moral standing even if it is very rare. The moral standing of individual pest animals means, for some people, that local eradication is unethical even if they are causing the decline and extinction of other species (Holland 2003, Rosenberger 1994). Unfortunately, the emphasis on individual rights almost always privileges animals over plants. At its extreme, this ethic maintains that it is unethical to kill any living thing, even to protect other living things (Varner 2002).

Moving the discussion from the language of rights to that of "respect" or "weighing of values or interests" can diffuse some of the tension between apparently competing "rights" and re-set the conversation. An individualist ethic can be modified to include the values of plants and to develop a hierarchy of values so that human rights to life are protected (Varner 2002). However, for a scientist interested in the protection of biodiversity, even a modified individualistic ethic may not reflect the importance of non-living goods such as diversity or ecosystem integrity (Leopold 1977). Alternatively Callicott (1990) has described a type of holism that assigns intrinsic value to the earth's biotic community. Sometimes this has been criticized as promoting the group to the harm of individuals (Armstrong and Botzler 2003b).[3]

Finally, controlling invasive species involves changes in human behavior that are inconvenient. This means that some humans may benefit and others be harmed by control. This opposition of stakeholders may lead to ambivalence about management (Lodge and Shrader Frechette 2003, Sagoff 2000). For example controlling ballast releases would entail cost to shippers and eventually cost consumers more for goods. Realizing the costs of cleaning up released pest species after introduction, however, provides some of the incentive to prevent species introductions (NISC 2003).

Relating Ethical World Views to NIS

In the conservation community, the movement from scientific problem (increase of pests and loss of biodiversity) to management solution (limitation of species invasions and removal of some species) may not always begin with the discussion of ethics. The conservation community is already dedicated to the protection of biodiversity (Patton and Erickson 2001). However, making ethical decisions about species management means we do need to ask basic questions about values.

One way to explore NIS as an ethical case study is to evaluate management decisions in the light of different ethical traditions described in typical environmental ethics texts.[4] An ethic that suggests some type of control of invasive species is likely to be a modified or mixed version of an anthropocentric (human centered), ecocentric (ecosystem centered) and possibly theocentric (God centered) view. But it is unlikely to include the extremes of sentience-centered or biocentric individualistic ethics. An anthropocentric point of view, for example, could advocate for control of those NIS that cause loss of life or livelihood for humans. Indeed, this is one of the primary concerns about exotic species such as West Nile Virus or plant pests (NCIS 2003, Pimentel 2000). Likewise, anthropocentrism could support control of NIS that lower the aesthetic value of nature (possibly by removing endangered species) even if economic and health costs were minimal.

An ecocentric point of view would be concerned about the integrity of ecosystem functions, including the stability of populations and maintenance of biodiversity and therefore would encourage control of exotic species. Both perspectives derived from Leopold's land ethic and from the deep ecology movement would emphasize the good of protection of ecosystem processes, though they might differ in their expression of the relationship of humans to nature or the tension between individualistic and corporate values (Armstrong and Botzler 2003).

Some people interpret theocentrism as another version of anthropocentrism. That is, God has made humans to have a special relationship with him; thus, human interests preempt all other interests. Indeed, this interpretation has been a major criticism of Christianity (White 1967). In fact, while that interpretation may be one many religious persons have, it is not necessarily theocentric. A theocentric view is that animals and plants have value in some way determined by the value God places on them. This is the foundation of the stewardship principle found in a number of monotheistic religions (Rolston 1993). For students who belong to one of the monotheistic religious groups, a theocentric environmental ethic demands protection of native and endemic species from loss, even if such protection demands inconvenience and sacrifice for humans (though it should be noted that theocentric positions vary widely within this broad outline [Gustafson 1981, Devall and Sessions 1985]).[5]

Individualistic points of view generally support individual rights of animals, particularly sentient animals, sometimes maintaining animal rights equal to human rights (Regan 1983). While this is an effective approach to the protection of endangered higher mammals such as cetaceans and great apes, it is problematic when it is applied to sentient animals that are overabundant such as white tailed deer, beaver,

nutria, or feral pigs and which can cause the extinction of other
species (Kenney 1990, Simberloff and Strong 2000).

A modification of the individualistic biocentric view to include
respect and care for non-sentient beings and aggregate goods such
as species (Varner 2002) might end up being similar to a modified
ecocentric view with an emphasis on individual rights (Armstrong
and Botzler 2003). Likewise, a theocentric view with a strong emphasis on the goodness of non-human creatures would lead to a respect
of the rest of nature similar to that of ecocentrism, while maintaining the value of individuals.

Thus, as a basis for environmental ethics, anthropocentrism can
be useful in suggesting a reason for limiting species introductions—
the negative costs of such introductions to humans. Ecocentrism, and
theocentrism albeit for completely different reasons, also suggest that
humans limit human activities to lower the effect of NIS introductions. Biocentric individualism at its extreme has little to offer a discussion where individual rights are pitted against entire populations,
species and ecosystems. However, modified versions of biocentric
individualism do maintain value of non-individuals and might inform
a discussion on NIS.[6]

In the Classroom

The introduction of NIS, then, raises a whole series of philosophical
and ethical issues for discussion in the classroom. Although I do not
teach an entire course in environmental ethics, I include discussions
on environmental ethics in at least three courses, all upper level
courses for biology majors with an ecological bent: two field courses
in ecology and techniques and one seminar course. One of the field
courses is the one described in the introduction. We see NIS in the
field and later discuss these real examples (such as Japanese knotweed)
and how our assumptions (e.g. assuming it ought to be removed)
affect our decision-making. The discussion of such assumptions leads
students to explore exactly the kinds of conceptual and ethical issues
about human relations with nature and ethical conflicts in ecological management I have considered in this paper. Another field course
uses vernal pools as a model habitat and we focus more on how to
protect rare species. Although this centers less on how to respond
to NIS, the two issues are inevitably related, especially as the NIS

examples we encounter in this course sometimes include bait fish placed in pools.

In the seminar course, we discuss environmental issues and use the text *Taking sides: Controversial Issues in Environmental Science* (Easton and Goldfarb 2003). Students undertake a major project and make a presentation of their own choice. Their presentations often include NIS (such as feral pigs) or native species management issues (such as control of white-tailed deer) and in the context of their topics, we discuss as a group the ethical bases for different actions, looking at the different worldviews and ethical approaches discussed above. I have found both my field and seminar students open and eager to discuss ethical issues and better able to understand the points of view of others when they have done so.

One text that would work well in conjunction with a discussion of specific case studies of NIS in a class would be *Environmental Ethics: divergence and convergence* (Armstrong and Botzler 2003). This text covers the roots of environmental ethics and the major world-views informing ethical decisions as well as some applied ethics. It is an appropriate text for use either for a course in environmental ethics, with management NIS as one type of applied case study, or as a source of supplemental readings in a course where ethics constituted just one part. One NIS case study my students have found engrossing is the case of the cane toad (*Bufo marinus*) imported into Australia to control the cane beetle in the 1930s. Unfortunately, no beetle control occurred and the cane toad, which is a voracious generalist predator, has spread rapidly, both eating and poisoning wildlife. This story is described in a humorous and scientific documentary, *Cane Toads: an Unnatural History* (Lewis 1987). I have found this film and discussion about it in the classroom to be a spring-board for deeper discussion on environmental ethics in the context of NIS. In particular, the case raises ethical questions concerning how one should weigh the competing interests of individual organisms with ecosystems and species.

Thus, in classes either on environmental ethics or ecology, the question of how to respond to NIS can provide a fertile ground for an exploration of basic environmental ethics concepts including at fundamental questions about human-nature interactions, ethical conflicts and human behavior; and several basic world views including the anthropocentric, biocentric, theocentric and ecocentric. Here I have been able to offer only a brief overview of the main components of such a discussion. However, I have found such a discussion in the context of specific NIS case studies helpful for students unfamiliar with the problems of NIS and for those who are planning a career in ecology or conservation biology, where management decisions informed by environmental ethics will inevitably have to be made.

NOTES

1. Thanks to two anonymous reviewers for *Worldviews* for their helpful comments.
2. A discussion on the definition of "nature" and "natural" and the relationship of humans to nature is too substantial for this short essay. I have described a couple of divergent alternatives. See Botkin (2001) for one application of the concept of "natural" to NIS. See the section "Are humans a part of nature or separate from it"? in *The Ethics of the Environment* (Brennan 1995) for several papers on the topic.
3. In relation to NIS, one difficulty with couching the discussion in terms of rights is that one could argue that if humans move species from one place to another, humans take on responsibility for the welfare of those individuals. Certainly, some would feel that about wild horses in the U.S. for example (Hawes-Davis 2001).
4. Such as *Environmental Ethics: Divergence and Convergence* Third Ed. (Armstrong and Botzler 2003).
5. The tension between group and individual protection, and the interests of non-beings such as ecosystems, is a central point in environmental ethics. Each of these approaches has a broad range of adherents that are more complex than can be described here. See overview in Brennan and Lo (2002) and deeper consideration in Devall and Sessions (1985), Rolston (1988), and Varner (1998). Gustafson (1981) defines a different theocentric view than that briefly summarized here. His work is reviewed in Beckley and Swezey (1988).
6. There was not enough space to address the connection of ecofeminism or pantheism to NIS. However, ecofeminism focuses on individuals and would have some of the issues of biocentric individualism. It is difficult to tell how pantheism would work itself out as a basis for management decisions about exotic species.

REFERENCES

Allendorf, F.A. 2003. "Introduction: population biology, evolution, and control of invasive species". *Conservation Biology* 17(1) 24-30.
Armstrong, S. and R.G. Botzler. 2003. "Chapter Eight, Ecocentrism" *Environmental Ethics: Divergence and Convergence* 3rd edn. Boston: McGraw-Hill. pp. 371-373.
Beckley, H. and C. Swezey. (eds) 1988. *James M. Gustafson's Theocentric Ethics: Interpretations and Assessments*. Macon, GA: Mercer University Press.
Brennan, A. (ed.) 1995. *The Ethics of the Environment*. Aldershot, Hampshire, U.K.: Dartmouth Publishing.
Brennan, A. and Y. Lo. 2002. "Environmental Ethics" in E. Zalta (ed.) *The Stanford Encyclopedia of Philosophy*. Summer 2002 ed. Available from: http://plato. Stanford. edu/archives/sum2002/entries/ethics-environmental/>. Accessed July 2004.
Brewer, C.A. 2001. "Cultivating conservation literacy: 'trickle down' is not enough". *Conservation Biology* 15:1203-1205.
Botkin, D.B. 2001. "The naturalness of biological invasions". *Western North American Naturalist* 61(3) 261-266.

Callicott, J.B. 1990. "Aldo Leopold's concept of ecosystem health" in, R. Constanza, B.G. Norton and B. Haskell (eds) *Ecosystem Health: New Goals for Environmental Management*. Washington, D.C.: Island Press, 1992.
Callicott, J.B. 1992. "The land aesthetic" in S. Armstrong and R. Botzler (eds) *Environmental Ethics: Divergence and Convergence*. 3rd edn. Boston: McGraw-Hill, pp. 176-179.
Cornell Lab of Ornithology. 1999. "Brood parasite: brown-headed cowbird (*Molothrus ater*)". *Birds in Forested Landscapes*. Available from http://birds.cornell.edu/bfl/species-accts/bnhcow.html. Accessed March 2004.
Curtis, P.D., and M.E. Richmond. 1992. Future challenges of suburban white-tailed deer management. Transactions of the North American Wildlife and Natural Resources Conference 57:104-114.
Devall, B. and G. Sessions. 1985. *Deep Ecology*. Salt Lake City: Peregrine Smith Books.
Dunn, E.H., Hussell, D.J.T. and D.A. Welsh. 2001. "Letter". *Conservation Biology*. 15(4) 2001.
Easton, T. and T. Goldfarb. 2002. *Taking Sides: Clashing views on Controversial Environmental Issues*. 10th edn. McGraw Hill Higher Education.
Ehrlich, P.R. 2002. "Human natures, nature conservation, and environmental ethics". *Bioscience* 52(1) 31-44.
Environmental Protection Agency (EPA). 2004. "Invasive non-native species". *Watershed Academy Web*. Available from http://www.epa.gov/OWOW/watershed/wacademy/acad2000/invasive.html. Accessed March 2004.
Gustafson, J. 1981. *Ethics from a Theocentric Perspective. Vol. 1. Theology and Ethics*. Chicago: University of Chicago Press.
Hawes-Davis, D. 2001. *El Caballo*. Film. Missoula: High Plains Films.
Holland, J.S. 2003. "Kill a cat, save a numbat?" *National Geographic* 204(6) 1.
Humphrey, M. 2000. "Nature in deep ecology and social ecology: contesting the core". *Journal of Political Ideologies* 5(2) 247-268.
Kenney, J. 1990. "The control of the wild". *National Parks* 64 (9-10) 20-26.
Kirby, A. 2003. "Alien species cost Africa billions" *BBC News World Edition*. 5 February, 2003 Available from: http://news.bbc.co.uk/2/hi/science/nature/2730693.stm Accessed June 2004.
Krasny, M.E. and S.K. Lee. 2002. "Social learning as an approach to environmental education: Lessons from a program focusing on non-indigenous, invasive species". *Environmental Education Research* 8(2) 101-119.
Leopold, A. 1977. "The land ethic" In *A Sand County Almanac: And Sketches Here and There*. New York: Oxford University Press, pp. 201-26.
Lewis, M. 1987. *Cane Toads: an Unnatural History*. Film. First Run Features.
Lodge, D.M. 2003. "Introduction to special issue: from the balance to the flux of nature: The power of metaphor in cross-discipline conversations". *Worldviews: Environment, Culture and Religion* 7(1-2) 1-4.
Lodge, D.M. and K. Shrader-Frechette. "Non-indigenous species: ecological explanation, environmental ethics, and public policy". *Conservation Biology* 17:31-37.
National Invasive Species Council (NISC). 2001. "Meeting the invasive species challenge: national invasive species plan". NISC: Washington DC. Available from https://www.denix.osd.mil/denix/Public/News/OSD/NIWAW/Invasive_Species/cover.html#toc Accessed March 2004.
Office of Technology Assessment. (OTA). 1993. *Harmful Non-Indigenous Species in the United States*. U.S. Congress. Available from http://www.wws.princeton.edu/~ota/disk1/1993/9325_n.html Accessed March 2004.
Patten, M.A. and R.A. Erickson. 2001. "Letter". *Conservation Biology* 15(4) 817.
Pimentel, D., Lach, L., Zuniga R. and D. Morrison. 2000. "Environmental and economic costs of non-indigenous species in the United States". *Bioscience* 50(1): 53-66.

Regan, T. 1983. "The case for animal rights". Excerpted in S. Armstrong and R.G. Botzler (eds) *Environmental Ethics: Divergence and Convergence*. 3rd edn 2003. Boston: McGraw-Hill, pp. 314-330.

Remaley, T. 1997. "Japanese knotweed: *Polygonum cuspidatum* Sieb and Zucc" *Alien Plant Invaders of Natural Areas Fact Sheets* Available from http://www.nps.gov/plants/alien/fact.htm Accessed March 2004.

Rolston, H., III. 1993. "Environmental ethics: some challenges for Christians". In S. Armstrong and R. Botzler (eds) *Environmental Ethics: Divergence and Convergence*. 3rd edition 2003. Boston: McGraw-Hill, pp. 231-234.

———. 1988. *Environmental Ethics*. Philadelphia: Temple University Press.

Rosenberger, J. 1994. "Attack of the feral pigs". *Emagazine: The Environmental Magazine*. 5(5)22-25.

Sagoff, M. 1999. "What's wrong with exotic species?" *Institute for Philosophy and Public Policy*. School of Public Affairs, University of Maryland, College park. Available from http//:pauf.umd.edu/IPP/fall 1999/exotic_species.htm Accessed March 2004.

———. 2000. "Why exotic species are not as bad as we fear". *The Chronicle of Higher Education*. 23 June B7.

Shrader-Frechette, K. 2001. "Non-indigenous species and ecological explanation". *Biology and Philosophy* 16:507-519.

Simberloff, D. and D.R. Strong. 2000. "Counterpoint: exotic species seriously threaten our environment". *Chronicle of Higher Education* 8 September B20.

Steele, F.L. and Hodgdon, A.R. 1968. *Trees and Shrubs of Northern New England*. Concord: Society for the Protection of New Hampshire Forests.

Union of Concerned Scientists. 2004. "Invasive species". *Global Environment*. Available from http://www.ucsusa.org/global_environment/invasive_species/index.cfm. Accessed March 2004.

Varner, G. 2002. "Biocentric individualism" In S. Armstrong and R. Botzler (eds) *Environmental Ethics: Divergence and Convergence*. 3rd edition 2003. Boston: McGraw-Hill, pp. 356-362.

White, L. Jr. 1967. "The historic roots of our environmental crisis". *Science* 155: 1203-1207.

ENVIRONMENTAL ETHICS FROM AN INTERDISCIPLINARY PERSPECTIVE: THE MARQUETTE EXPERIENCE

Jame Schaefer

Abstract

Marquette University's new Interdisciplinary Minor in Environmental Ethics moves beyond a multidisciplinary approach to learning by integrating and applying the knowledge and skills acquired in ecology, natural resource economics, environmental philosophy, earth physics, and theology courses. The first two years of this interdisciplinary program provided an opportunity for faculty and students to experiment with collaborative methods in their individual courses to integrate their efforts in a capstone seminar that focused on the ethical implications of electricity generation and use in the United States. From this experience, a more comprehensive approach to addressing environmental problems from an ethical perspective was developed, and more effective ways of teaching and learning were identified to improve the program.

Keywords: environmental ethics, multidisciplinary, interdisciplinary, environmental education, electricity generation

Introduction

Marquette University is a Catholic, Jesuit institution "dedicated to serving God by serving our students and contributing to the advancement of knowledge."[1] Through academic and co-curricular programs, Marquette strives "to develop men and women who will dedicate their lives to the service of others, actively entering into the struggle for a more just society."[2] The University's curriculum is structured around offering students the skills, knowledge, experience, and ethical orientation to be informed and effective citizens engaged in this struggle.

In recent years, faculty members have recognized that the pursuit of knowledge and the struggle for justice have a wider compass than has been understood traditionally. Whereas the traditional approach to advancing knowledge has been departmentalized, environmental issues touch on several different ways of knowing that need to be engaged if these issues are to be addressed effectively. Furthermore, whereas the traditional struggle for justice has centered on relationships among humans, the inseparable connections among *homo sapiens*, other

Clare Palmer (Ed.), *Teaching Environmental Ethics*, 173-189.
© *2006 Koninklijke Brill NV. Printed in the Netherlands.*

species, and the natural environment need to be factored into the concept of justice from which actions aimed toward achieving justice in the world can be discerned.

Cognizant of the need to move toward more inclusive ways of learning about the natural environment, Marquette professors initiated dialogue in 1999 to consider how they could offer students an opportunity to reflect comprehensively on the ethical implications of environmental concerns. These gatherings led to the development of a proposal to establish an interdisciplinary minor in environmental ethics through which undergraduate students could draw upon and integrate the knowledge and skills learned through multiple disciplines.[3] After nearly two years of collaboration and successful advancement of a proposal through the University's approval process, the Interdisciplinary Minor in Environmental Ethics was launched in Fall 2001. Eight students completed the program by December 2003 while others proceed towards various stages of completion.

The purpose of this article is to share the Marquette experience and to welcome suggestions for improving upon it. In the first part, I cover the rationale, goals and requirements of the minor. Focus is placed subsequently on the capstone seminar offered for the first time during the Spring 2003 semester. I conclude with lessons learned that are now being implemented in order to make the program more effective.

The Interdisciplinary Minor in Environmental Ethics

Two fundamental and interrelated goals guide Marquette's environmental ethics minor. One is to enhance student understanding of environmental issues by drawing upon and integrating the knowledge and skills provided by several pertinent disciplines. The second is to prepare students to consider more thoughtfully, and to address more effectively, the serious ethical questions pertaining to the natural environment today. Going beyond the multidisciplinary approach, in which each discipline deals with the natural environment from the perspective of its own data, methods and purviews, to integrating the disciplines for reflection, discussion and application by the students is deemed essential for a comprehensive approach to complex environmental concerns.[4]

These two goals are advanced by five specific student objectives:

(1) To acquire the basic scientific knowledge needed for a sound understanding of existing and projected environmental problems;

(2) To become aware of the political and economic contexts within which environmental problems emerge and the means offered by the social sciences for addressing them;

(3) To be familiar with theological and philosophical traditions and methods that ground and guide reflection on the ethical implications of environmental concerns;

(4) To learn how literature and the humanities help people understand their relationship to the natural environment and the responsibilities that spring therefrom; and,

(5 To discern how the various disciplines can contribute to addressing environmental problems from an ethical perspective.[5]

Inherent in these objectives is the recognition that each of the disciplines has distinctive data, methods, purviews, and limitations when approaching environmental issues. No one or two can address environmental issues adequately in light of their complexities, and all are needed for their comprehensive resolution.[6]

The Minor strives to integrate studies in the fields of ecology, physics, economics, philosophy, and theology. Four already active courses were incorporated into the program, one course that had been offered under a generic Department of Theology number was given a dedicated number, and a capstone seminar was created as a culminating experience aimed at integrating the disciplines on an environmental issue. While the five core courses approach the natural environment from diverse disciplinary perspectives, the faculty members who teach these courses advance the two program goals explicitly and implicitly in course lectures, discussions, and assignments. The capstone seminar builds upon the knowledge and skills learned in the core courses by bringing them together to address one ecological problem as described below.

Specifically, the five core courses introduce students to the knowledge and skills offered by each discipline. The required biology course, Biology 040 *Ecology*, focuses on the complex interactions of living organisms and their physical and chemical environment. Physics 009 *Earth and Environmental Physics* explores the effects of human population and activities on the environment, placing emphasis on energy exchanges, the energy balance of the earth, land and water use, the water cycle, and the effects of chemical and physical pollution on water and the atmosphere. Economics 163 *Environmental and Natural Resource Economics* guides student investigation of the linkage between economic growth and environmental change when the natural capacity of an ecological system to provide services to humans, other animal species, and plants is affected.

While studies in physics, biology, and economics expose students to ways in which the physical and social sciences approach ecological realities, the Minor as a whole is geared toward grappling with philosophical and religious foundations for addressing ecological concerns. Philosophy 132 *Environmental Philosophy* considers the philosophical bases of ecological theory, including the relationship between humans and the physical world, the value standing of natural entities and systems, the morality of making tradeoffs between species, and the ethics of limiting consumption and population. This course is crucial for training students to reflect logically on the ethical dimensions of environmental matters.

Theology 171 *Foundations for Ecological Ethics* explores religious bases for valuing and acting responsibly toward other species, ecological systems, and the biosphere. The course examines carefully and critically some concepts found in the Bible, texts by eminent Christian theologians, and Catholic social teachings to determine the extent to which they can be helpful when responding to ecological degradation. Among these concepts are the goodness, beauty, sacramentality, and integrity of creation, caring for creation, its restrained and grateful use, the kinship of creatures, living virtuously on Earth, and demonstrating preference for the poor. Because some of these concepts surface in the works of writers whose views of the world differ vastly from our current scientific understanding of the cosmological development of the universe and the biological evolution of species, promising concepts are critically retrieved and reformulated to reflect basic contemporary scientific findings. This "critical-creative" approach to reworking pre-scientific theological ideas so they reflect basic findings by the scientific community today provides a realistic understanding of humans in relation to other species and ecological systems. This approach also facilitates more plausible theological discourse rather than falling into the anthropocentrism that permeates patristic and medieval texts, albeit from a theocentric perspective.[7] Students subsequently work out principles of normative behavior from these revised concepts, and apply the norms to ecological problems they select and research from scholarly, governmental, and advocacy literature. Also examined critically are concepts in other major religious traditions (e.g., Judaism, Islam, Hinduism, Jainism, Buddhism, and Native American tribal religions). This exercise provides the additional benefits of raising student awareness of and appreciation for other cultures and of identifying some shared concepts that can serve as the basis for a global system of environmental ethics.[8] The application of principles from various religious foundations to current ecological problems has proven to be especially instructive for students, not only in understanding concrete situations but also in determining how they can be addressed at various levels of society.

The achievement of interdisciplinarity is promoted by contact between professors in the different core areas. Professors who offer the required philosophy and theology courses emphasize links to the subject matters of ecology, physics, and economics. Those who teach the philosophy and theology courses invite the ecology professor into class sessions early in the semester to lecture on the basics of ecology. In the required theology course, the ecology professor also identifies scholarly sources for students to peruse when researching the ecological problems they track in connection with the various theological themes (e.g., the goodness, beauty, and integrity of creation). The philosophy course usually incorporates readings on the economic dimensions of environmental problems. Both philosophy and theology courses address environmental justice concerns from the perspectives of their disciplines, and experts outside of the immediate Marquette community are invited occasionally into class sessions. When visiting professors are on campus to give public lectures on issues relating to the natural environment, students are alerted to these opportunities and, whenever possible, visiting professors are invited into class sessions of courses required for the Minor to discuss issues in greater depth. Special gatherings with visiting professors are arranged for students who are undertaking the Minor so that they are exposed to leading scholars in the field.

Recognizing that other disciplines provide knowledge and skills that are significant to understanding and addressing environmental concerns, faculty members have identified additional courses that complement those required for the Minor. They include anthropology, the environment of municipalities, chemistry, environmental literature, journalistic reporting on the natural environment, and the constructive relationship between religion and science. The anthropology course provides students with a realistic understanding of the evolution of the human species and the human connection with other species from and with whom humankind evolved over time. In the chemistry course, students gain an intricate understanding of chemical composition, the interconnections of natural chemicals in the physical world, the effects that chemicals manufactured by humans have on living beings and ecological systems, and the unknowns about manufactured chemicals and their interactions that require additional research. The religion-science course engenders an understanding of the complementarity of theology and the natural sciences on issues at their boundaries when the data, methods, purviews, and limitations of the disciplines are recognized and respected. Focus on the city and the natural environment can be particularly helpful to student understanding of environmental problems that are unique to municipalities, how they are being addressed, and complications as well as impediments to addressing complex issues. The course on environmental literature develops student sensitivity to discerning the innuendos of literary expressions about the natural environment, while the journalism course facilitates informed writing about environmental issues. The capstone seminar draws upon the knowledge and skills learned in the required and complementary courses.

The Capstone Seminar: Electricity Generation and Use

At the culmination of the Interdisciplinary Minor in Environmental Ethics, the capstone seminar offers students an opportunity to integrate the knowledge and skills already learned and to collaborate in exploring the ethical dimensions of one particular problem. Complementary courses that students have completed in disciplines recommended, but not required, for the Minor are also identified and drawn upon during seminar discussion and designation of research tasks.

Conceived originally as a cooperative learning experience, students are required to identify research needs, report periodically on research findings, point to additional areas needing investigation, reflect as a group on the ethical implications of their findings, and make decisions together about the most promising ethical approach to the problem studied. The final demonstration of a student's achievement of the Minor's goals and objectives is the student's contributions to a written report on an ethical response to the problem.[9]

The first capstone seminar was conducted during the Spring 2003 semester and engaged ten students in addressing the generation and use of electricity in the United States. This topic was selected from several possibilities by the capstone professor, in consultation with students who preregistered for the seminar and with faculty members who taught required and complementary courses. As the Director of the Interdisciplinary Minor and designated capstone professor, I had extensive experience of this topic,[10] and the other professors indicated their preparedness to deal with it from the perspectives of their disciplines. Also significant in the selection of this topic was the fact that the U.S. Congress was in the process of considering several versions of an energy policy for the nation, and the faculty hoped that this process might stimulate increased student interest in an issue into which they might have some input.[11]

Six Marquette scholars representing the departments of Biology, Economics, Philosophy, Physics, Electrical Engineering, and English participated in the capstone seminar. Representatives of state and federal governments and officials from the Wisconsin electric utilities, energy efficiency companies, environmental advocacy groups, and religious organizations were involved at appropriate times. Though the topic was overly ambitious in scope and scale, the seminar was judged a highly engaging, stimulating, and productive educational experience by students and faculty.[12]

Students sought and achieved the primary program goals and student objectives established by the College of Arts & Sciences for the environmental ethics Minor[13] by (1) applying the knowledge and skills learned in other courses required for the Minor when researching the facts, problems and ethical concerns pertaining to electricity generation and use in the United States, (2) identifying ethical principles that flow from religious foundations for guiding the generation and use of electricity, (3) listening carefully and engaging thoughtfully in conversations with one another, Marquette scholars, and representatives of government, electric utilities, environmental advocacy groups, and religious organizations about electricity generation and use, and (4) working cooperatively to develop a seminar strategy for addressing the topic informed by the disciplines pertinent to the Minor. The students were evaluated on the basis of their participation in seminar discussions on assigned readings and review of proposal drafts (30%), presentations and reports on energy sources (30%), draft and final versions of assigned sections of the proposal (30%), and final reflection on the seminar (10%).

Texts consulted included Thomas Casten's *Turning Off the Heat* (1998), *Energy: Science, Policy and the Pursuit of Sustainability* edited by Robert Bent, Lloyd Orr, and Randall Baker (2001), and Donald Brown's *American Heat: Ethical Problems with the United States' Response to Global Warming* (2002). Bent, Orr and Baker's anthology provided a basic interdisciplinary perspective on global energy problems from which students drew when addressing electricity generation and use in the United States. Brown's text proved indispensable for identifying key ethical concerns that have been absent in positions advocated by the United States government during global warming negotiations. Casten's market-based solution for decarbonizing the United States' economy, promoting energy efficiency, and establishing a renewable energy future sparked critical and creative dialogue among the students. A plethora of articles and documents from federal and state governments, electric utilities, private renewable energy contractors, and advocacy groups were also assigned for full seminar discussion or consideration by teams. An on-line learning program[14] was used for additional dialogue among the students and for downloading team-generated presentations and drafts of reports.[15] The seminar met formally for two hours once a week with team sessions held in between.

At the commencement of the seminar, students reviewed current statistics issued by the United States Department of Energy on national and sector electricity consumption and types of generation that a professor in Marquette's Department of Electrical Engineering had prepared for their use. Also examined were the Energy Policy Proposal formulated under the leadership of the Vice President of the United States and the latest versions of energy bills in the U.S. House of Representatives and Senate. The students considered several ways of organizing their research project and began to draft an outline for the final seminar report. Components needed for each report were identified in seminar, and the desire for uniformity was upheld in order to produce a cohesive report. Categories of various types of information and sources were specified after deliberation on the possibilities, and the students opted for a combination of scholarly sources from the pertinent disciplines, federal and state documents, information from non-governmental organizations, including religious and environmental advocacy groups, public utilities that generate electricity, and official statements by the hierarchy of the Catholic Church and the Society of Jesus. For their first research tasks, the students selected the areas of generating electricity from non-renewable sources—coal, nuclear, oil, and natural gas.

Seminar sessions turned to the knowledge, skills, and insights on electricity generation and use available through the Minor's core disciplines. After reviewing the characteristics of their disciplines, professors from the departments of Philosophy, Physics, Biology, Economics and Electrical Engineering presented their perspectives on the topic and discussed key points of the articles assigned in advance for students to read.[16] Each professor pointed to the scope and limitations of their own discipline, what it offered toward understanding the topic, and the need for other types of knowledge. The philosophy professor laid out alternate theoretical approaches to ethical principles that can be helpful to the seminar task, including Aldo Leopold's "land ethic."[17] When prompted by the students, the professors shared their reactions to proposals for constructing a coal-fired electricity generation park south of Milwaukee, calls for more nuclear power plants now that the Nevada waste disposal site for spent nuclear fuel has been approved by federal officials, and renewable energy sources. Students probed with considerable interest the professors' rationales for the positions they took on these issues and the ethical principles they were following. The five professors graciously welcomed additional student inquiries for the remainder of the semester.

As the theology professor, I covered the religious foundations from which moral principles pertinent to the topic could be drawn. All of the students but one had completed Theology 171 *Foundations for Ecological Ethics* the semester before, so they were quick to discern some of the most salient Christian concepts to retrieve when dealing with electricity generation and use now and into the future. They chose to stress reformulated concepts pertaining to the integrity of creation and the need for humans to cooperate with other species and abiota for their common good.[18] They also decided to draw upon the moral virtues in the teachings of Thomas Aquinas;[19] his treatment of the virtue of prudence was especially appealing as the step-by-step approach to decision-making that is needed when dealing with future electricity generation and use. They construed the virtue of justice more broadly to include other-than-humans, the virtue of temperance as a basic principle for constraining the use of electricity, and the virtue of fortitude as the inclination needed to enable individuals to remain steadfast with their ethical stances. The students also reviewed new materials that conveyed the views of the

Society of Jesus on environmental issues,[20] and they decided that
the sacramentality of the physical world as the mediator of God's
presence and character and the Jesuit call to justice would be guiding foundations for their deliberations. Two students agreed to draft
the theology report which was slated to be considered subsequently
by the others during a seminar session.

The seminar turned to team presentations on non-renewable sources
of generating electricity. Using audio-visual programs, the students
shared their research on natural gas, oil, coal, and nuclear generation. Each covered the national and regional statistics on using that
source, the stages of the fuel cycle from extraction to disposal, environmental problems at each stage, limitations and advantages, alternate or improved ways of generating electricity than that under
consideration, and initial ideas for addressing the source from an
ethical perspective. The reports were lively, engaging, and sometimes
humorous. Questions and challenging comments followed each presentation in a spirit of "shared inquiry" and desire to produce a
worthwhile and meaningful report. Considerable attention was given
to the initial recommendations proffered by the various teams, and
recommendations were challenged and reworked after serious deliberation about what should be done and why. For example, the recommendation by the research team to encourage the generation of
electricity by nuclear fission was contested for ethical and economic
reasons, the need for more information was identified, and an eventual consensus was reached to discourage the building of new nuclear
power plants in the United States "until radioactive waste/spent fuel
disposal is available for current plants and wastes slated for disposal
are sufficiently minimized to preclude the need for a second high-
level radioactive waste repository."[21] The research teams for each of
the non-renewable areas of investigation proceeded to draft their
reports based on the agreements reached during seminar discussions.
I commented in writing on their drafts, the reports were revised
accordingly, and, if acceptable, they were added to the project's electronic file.

A similar process was followed when addressing the generation of
electricity from renewable sources—biomass, geothermal, hydrogen,
hydropower, solar, and wind. In addition to assigned readings on these
sources, national statistics on energy generation from renewables, and
other sources the students identified via the www, the students learned
from a panel of representatives of organizations advocating the move-

ment to renewable sources, and from small businesses that manufacture and service wind generators, solar panels for collecting heat, solar cells for producing electricity, and hydrogen fuel cells. Equally important were the reasons these people gave for working in their field. Some were solidly religion-based, and most were idealistic and inspiring while remaining realistic about obstacles to achieving the ideal. The students' subsequent presentations in seminar on wind, solar, geothermal, biomass, and hydrogen sources for generating electricity demonstrated how positively impressed they were with their findings.

While the students were in the process of completing their research on renewable sources for generating electricity, the President of Wisconsin Energy Corporation presented the industry's perspective on electricity generation through non-renewable and renewable sources. He emphasized coal as the most proven and promising near-term source. Students who had researched this non-renewable source asked pointed questions and pursued the need for implementing co-generation and distributed electricity (the small-scale production of electricity at or near customers' homes and businesses) techniques so the by-products of electricity generation would be put to efficient use. A representative of one of the leading non-governmental advocacy groups in the State of Wisconsin, Wisconsin's Environmental Decade, followed and encouraged moving toward renewable sources and more efficient use of electricity in all sectors of the economy.

The students proceeded to research options for using electricity more efficiently in all sectors of the economy—residential, commercial, industrial, public utility, government, and education. Receiving considerable attention was the importance of striving for "sustainable development," which the students construed within the context of their project as using electricity efficiently and appropriately in all sectors of the economy, producing electricity in ways that minimize environmental degradation, avoiding the depletion of non-renewable sources at the expense of future generations, relying on renewable sources as the "mainstay" of the United States' economy, and assuring that the electricity *needs* of all people are met while maintaining a stable global climate.[22] Student interaction was lively when questioning why electricity should be used more efficiently from ethical and religiously-grounded perspectives.

A representative of Franciscans International stirred student interest in religious motivation for advocating more wise and efficient generation and use of electricity. The sacramental and justice perspectives she

shared bolstered the rationale of the theology report that two students had drafted around the themes of the unity of creation, human
collaboration with God by living virtuously, solidarity with the poor,
and the principle of subsidiarity which requires appropriate action
from the individual to the international community.[23] After an iter-
ative process of reviewing and revising their work, the students produced an excellent report that provided solid religious foundations
for subsequent deliberations on the recommendations that had been
drafted by the various teams.[24] The students recognized that their
recommendations had to flow from these foundations if they desired
a logical and cohesive report, and they worked assiduously toward
this goal.

The remainder of the seminar centered on in-depth discussions of
the draft student recommendations for electricity generation by sources
and use by sectors. With these draft recommendations in hand, members of each team took turns leading discussions, listening to suggestions, mediating differences, coming to a consensus whenever
possible, and resorting to majority vote where reaching a consensus
proved impossible. An especially poignant and anguished discussion
occurred when students grappled with the economic circumstances,
adverse direct or indirect effects from all methods of generating electricity, and impediments to more efficient use of electricity in all sectors. Their discussion resulted in a decision to strive for an ideal
future with interim measures to achieve it. The "trajectory" of their
proposal speaks well for itself:

> We look to a future in which electricity is produced in ways that envi-
> ronmental degradation is minimized, non-renewable sources are not
> depleted at the expense of future generations, renewable sources are
> the mainstay of our economy, electricity is used efficiently and appro-
> priately in all sectors of our economy, the basic electricity needs of all
> people are met, and the global climate is stable. In our vision for the
> future, a balance exists between the desires of the consumer and the
> needs of the global biotic community, and ecological diversity provides
> the natural defense against devastating catastrophes.
>
> To facilitate the realization of this future, we encourage improvement
> in the efficiency in which electricity is produced and used. The most
> efficient methods possible should be employed when generating electricity
> from traditional fuels. Consumers of electricity should use efficient
> appliances and lights, and they should embrace simple methods of sav-
> ing electricity. Fuel sources for the production of electricity should shift
> from primarily non-renewable to renewable sources, with renewables
> subsidized at levels at least comparable to non-renewables. This shift

should be accompanied by an orientation toward distributed generation and comprehensive co-generation of heat and electricity. Greenhouse
gas emissions should be decreased dramatically to ensure that future
generations inherit a stable climate in which adequate food production and standard of living are possible for all. The present array of
traditional means of producing electricity cannot be sustained far into
the future, and modifications need to be made so more varied and
renewable types of generating electricity become available. Within the
varied contexts of the diverse regions of the United States, a portfo-
lio of generation methods should be implemented in order to moderate the negative consequences of each form of production.[25]

Conscious of the need for action at all levels of society, the students
appealed to "all who can bring about changes in their homes, in
their businesses, in manufacturing products, in generating electricity,
in government at all levels, in educational institutions, and in places
of worship." They reasoned:

> Every member of society engages in behavior that affects electricity
> use and its effects on the environment to a greater or lesser extent,
> so we wish to address individuals and groups in their respective deci-
> sion-making capacities about the ethical implications of the production
> and consumption of electricity. We are especially cognizant of the
> efforts currently underway in the United States Congress to develop
> an energy plan, and we hope our elected representatives will consider
> our vision for the future and how to arrive there.[26]

Altogether, the students made ninety-two recommendations for more
ethically responsible electricity generation and use.[27] Thirty-two focused
on electricity use in the various sectors of the economy, thirty-five on
generating electricity by renewable sources, and twenty-five on using
non-renewable sources for electricity generation.

For the culminating session, U.S. Senator Russell Feingold from
Wisconsin sent his Washington, D.C.-based energy and environment
aide to Marquette to inform students about the legislative process,
to listen to the presentation of their report, and to comment on their
recommendations.[28] This visit was indeed timely since she left the
U.S. Senate while a Senate-House conference committee was in the
process of marking up the legislators' energy bill, and she took back
for their consideration some of the Marquette students' recommendations that she thought would be appealing and acceptable from a
budgetary perspective.[29] This affirmation of their thinking was grat-
ifying for the students. Students, faculty, parents, friends, and visitors from Northwestern University who were interested in tackling

a similar project attended the session and cheered the Marquette students for their seminal efforts. Several were also awarded certificates acknowledging their completion of the Interdisciplinary Minor in Environmental Ethics.

Conclusions

Marquette's experience with teaching environmental ethics from an interdisciplinary perspective has yielded many benefits for students and faculty. The capstone seminar provided an invaluable opportunity for students to integrate and apply the knowledge and skills they had learned through their studies in their various courses to addressing the problem of electricity generation and use in the United States from an ethical perspective. Student integration of the various disciplines' approaches yielded a more comprehensive and effective proposal than one or two disciplines could have provided. Reflecting in depth from solid philosophical and religious foundations, the students were able to reason systematically to the types of behavior that should be demonstrated. They learned to balance the ideal solution against the economic circumstances, direct and indirect effects of the various methods of generating electricity, and impediments to more efficient use of electricity in all sectors of the economy. They argued for a trajectory within which reasonable means would be used to achieve an ideal future.

The students also learned how to work cooperatively with one another, to lead discussions, to negotiate toward a consensus, and to reach a majority conclusion when a consensus could not be achieved. The faculty involved in this process were enriched by the students' questions, impressed by the seriousness with which they probed for solutions, and delighted with the appreciation they demonstrated when considering team reports and recommendations.

Despite the fact that this seminar proved to be an outstanding learning experience, it was overly ambitious. Focusing on electricity use by sector or the generation of electricity by non-renewable or renewable sources would have been more manageable and perhaps more intellectually satisfying, since several students commented that they did not feel sufficiently "expert" from their research to make the informed case they would have preferred to have made. The topic of the next capstone seminar is under careful consideration to assure that the work can be accomplished during one semester and that students can experience greater confidence in their research and ethical reflections. Finally, the need to engage political science professors in the next capstone and in the program overall is crucial to its success, since most environmental concerns translate one way or another into policy decisions.

NOTES

1. Marquette University (1998).
2. Ibid.
3. Environmental Ethics Facilitating Committee (August 2000).
4. On Marquette's campus and elsewhere, the lines between traditional fields of study have proven to be permeable as scholars recognize the limitations of their disciplines in providing perspectives on complex issues and realize that more comprehensive learning can be provided when multiple disciplines are tapped and integrated. The emergence of a variety of new, integrative fields of study (e.g., interdisciplinary minors and/or majors in Women's, International, African-American, Justice and Peace, Urban and Environmental Affairs, Medieval, Applied Mathematical Economics, and Family Studies) attests to the University's movement toward multidisciplinary and interdisciplinary learning. An informative overview of interdisciplinary learning at other institutions is provided by Hutchins Center for Interdisciplinary Learning at www.sonoma.edu/virtcomm/hutchcent.html. Among the promising analyses of interdisciplinary efforts are Ivanitskaya, Clark, and Montgomery (2002), Kimskey (2002), Klein (1996), Klein and Newell (1996), and Newell (1990). Particularly encouraging of outcomes are Lewis and Shana (2003) and Newell (1996). The National Endowment for the Arts offers grants for multi-disciplinary and interdisciplinary projects (www.nea.gov/grants/apply/GAP05.Multi.html).
5. These student objectives are paraphrased from "Proposal to the College of Arts & Sciences to Establish an Interdisciplinary Minor in Environmental Ethics" (August 2002) submitted by the Environmental Ethics Facilitating Committee comprised of faculty from Biology, Communications, Economics, English, Philosophy, Physics, Political Science, and Theology. See http://www.inee.mu.edu.
6. This perspective accords with the burgeoning literature on the constructive relationship between religion and science. Among a plethora of examples, see Barbour (1997), Haught (1995), and Polkinghorne (1994).
7. See Schaefer (2001) for an explanation and demonstration of this "critical-creative" approach to retrieving patristic and medieval notions in the Christian tradition. See further Schaefer (2002) and (2003). An overview of these notions is provided in Schaefer (2004).
8. When working with these shared concepts, students have recognized that the impetus for acting morally may be dulled if the particularities of a religion are not evident to those who profess it.
9. Environmental Ethics Facilitating Committee (2000).
10. Among my experiences with electricity generation and use issues are serving on energy task forces by appointment of the Governor of the State of Wisconsin and the Archbishop of the Archdiocese of Milwaukee, chairing the State of Wisconsin's Radioactive Waste Review Board when the U.S. Department of Energy was searching for a crystalline rock formation in which to store highly radioactive spent fuel from commercial nuclear power plants, and serving as a member of the State of Wisconsin's Low-Level Radioactive Waste Commission by appointment of the State Legislature.

188   JAME SCHAEFER

11. Toward that end, I worked closely with staff in the offices of the Senators and Members of the House of Representatives in the U.S. Congress to keep informed about pending legislation.

12. INEE Capstone Seminar Students (2003).

13. Environmental Ethics Facilitating Committee (2000).

14. Blackboard, accessible from http://bb.mu.edu.

15. Early in the semester, environmentally sensitive ways in which the seminar could proceed were identified, and minimizing the use of paper was adhered to throughout the seminar deliberations.

16. Three sessions were dedicated to these presentations so the students had a reasonable amount of time to sift out the differences in the disciplines and to think about how they contributed in unique but complementary ways to the seminar topic.

17. Leopold (1966), 262.

18. This theme is explored thoughtfully by Van Till (1996). Also see Schaefer (2002).

19. See Schaefer (2003) for a reformulation of Aquinas's thinking about the moral virtues and application to environmental problem-solving.

20. The students were particularly impressed with the discussions by the General Congregation of the Society of Jesus (1999) and the Society's Superior General Kolvenbach (1997).

21. INEE Capstone Seminar Students (2003).

22. The students decided on this pointed use of the contested phrase "sustainable development" after considering several versions of its use. The most extensive sustainable development program is advanced by the United Nations through its Department of Economic and Social Affairs (http://www.un.org/esa/sustdev/sdissues/sdissues.htm).

23. Graduating seniors Laura Blazer and Joseph Rowley penned this report, which is accessible through INEE Capstone Seminar Students (2003).

24. The principle of subsidiary requires taking action appropriate to one level of responsibility (e.g., the family) before moving to or appealing for action at another level (e.g., the neighborhood or the civil community). See Verstraeten (1998) and Leys (1995).

25. INEE Capstone Seminar Students (2003).

26. Ibid.

27. Ibid.

28. Senator Feingold's aide received an electronic copy of the students' report before arriving on campus and demonstrated through her questioning and reference to the report that she had read it. The students were impressed with her attention to their efforts.

29. Including in electric bills an estimate of the effects on the environment by the amount of electricity used appealed to the fiscally conservative Senator from the State of Wisconsin. The students wished to underscore the need for people to be educated about the adverse effects of electricity generation and the need to use electricity more efficiently.

REFERENCES

Barbour, Ian. 1997. *Religion and Science: Historical and Contemporary Issues*. San Francisco: HarperSanFrancisco.

Bent, Robert, Lloyd Orr and Randall Baker (eds). 2001. *Energy: Science, Policy and the Pursuit of Sustainability*. Washington D.C.: Island Press.

Brown, Donald A. 2002. *American Heat: Ethical Problems with the United States' Response to Global Warming*. Lanham, Md: Rowman and Littlefield.

Casten, Thomas R. 1998. *Turning Off the Heat: Why America Must Double Energy Efficiency to Save Money and Reduce Global Warming*. Amherst, NY: Prometheus Books.

Environmental Ethics Facilitating Committee. 2000. "Proposal for Establishing an Interdisciplinary Minor in Environmental Ethics". http://www.inee.mu.edu/Proposal%20for%20INEE.htm.

General Congregation of the Society of Jesus. 1999. "We Live in a Broken World: Reflections on Ecology". *Promotio Justitiae* 70 (April).

Haught, John F. 1995. *Science and Religion: From Conflict to Conversation*. New York: Paulist

INEE Capstone Seminar Students. 2003. "Generating and Using Electricity in the United States". ARSC 110 Capstone Seminar Proposal, Interdisciplinary Minor in Environmental Ethics, Marquette University, 29 April. http://www.inee.mu.edu/Capstone%202003/Proposal.htm.

Ivanitskaya, Lana, Deborah Clark and George Montgomery. 2002. "Interdisciplinary Learning: Process and Outcomes". *Innovative Higher Education* 27.2: 95-102.

Kimskey, William D. 2002. "General Education, Interdisciplinary Pedagogy and the Process of Content Transformation". *Education* 122.3: 587-94.

Klein, Julie Thompson. 1996. *Crossing Boundaries: Knowledge, Disciplinarities, and Inter-disciplinarities*. Charlottesville: University Press of Virginia.

Klein, Julie Thompson and William H. Newell. 1996. "Advancing Interdisciplinary Studies" in Jerry Gaff and James Ratcliff (eds) *Handbook of the Undergraduate Curriculum*. San Francisco: Jossey-Bass, pp. 393-415.

Kolvenbach, Peter-Hans. 1998. "Our Responsibility for God's Creation". Address at the Opening of Arrupe College, Zimbabwe, 22 August.

Leopold, Aldo 1966. *A Sand County Almanac: With Essays on Conservation from Round River*. New York: Ballantine.

Lewis, Valerie K. and Steven H. Shaha. 2003. "Maximizing Learning and Attitudinal Gains Through Integrated Curricula". *Education* 123.3: 537-47.

Leys, Ad. 1995. *Ecclesiological Impacts of the Principle of Subsidiary*. Kampen: Kok.

Marquette University. 1998. "Mission Statement". http://www.marquette.edu/pages/home/about/wearemu/mission.

Newell, William H. 1990. "Interdisciplinary Curriculum Development". *Issues in Integrative Studies* 8: 69-70.

Polkinghorne, John. 1994. *The Faith of a Physicist: Reflections of a Bottom-Up Thinker*. The Gifford Lectures for 1993-4. Princeton: Princeton University.

Schaefer, Jame. 2001. "Appreciating the Beauty of Earth". *Theological Studies* 62: 23-52.

——. 2002. "Grateful Cooperation: Cistercian Inspiration for Ecosystem Ethics". *Cistercian Studies Quarterly* 37.2: 187-203.

——. 2001. "Acting Reverently in God's Sacramental World," in Francis A. Eigo (ed.) *Ethical Dilemmas in the New Millennium II*. Villanova: Villanova University, 37-90.

——. 2003. "The Virtuous Cooperator: Modeling the Human in an Age of Ecological Degradation". *Worldviews: Environment, Culture, Religion* 7.1-2: 171-95.

——. 2004. "Catholic Foundations for Environmental Ethics: A Critical-Creative Approach to Patristic and Medieval Notions". *Current Issues in Catholic Higher Education* 24.1: 31-67.

Van Till, Howard J. 1996. "Basil, Augustine, and the Doctrine of Creation's Functional Integrity". *Science and Christian Belief* 8: 21-38.

Verstraeten, J. 1998. "Solidarity and Subsidiarity", in David A. Boileau (ed.) *Principles of Catholic Social Teaching*. Milwaukee: Marquette University, pp. 133-148.

TEACHING THE LAND ETHIC[1]

Michael P. Nelson

Abstract
This paper discusses the teaching of the Leopoldian Land Ethic in an environmental ethics class. The Leopoldian Land Ethic is arguably the most fully formulated and developed environmental ethic to date. Moreover, at least in North
America, it is also the ethical reference point of choice for conservation workers
both within and outside of government service, and thus it is particularly important that students who will pursue such careers are exposed to it. Although there
are a number of ways to unpack the Land Ethic in a university environmental
ethics classroom, and for more public audiences, this paper outlines one method
that has been highly effective in both teaching settings over a long period of time.

Keywords: Land Ethic, Aldo Leopold, environmental ethics, evolution of ethics, environmental education

Introduction

For well over a decade now my undergraduate environmental ethics
class has culminated with a philosophical exegesis of the Land Ethic[2]
of Aldo Leopold. This is a class that I have taught every semester
to over 150 students who are predominately from our College of
Natural Resources. These students generally self-identify as "science-
and practically-minded"; they study forestry, water and soil science,
environmental education, general resources and land management,
and the like; and most will go directly from their undergraduate edu-
cations to entry-level natural resource work for both government and
private agencies. Only a handful of philosophy majors or philosophy majors with a concentration in environmental ethics take the
course each semester. The course also satisfies the university's manda-
tory "Environmental Literacy" requirement and therefore attracts
many students who need to satisfy this General Degree Requirement.
In short, this large course is predominately made up of students who
are required to take it. This course is also the legacy of the first
course in the world taught in environmental ethics by J. Baird Callicott
beginning in 1971.

Clare Palmer (Ed.), *Teaching Environmental Ethics*, 190-201.

Leopold's Land Ethic, I tell my students, is arguably the most fully formulated, developed, and debated environmental ethic to date. In my frequent interactions with colleagues from other academic disciplines and with US conservation organizations from both the private and government sectors, I have also become keenly aware that "Leopoldian" is the language that can bridge gaps between academia and public service, between academic disciplines, and between narrowly anthropocentrically motivated conservationists and those whose environmental concern is prompted by other, more non-anthropocentric, sensibilities. In addition to the purely pedagogical, philosophical, and intellectual reasons to prescribe a heavy dose of Aldo Leopold in my course, given that many of my students will become professional conservationists, I view teaching the Land Ethic as a way to instill within them something that will serve them professionally. This essay serves as at least a rough outline of how I teach the Land Ethic in such a course.

Recently, on the first day of a one week graduate Environmental Education course in Environmental Ethics, students handed in an assignment in which they were asked to indicate what familiarity they already had with topics that were going to be covered during the course. I was especially struck by the comments made by one student:

> While I have some familiarity with nearly all of the topics on the syllabus, I'm not sure what the land ethic is. Don't get me wrong, of course I have heard of the land ethic and of Aldo Leopold, and I have heard over and over how we need to begin to live according to the land ethic, blah blah blah. But what does that mean, I mean what *is* the land ethic and how does it work? I hope we cover that in detail in this course and we don't just gloss over it like I see done most of the time.

When I spoke with her about her comments I found that she was upset by what she thought to be a lack of critical reflection and philosophical development of the Land Ethic in both the environmental literature with which she was familiar, and the natural resources courses she had already taken at the university. Likewise, she seemed convinced that in order to do anything other than preach to the choir of "Land Ethic or Leopold faithful", more had to be said. "How can we respond to those who don't think nature merits moral consideration?", she asked. This seems a serious concern not only worthy of, but demanding, a response; a response, I assured her, that would be forthcoming during the course.

Teaching the Leopold Land Ethic: Moral consideration

In its most basic manifestation it is obvious what the Land Ethic is. Leopold makes this very clear. In fact, Leopold even goes so far as to provide us with a summation of his Land Ethic. Leopold's summary moral maxim states that "A thing is right when it tends to preserve the integrity, stability, and beauty of the biotic community. It is wrong when it tends otherwise" (1949: 224-5, 1966: 262).[3] This is one of the most oft-quoted two sentences in all of conservation literature. It emblazons t-shirts, bumper stickers, and park benches. It has become almost a holy mantra among environmentalists. According to the summary moral maxim of the Land Ethic, actions (individual or collective—always a point worth pausing for and asking about in class) ought to be judged right or good if they promote the health of the biotic community and wrong or bad if they harm the biotic community. Voila! . . . notoriously difficult ethical decisions made simple.

However, summary moral maxims of ethical positions are just that: boiled-down, intentionally understated attempts to wrap up a more robust moral position. As a result, they often fail to capture the true and complete essence of the author's intentions. However, we surely know that there is more to Jeremy Bentham's utilitarianism than just "actions are right if they produce the greatest amount of happiness for the greatest number of people", more to Immanuel Kant's theory of rights than "do that action that you would be willing to have made into a universal law", and, likewise, there is more to Leopold's Land Ethic than "A thing is right . . .". Simple reliance on slogans, mantras, and summaries either are no replacement for the understanding of an ethical position at all, or, at best, they are only persuasive to someone who already believes in the ethical position to begin with. Reliance only upon the summary moral maxim of the Land Ethic to convey the meaning of Leopold's ethical position does not allow us to respond to dissenters, nor to articulate why it is that the moral inclusion of the biotic community is called for.

It is this fundamental point—concerning inclusion in the moral community and the nature of ethical systems—that is central to my teaching of the Land Ethic. All ethical systems, including the Land Ethic, address the concept of the moral community, which can be represented by a circle. Those within the circle are included as members of the moral community, and are due direct moral consideration; those outside of the circle are not. This basic—and arguably oversimplified—model of moral discourse serves the course throughout the semester as a way to illustrate the different moral theories that we encounter (environmental ethical theories that generally become more inclusive); hence it is nothing new by the time we get to Leopold.

One useful way to have students think of ethical systems is that said systems are concerned with who or what belongs inside this circle or with who or what merits direct moral consideration; or, conversely, with who or what should be left outside of the circle or with who or what nets either indirect moral consideration, or none at all. This involves asking what it is that determines a position within the circle, what determines where the line is to be drawn, or what the key to moral consideration should be. When one attains membership in the moral community one attains what might be called *direct* moral standing. In other words, moral community membership implies that one counts for reasons greater than one's value as a means to some other end, or that one possesses value beyond mere instrumental value (intrinsic value, that is). When one is left outside of the scope of the moral community one either possesses no value at all (and hence no moral standing at all) or only instrumental value (value as a means to some other end) and only indirect moral standing.

Historically, given that the keys to moral inclusion have been offered as traits that humans were thought to possess to the exclusion of the non-human world, such direct moral standing has only been (more or less) human-inclusive. Many of these "keys to moral consideration" come out in the course of the semester during discussion of other environmental ethical theories, so by this point the students are familiar with this concept and with the history of proffered keys.

However, by claiming that the key to moral consideration is not some single quality but rather that it lies in membership of the biotic community—and that the rightness or wrongness of an action is judged by the contribution it makes to the health of the biotic community—the Land Ethic significantly and radically alters the makeup of the moral community. In Leopold's own words (1949: 204), "the land ethic simply enlarges the boundaries of the [ethical] community to include soils, waters, plants, and animals, or collectively: the land".

So far, then, we know what the end result of the Land Ethic is: a vastly more inclusive moral community. But how does this come about, why should our moral community become more inclusive and with what problems does this present the class?

Teaching the Leopoldian Land Ethic: Evolution and Ethics

Ethics, for Leopold, are—as are other ecological and evolutionary traits—located in a context and always changing or evolving. The Land Ethic builds upon the notion that there is an historical process of ethics—an origin, a growth, and a development—and that we can explain ethics and the development of ethics biologically. For many students, this seems strange (even counter-intuitive) given that they accept a distinction between what we usually view as a neutral and purely objective scientific discipline (biology) on the one hand, and ethics as a more (or totally) subjective humanities discipline on the other; and they think of these two realms as having little or nothing to do with one another. However, a discussion of the is/ought problem at the beginning of the semester usually goes a long way toward at least allowing for the possibility that these two realms are not entirely distinct by the time we reach Leopold.

Interestingly for these particular students, Charles Darwin (1981: chapter III) was the first person to give a biological-progression sort of accounting of ethics. Since Darwin is perceived by the students as a "hard" scientist, they are always willing to at least consider what he might have to say about something like ethics. Darwin wants, even needs, to show that everything about humans is a product of evolution: everything including our ethical characteristics and systems. Clearly, Leopold (and, indeed, most of the students in the course) is more familiar with this sort of a biological or scientific account rather than with a similar philosophical account.[4] So it is no wonder that Leopold uses the Darwinian model to explain the development of ethics, and no wonder that the students in this particular course fight this approach to ethics less than they might some other.

Darwin claims that ethics evolve, and that this evolution is social (we might then refer to such an approach to ethics as a "biosocial" evolution of ethics). In Darwinian fashion, Leopold also speaks of an evolution of ethics when he states, at the very beginning of the "Land Ethic", that the area governed by ethics has grown larger over time. As Leopold (1949: 201) writes "during the three thousand years which have since elapsed [from the era of Odysseus], ethical criteria have been extended to many fields of conduct, with corresponding shrinkages in those judged by expediency only. This extension of ethics . . . is actually a process in ecological evolution". This phenomenon demands explanation.

However, students quickly pick up on a potentially serious problem with this approach to ethics. Darwin is attempting to provide us with a biological account of the existence of ethics, but ethics at first seems to present a significant hurdle for Darwin, and hence for Leopold: How are ethics possible from the point of view of the theory of evolution? At first glance even Leopold admits that they seem to be impossible from an evolutionary perspective. In fact, he defines ethics such that they seem to be impossible. "An ethic, ecologically", he writes (1949: 202) "is a limitation on freedom of action in the struggle for existence". However, since, from an evolutionary point of view it would seem that only the most ferociously competitive of the world would survive and, hence, reproduce and pass on their ferociously competitive tendencies, limiting one's freedom of action in the struggle for existence would apparently be a sure-fire way to eradicate oneself. It would seem that from an evolutionary point of view that ethics would not evolve, that cooperation would get cut off, that those who were altruistic would die off (and altruism would die out), and that only those who out-competed their fellows would survive. I gather that a large part of the problem for my students is a conflation between the notion of "fitness" as found in Darwin, and the notion of "strength" as in the Social Darwinian notion of "only the strong survive". Clarifying the notion of natural selection and the concept of fitness (as different than strength—something that needs to be clarified in class given some very common confusions about the basics of Darwinian natural selection theory that the students often reflect) goes a long way here, but not all the way.

How could "limitations on freedom of action" ever have originated and evolved, ever have been a trait that improved the fitness of an individual or group of individuals? Of course we can explain the occurrence of instances of ethics, benevolence, and altruism as mutations since any mutation is possible; but why and how was ethics as a limitation of freedom of action a successful mutation? How did it get selected for and develop over time?

Darwin's answer: the key to ethics, ethical behavior, and the process of ethics is found in *society* and *sociability* or *community*. Ethics come into being in order to facilitate social cooperation. Hence, ethics and society are *correlative*, they change in relation to one another.

Many animals are in some respect social animals, and humans are intensely social. For these social animals, life's struggle is more efficiently conducted in a society; there is a survival advantage to

living in a social setting. According to Darwin, at this point, or
because of this point, ethics come into being since we cannot live
in a social setting without some sort of limitations on our freedom
of action, or without ethics. I sometimes summarize this in blackboard shorthand as follows:

No Ethics → No Society → No Survival

Not only are we are ethical creatures *because* we are social creatures,
but we are ethical creatures *to the extent* that we are social creatures
as well. That is, the more intensely social we are as animals, the
more complex are our ethical structures (in fact, those with more
intense societies even have bigger neo-cortexes).[5] Again, continuing
to root this explanation of ethical development in what the students
think of as science seems to command their attention even though
they were previously unfamiliar, and even uncomfortable, with ethical discourse.

Leopold (1949: 203-4) writes:

> All ethics so far evolved rest upon a single premise: that the individ-
> ual is a member of a community of interdependent parts. His instincts
> prompt him to compete for his place in the community, but his ethics
> prompt him also to co-operate (perhaps in order that there may be a
> place to compete for).

In short, given the kind of creatures that we are, our continued existence is more likely given the presence of a society, and for societies to flourish there must be some sort of rule, some sort of limitation
on the freedom of action, some sort of ethics.

Teaching the Leopoldian Land Ethic: Sentiment and Ethics

Students often want to know how ethics originate. Darwin asserts
that ethics emanate from the natural *parental* or *filial* affections, or in
the biologically ingrained emotional bond of caring for young. This
means that, biologically, we all possess the ability to extend moral
consideration to others, or that our moral sentiments are malleable.
The notion of a shared ethical capacity here butts up against students' preconceived, but not reflected on notion that ethics are wildly
subjective and fickle (although many have no problem making very

universal and absolutist moral claims at the same time), while the notion that ethics are amenable to change is at first a confusing and uncomfortable idea that I eventually attempt to make an empowering idea: if we are morally adrift with regard to the environment, we can change course; we do have that ability.

But how do ethics develop and spread? How did larger societal ethics evolve? The answer: We extend ethical consideration (feelings of moral sympathy) to those we perceive to be within our community—again, ethics and society are correlative. Therefore, *ethical inclusion spreads as our sense of community spreads*. At this point, referring back to *A Sand County Almanac* as Leopold's own attempt to foster this sort of enlarged ecological literacy not only illustrates this point but adds another dimension to their experience with the book.

As we extend sentiment (and thus moral inclusion) from offspring and family, towards friends, relatives, etc. we include them, also, within our realm of morality. In teaching, I illustrate this by using the example of the (admittedly overly-simplistic) history of civilization. Aboriginal societies consisted of fifty or so closely related individuals called clans or gens. The moral community at that time included members of one's clan (i.e., there existed a clan ethic, or many clan ethics). However, those outside the social community of the clan were not ethically considered or included. Eventually there was a recognition that it would be advantageous to live in a larger group (coupled, I would imagine, with contact with those "others" and the realization that they were not significantly different than us—or that the differences that they did have were not morally relevant). Hence, there was a banding together of clans into tribes, and here ethics varied and became more inclusive (they had to for the tribe to survive—the ethic has to match the social community realization or it all falls apart. For example, if we did not have a "classroom ethic" of sorts, we could not have a class).

Historically this process of moral expansion is repeated. As tribes merge into nations, which in turn develop into nation states or countries, ethics extend as society does and the boundaries of the moral community continuously enlarge. And always, the fuel that powers this system is empathy (a sentiment) based on a sense of community (prompted by reason). I often employ some version of the following diagram to represent this point:

Historical Social Evolution

Clan → Tribe → Nation → Nation State → Global Village → Biotic Community

Corresponding Ethical Change

Clan Ethic → Tribal Ethic → Nation Ethic → Patriotism → Human Rights
→ Land Ethic

→ = rationality on the first level, sentimentality on the second, and an arrow between rows can be used to illustrate the correlative nature of the relationship between the level of social realization and the corresponding ethic.

At this point some caution needs to be exercised. Students often react skeptically to the emotion/moral sentiment approach to ethics.[6] Although the tradition Leopold is reflecting here does claim that we are ethical creatures primarily because we are emotional creatures, that is not the whole of the picture. Human reason drives the community realization. The Land Ethic is, then, an attempt to ground a moral theory on the dialogue between what we think of as reason and what we think of as emotion: two dramatic components of our lived world. As reason prompts me to enlarge my social community, my moral sentiments are now triggered to morally enfranchise that new community; if they are not, then that level of social realization cannot be facilitated. Certainly this interplay merits teasing out in the classroom in greater detail. I have actually found that a short series of fairly mundane examples from one's daily life go a long way toward demonstrating that there may be some problem with trying to sever emotion and reason entirely. For instance, when a friend is upset (emotion) we are often offered—or expect to be given—an explanation (reason) for this emotional state. When we try to calm an angry friend (emotion) the tonic we use is often a re-examination of the facts that lead to the anger (reason), and so on.

There are a number of examples, I explain to students, of the enlargement of the global moral community today. The idea of universal human rights is one such case; and it is widely accepted now that country of origin, race, sexual orientation and so on, are not morally significant qualities. We are all part of a single human, moral, community. Leopold's Land Ethic moves one step further on: to the idea of the whole biotic community as a moral community. So, for the biotic community to become a moral community to which the Land Ethic applies, those previously conceived of as being outside the moral community must be brought in. The key to this social and moral expansion is the science of ecology, which allows us to see the world as a biotic community.[7]

Leopold seems convinced that once we begin to see the world as a biotic community, the Land Ethic will follow naturally—a leap of faith that is always interesting to bring up and question in class. Our inherited social and ethical instincts, for Leopold, will be activated when we begin to see plants and animals, soils and waters as fellow-members of a biotic community. Therefore, ethical change is intimately entwined both with knowledge of ecology and with metaphysics, or worldview remediation. Thus, the key to moving from a humanitarian ethic to the Land Ethic is *universal ecological education*—part of which I hope is happening in the classroom where this is being studied!

For Leopold the acceptance of the Land Ethic is clearly feasible. As he puts it (1949: 203) "the extension of ethics to this third element [the biotic community] is, if I read the evidence correctly, an evolutionary possibility". So, the *possibility* of a Land Ethic is clear—again, ethics are malleable. However, Leopold's message also contains a warning. The Land Ethic is not just an evolutionary possibility, but also an "ecological necessity". It is not just that an adaptation of the Land Ethic is possible or that it would be nice, but that it is a necessity if that level of social organization is to hold together; just as every ethical extension is necessary for that level of social inclusion to hold together. There is no clan without a clan ethic, no country without some level of love for one's country or patriotism, and no biotic community without a Land Ethic. For the biotic community (which now includes us) to flourish, the adaptation of a system of moral thought that attributes direct moral standing to the land is an absolute necessity.

Conclusion: Developing Teaching about the Land Ethic

In addition to this basic framework, the exciting thing about teaching the Land Ethic is that there are numerous important and interesting further paths that an instructor might take. In fact, some of these are quite crucial for a fuller understanding of Leopold's theory.

First, after the foundation of the theory is laid out, a series of objections and responses not only helps students to see the Land

Ethic as a contested theory, but also allows the theory to unfold in more detail. To this end, I begin with those from Callicott (esp. 1999: 99-115) as well as with my own work on the charge that the land ethic can lead to "environmental fascism" and I explore further issues that arise from such questions (esp. Nelson 1996). In fact, I work through a series of ten objections and possible responses to the Land Ethic. Although I do not have the space here to develop that discussion in any detail, I would be happy to provide a handout to anyone interested.

Second, it often serves the students to explore how the rest of Leopold's *A Sand County Almanac* provides the reader with a subtle lesson in ecological literacy: the very lesson he believes triggers our biotic community social instinct.

Third, it is important to discuss how ecology has dramatically changed since 1949 and how it is that this change may complicate the foundations of the land ethic beyond Leopold's own discussions. Callicott's essays "The Metaphysical Implications of Ecology" (1989) and "Do Deconstructive Ecology and Sociobiology Undermine the Land Ethic?" (1999) provide a solid background for this topic.

In my experience the Land Ethic is also the environmental ethical position that seems to translate best to more general audiences. This is not just because these audiences are familiar with Leopold's work or words, but because the theory appears to resonate quite deeply with the foundations of the moral experiences of those audiences. While they might disagree, at least at first, with the extent to which Leopold and "Leopoldistas" such as Callicott attempt to morally enfranchise the human and more-than-human worlds, they find resonance with the essential form of ethical assumptions and possible extensions. This, it has always seemed to me, is a hugely powerful connection, a place to start from, and a common tongue from which to begin what are perhaps the most important conversations in which the world is currently engaged.

NOTES

1. This paper reflects the author's experiences while teaching at the University of Wisconsin-Stevens Point, a position which he has since vacated.

2. Because the theory of environmental ethics formulated by Aldo Leopold (1949, 1966), and later developed by J. Baird Callicott (see especially 1989, 1999) is a specific type of environmental ethic, it seems proper to capitalize it. Hence, the Land Ethic is that environmental ethic defended by Leopold and Callicott (and

myself (1993, 1996)). This avoids the common confusion associated with using "land ethic" as a synonym for "environmental ethic."

3. The 1949 edition of *ASCA* is preferable. The 1966 edition includes added essays, the order of the essays within the volume has been rearranged, and over the years I have even discovered rearranged, added, and missing wordings.

4. A philosophical account does exist and can be found (for example) in the works of Scottish Enlightenment philosophers David Hume (1957, 1978) and Adam Smith (1982), both of whom Darwin actually cites. If I had the time in my own class I certainly would go even further into this account of ethics. If the course were, for instance, less of a massive service course for the College of Natural Resources, and more of a typical upper division philosophy course, then reading Hume and Smith would be a must.

5. See Ridley (1996: 69) and Humphrey (1983).

6. The reason/emotion dualism that has to be addressed here is just one among (what the reader has probably by now realized) a series of preconceived and entrenched dualisms that students bring to the course: is/ought, science/humanities, nature/human, etc. In some ways, a substantial sub-theme of the course is to challenge their preconceptions about dualisms, or at least to demonstrate where it is that these come from and how that might be reconsidered, and what that reconsidering might mean.

7. Admittedly, ecology is not the only scientific theory that might prompt this expansion of the social community. Evolutionary theory and quantum theory (among others) might also do this, and therefore might also be worth exploring while discussing the Land Ethic.

REFERENCES

Callicott, J. Baird. 1989. *In Defense of the Land Ethic: Essays in Environmental Philosophy.* Albany, NY: State University of New York Press.
——. 1999. *Beyond the Land Ethic: More Essays in Environmental Philosophy.* Albany, NY: State University of New York Press.
Darwin, Charles. 1981 [1871]. *The Descent of Man, and Selection in Relation to Sex.* Princeton, NJ: Princeton University Press.
Hume, David. 1957 [1751]. *An Inquiry Concerning the Principles of Morals.* New York: Macmillan.
——. 1978, vol. I originally published in 1739, vols. II and III in 1740. *A Treatise of Human Nature.* Oxford: The Clarendon Press.
Humphrey, Nicholas. 1983. *Consciousness Regained: Chapters in the Development of Mind.* New York: Oxford University Press.
Leopold, Aldo. 1949. *A Sand County Almanac: And Sketches Here and There.* New York: Oxford University Press.
——. 1966. *A Sand County Almanac: With Essays on Conservation from Round River.* New York: Ballantine Books.
Nelson, Michael P. 1993. "A Defense of Environmental Ethics: A Reply to Janna Thompson", *Environmental Ethics* 15:147-60.
——. 1996. "Holists and Fascists and Paper Tigers ... Oh My!", *Ethics and the Environment* 1: 103-17.
Ridley, Matt. 1996. *The Origins of Virtue: Human Instincts and the Evolution of Cooperation.* New York: Penguin/Viking.
Smith, Adam. 1982 [1759]. *A Theory of Moral Sentiments.* Indianapolis: Liberty Fund.

PLACE AND PERSONAL COMMITMENT IN TEACHING ENVIRONMENTAL ETHICS

Philip Cafaro

Abstract

This essay, a personal account of teaching environmental ethics, advances two main points. First, focusing on local environmental issues makes for better classes. Teachers can take advantage of local environmental expertise at their institutions and in the wider community; local focus provides a good balance given philosophy's tendency to abstractness; students tend to feel more engaged and excited about the class. Second, environmental ethics classes should spend more time helping students articulate their own ethical positions and showing them how to act upon them. In this way, our classes will better prepare and inspire students to do right by nature.

Keywords: environmental ethics, teaching, place, consumption, commitment

Introduction: First Experiences in Teaching Environmental Ethics

My first two opportunities to teach a full course in environmental ethics were at Southwest Minnesota State University, a small school (about 2500 students) out on the prairie near the South Dakota border. In the first class we covered many interesting and important topics: whether nature has intrinsic value; the proper-role of cost/benefit analysis in policymaking; duties to future generations; and more. The focus, as in most philosophy classes, was on general principles and (to a lesser extent) their application. The class was fun to teach and fairly well received by the students. But I had a sense that it could be better, if I could help my students—many of whom had little background in philosophy—tie our theoretical discussions more clearly to practical, tangible concerns.

The second time I taught the class, I gave it a much more local focus. We began by reading Kent Meyers' *The Witness of Combines* (1998) a memoir about growing up on a farm in southwest Minnesota in the 1960s. We finished the semester with Minnesota author Sigurd Olson's first book of north woods sketches, *The Singing Wilderness* (1997). In between, we treated many of the same issues as in the previous class, but I made a point of using local or regional examples to illustrate them (for example, we visited a local hog farm during

Clare Palmer (Ed.), *Teaching Environmental Ethics*, 202-212.

our discussions of animal rights). I brought in five local speakers to talk about environmental issues, including a state park supervisor, an organic farmer and a watershed management coordinator. And I assigned group projects, in which students analyzed local environmental issues.

The second class was a lot better! Starting with the Meyers' memoir allowed me to define some basic ideas—sustainability, intrinsic versus instrumental value—in simple and accessible terms. More important, it allowed the many students who had also grown up on farms in the area to relate environmental value issues to their own lives. Some of the students who most enjoyed the book were agribusiness majors, the kind of students who tend to tune out abstract, philosophical discussions and whom I had largely failed to reach in the first class.

Bringing in so many speakers meant less time to discuss assigned readings and topics in value theory. In exchange, my outside speakers brought greater emphasis on the actual values at work in environmental decision-making. They also conveyed a lot of basic information about local environmental issues. (In general, I have found that my university colleagues and local environmental experts are flattered to be asked to speak about their work, although sometimes they are a bit daunted by the idea of talking to a philosophy class.)

For their group projects, I had students visit five different state parks in the region. They learned about park topography and ecology, reviewed management plans and talked with park supervisors about environmental issues. They wrote reports analyzing the values upheld by current park management policies, and identified alternatives. These projects provided many benefits; for a start, some students who had grown up within a few miles of the parks visited them for the first time. Students learned what issues park managers deal with and the trade-offs they make between various interests. Their projects helped them connect the values held by park managers and park visitors to particular policies, and the policies to physical changes in the land around them. Thus general principles were made concrete and the importance of values to environmental outcomes made clear.

The message I took from these two classes was simple: tying environmental ethics classes into place creates better classes. Students are more engaged, abstract concepts are made clearer, and the consequences of particular theoretical positions are elucidated. Place-based classes appeal to more students and to difficult-to-reach students, including the guys with the baseball caps in the back row. They help students clarify their own environmental values and show them that those values make a difference.

Current Teaching in Environmental Ethics

When I took up my current job at Colorado State University, I backslid a bit from what I had learned in Minnesota. My first two environmental ethics classes had few local speakers and no group projects, and the focus returned squarely to general theoretical issues. There were some good reasons for this. I was new to the area, so knew fewer people to invite to class. Classes were larger, making it harder to fit in group projects. The students were also a more heterogeneous and less locally-focused group, and I thought that they were better prepared for rigorous philosophical discussion right from the start.

Still, the classes suffered from the change. Discussions of theoretical and policy issues were relatively lifeless. Some of our best sessions were group discussions of regional environmental issues, such as elk management in Rocky Mountain National Park and proposed emissions controls for cars along Colorado's Front Range. So once again and over several iterations, I revamped the course to give it more of a local focus.

I brought in more speakers. These included a local rancher working to restore a wetland on his property, the chair of the county planning and zoning board, the district ranger for the Canyon Lakes District of the Roosevelt National Forest (the US Forest Service manages much of the land to the west of town), and the director of the Colorado Heritage Program, which monitors populations of threatened species across the state. I try to find speakers with strong environmental values, who are working to instantiate those values. In addition to informing students about local issues, such speakers reinforce the idea that individual effort makes a difference.

At the same time, I look for speakers who voice different sides of environmental issues and model different ways to work to protect nature. I invite Forest Service employees largely because their positions on forestry issues are so different from my own. In my most recent class, I brought in two environmental activists with very different personal styles (in-your-face versus consensus building) and issue foci (political campaigns versus campus energy audits). Both have had great success, in changing local environmental policy and changing the university's facilities management practices, respectively. Comparing their efforts helped show my students that there is no one royal road to environmental success.

Teaching at a land-grant university with a strong focus on environmental research, I find I can bring in colleagues working on local environmental issues, without sacrificing rigorous discussion. For example, last year my colleague Ellen Wohl from the Earth Resources Department discussed her recent book *Virtual Rivers* (2001), which analyses the degree to which Colorado's Front Range rivers retain natural characteristics (in terms of hydrological function, native species diversity, etc.). Students found this discussion of their local landscape fascinating; I found it linked up nicely to discussions of "the social construction of wilderness" and the pros and cons of managing nature.

In addition to local speakers, I bring in local issues whenever possible, often to introduce or complement theoretical discussions. For example, for a number of semesters I have screened *Varmints*, an hour-long film about prairie dog shooting in the western United States, as a way to introduce issues of animal rights and endangered species management. Prairie dogs are a hot issue here: currently Colorado and other Plains states are changing management plans in an effort to stave off the listing of the black-tailed prairie dog under the federal Endangered Species Act. Some of my students have shot prairie dogs as kids, for fun; others have seen favorite colonies bulldozed to make way for tract housing. Showing *Varmints*—with plenty of breaks for students to air their own views—is a great way to initiate discussions regarding individual animal welfare versus holistic ecological health, good versus bad kinds of recreation, and other issues. I try to move from these examples to discuss the theoretical issues they suggest. I believe a key goal in teaching applied ethics is to find the right balance between detailed attention to practical issues and rigorous discussion of principles.

Future Plans for Teaching Environmental Ethics

In a recent class, I think I hit a good balance during a four-week long discussion of forestry issues. Helping me achieve this was Peter List's *Environmental Ethics and Forestry* (2000), an anthology with an unusually wide selection of material. Using readings from List's book, I first set out a range of possible ethical positions regarding forestry— including "resourcist" positions usually given short shrift in environmental ethics anthologies, but alive and well out in the real world. Then the class looked at two articles by Holmes Rolston attempting to identify ethical and aesthetic values in forests, thus bringing greater philosophical rigor and precision into the discussion. These articles proved successful in helping students articulate their own views regarding forest values. Next we discussed debates within the Society of American Foresters in the 1990s about whether to add a strong "land ethic" canon to their professional code. This led us into central issues about how to manage forests—and the connection between how managers manage forests and how the general public uses them. Finally, we reviewed correspondence between local Sierra Club activists and local Forest Service officials regarding a range of management issues on the adjacent Roosevelt National Forest, including ORV use, ski area expansion and fire policy.

I was quite pleased with these discussions, which ranged from the most general issues in value theory to particular decisions about whether or not to build roads or chair lifts. They did justice to the whole range of values that one finds behind natural resource management issues. And they showed the implications of particular consumption issues to land management decisions (no demand for more downhill skiing, no discussion about whether or not to build new ski lifts into roadless areas). A number of the issues we discussed were forest recreation issues; here in Colorado, discussing recreation is a good way to get at what people want from nature and what we take from it. So, a discussion of ethical theory and environmental policy did not just remain that, but also helped at least some students better understand their own environmental values and the consequences of their actions.

In the future, I'd like to move more in this direction of helping students make their own values explicit and explore new possibilities for making change. It is important to share the insights of philosophers who have thought long and well on these topics; it is important to debate policy issues and what "we all," as members of societies, should do to meet environmental challenges. But it is too easy for our students to discuss policy issues and theoretical positions impersonally, without ever connecting any of this up to their own beliefs and choices. Thus environmental ethics may remain "merely academic," even for students with some personal environmental commitment. I believe a combination of personal values clarification and discussion of wider social issues will lead to the deepest ethical understanding. It will also provide the strongest incitement to personal and social improvement.

How to help, or force, students to specify and then grapple with their own environmental values? Here are some possibilities I'm considering for future classes:

- Start by having students state their own environmental values, in some detail, in a short paper or exercise. Before they even hear the words "animal rights" or "intrinsic value," get them to write down their ethics in their own words. Then have them reflect back on this exercise at several points during the ensuing class. Perhaps have them specify their environmental ethics in the form of a credo, then see if they decide to change or reword it along the way.
- Have students keep a journal, both of their enjoyment of nature and their uses of it. Considering these two aspects of how they value nature should lead to a rather full picture of their environmental ethics, allowing them to reflect on it over the duration of the course. (I have found that collecting and commenting on student journals every few weeks works very well in small seminar classes. It allows shyer students to have their say and provides a new form of reflection for everyone. It is labor intensive, however.)
- Ask students to evaluate a series of environmental decisions at the start of class. Then have them reflect on their answers at the end of class to see how they justify, qualify, or change their earlier answers. I might also ask them to reflect generally on how or whether the class has deepened or changed their environmental ethics.

Consumption Issues and Teaching Environmental Ethics

Consumption decisions are particularly well suited to helping students articulate their own environmental values. Few of us work to restore wetlands, sit on planning commissions, or manage national forests. But we are all consumers whose consumption decisions affect the environment. Partly for this reason, consumption ethics has bulked larger in my environmental ethics classes over the years.

At first, I would bring in practical consumption issues toward the end of my classes. "OK," I would say to the students, "if you think there is something to these ideas of nature's intrinsic value, or preserving ecosystem health, here are some of the things you can do to limit the harm your consumption does to the earth." On successive days I might bring in a compact fluorescent bulb, some compost from my garden, or a pinwheel (to represent purchasing wind power from the local utility). I would start each class with a ten-minute discussion of the consumption option in question, then move on to the main issues for the day.

In recent classes, I have worked consumption ethics more fundamentally into the syllabus. This year, for instance, we read psychologist Tim Kasser's *The High Price of Materialism* (2003) moving through his book with what some students felt was excruciating thoroughness. Kasser summarizes well-known evidence that high material consumption and increased wealth do not correlate with happiness. He then spends the bulk of his book discussing the further thesis that a materialistic *orientation* correlates with *un*happiness, and that people who emphasize developing fulfilling personal relationships or pursuing intrinsically interesting activities tend to live happier lives. I found this book made a neat cross-disciplinary comparison to philosophy's traditional discussions of materialism. Students were challenged by it, grappling with the logic of Kasser's antimaterialist arguments and with his interpretations of the empirical data. His book helped them reflect on their own hopes for happiness and their own beliefs regarding the roles wealth and possessions play in achieving it.

During this semester, I also had students calculate their ecological footprints, using a simple program found at www.lead.org/lead-net/footprint/intro.htm. Fifteen to thirty minutes of calculations allowed them to come up with an estimate of the land needed to support them each year, in acres (other programs allow students to quantify their ecological footprints in terms of annual energy consumption or pollution generated; see www.rprogress.org for further discussion). This simple exercise allowed students to quantify the costs of their consumption, compare themselves to one another, and calculate which lifestyle changes would do the most environmental good. It gave them a sense of what is really important in their consumption decisions. I hope it helped a few of them move beyond the common stance that "it's all a mess, so what's the use of trying to change anything?"

In the future, I plan to do this exercise earlier in the semester. Then I will ask students to choose one or two changes to make in their consumption patterns and have them keep a record of their efforts for one month. At the end, I will have them calculate how much their efforts have accomplished in lessening their ecological footprint and the effects on their "quality of life." From there the discussion may branch out in a number of ways: for example, into questions about how much we have to give up in order to be good environmentalists, or whether lower consumption should be mandated by governments.

I anticipate that some students will find this exercise intrusive, or just not want to do it. I'll allow them to substitute a writing assignment on some consumption issue, without prejudice to their grades. Still, the contrast will be there, between those who choose to do something about their ecological footprint and those who just want to talk about it. Isn't this one of the most important distinctions we need to make in a class in environmental ethics? In any ethics class, for that matter? As Aristotle wrote over 2300 years ago, the end of ethical philosophy is action, not knowledge (*Nicomachean Ethics* I, 3).

For most of its history, right living was seen as essential to philosophy. Ancient ethical treatises engaged the most general issues in ethical theory *and* the most concrete suggestions for living better lives; more than one recent philosopher has noted that in this they resembled modern self-help books more than modern philosophy texts. I believe that environmental philosophers should take the hint from this comparison. In our environmental ethics classes, we should help students delve deeply into the philosophical issues surrounding how to live justly in nature *and* we should show them how to do so in some detail. Only this kind of comprehensiveness and commitment will achieve the promise of applied ethics and complete the rehabilitation of philosophical ethics from a lost century of arid, fruitless meta-theorizing. Only this sort of "doubly applied" ethics will give our students what they want and what they are right to want from us: guidance on how to fight environmental destruction and live just, meaningful and fulfilling lives.

Response to Concerns

In their helpful comments on an earlier draft of this essay, *Worldviews'* referees brought up four worries that some current readers might share. Let me conclude by addressing these worries.

Worry one. Focusing on actual, concrete environmental decisions and inviting in so many non-philosophers to lead discussions will "water down" the philosophical content of classes.

I answer that making these changes does leave less time for presenting and debating theoretical issues. But I think that on average, students come away with a better grasp of ethical theory when I spend less time hammering away at theory and more time tying theory to practice.

In my experience, philosophy majors tend to want more theory, agribusiness majors want more practical examples and English majors want more nature poetry. Since my environmental ethics classes include all of these kinds of students, I try to accommodate them all with some of what they like and are accustomed to—and to challenge them all with unfamiliar ways of approaching these issues. What philosophers preeminently bring into the educational mix are argumentative rigor and a focus on value issues. Students in applied fields can benefit greatly from exposure to our approach. But philosophy majors benefit from reminders that ethical ideas have real-world consequences.

Worry two. Focusing on local issues and "place" could make a course too narrow, leading it to neglect unfamiliar kinds of environments (urban environments if the school is in a rural setting, for example) or global issues.

I answer that it is possible that a local focus could lead to such narrowing. On the other hand, most colleges and universities are within striking distance of a variety of environments for study. Colorado State University, for example, has urban areas (large cities, small cities, towns), rural areas (croplands, ranchlands) and wild areas (national parks, national forests, national grasslands) all within a sixty mile radius. I believe classes in environmental ethics should illuminate issues facing all three kinds of areas and have found that a local focus can help accomplish this.

It is true that some problems, such as global climate change and the worldwide extinction of species, demand a comprehensive vision. Yet even here, starting locally has value. After exploring the ways their own happiness depends on appreciating local wildlife or connecting to particular places, students should be sensitized to the costs that other communities could pay due to climate change or species extinctions. After realizing the degree to which their own health and wellbeing depend on global ecosystem services, students should better understand the need to protect them.

Worry three. Demanding personal commitment in an ethics class inappropriately crosses the line from environmental ethics to environmental advocacy.

I answer that while requiring particular kinds of environmental commitment would be illegitimate, requiring students to explore their own environmental commitments through more open-ended assignments is pedagogically appropriate, given the potential for self-knowledge and personal values clarification. If such assignments are designed and implemented with respect for differing viewpoints, they need not be coercive. In addition, the move from ethical belief to effective action is at least as complicated as the move from ethical confusion to ethical belief; philosophers could make real contributions toward environmental protection by analyzing environmental action.

We cannot require environmental commitment. On the other hand, we should nurture it where it exists. Many of our students arrive in class with strong environmental values; academic philosophers generally do a poor job of inspiring them and helping them act on those values. This is no minor failure, given that right action is the proper goal of philosophical ethics.

Worry four. This approach assumes that there are "right answers" to questions in environmental ethics, which could lead to intellectual complacency and dogmatism.

I answer that these are real dangers, but that they must be met honestly, not by pretending to ethical uncertainty in cases where it doesn't exist. Just as we discuss interpersonal ethics without us or our students believing that it is an open question whether murder or rape are morally acceptable, so we can discuss environmental ethics without us or our students believing it is morally acceptable to piss in a neighborhood pool or dump untreated toxins into a local river. We need not assume that there is one right answer to how people should live in nature. We may assume that there are better and worse answers to this question, and that part of the job of environmental philosophy is to encourage people to *live* better answers.

Philosophical analysis is only part of philosophy. When it helps people better understand their ethical choices, it performs a useful service. It is more likely to achieve this when it focuses on real ethical uncertainty, unlikely to achieve it when philosophers assume uncertainty in order to motivate theoretical discussion. And when philosophical analysis sets itself up as the whole of ethics, it typically leads to logic-chopping and passivity among philosophers and our students. Human life and human impacts on nature are too important to trivialize in this way. Classes in *applied* ethics, at least, should avoid such trifling.

REFERENCES

Aristotle. 1998 ed. *Nicomachean Ethics*. Oxford: Oxford University Press.
Kasser, Tim. 2003. *The High Price of Materialism*. Cambridge: MIT Press.
List, Peter. 2000. *Environmental Ethics and Forestry: A Reader*. Philadelphia: Temple University Press.
Meyers, Kent. 1998. *The Witness of Combines*. Minneapolis: University of Minnesota Press.
Olson, Sigurd. 1997. *The Singing Wilderness*. Minneapolis: University of Minnesota Press.
Rolston, Holmes. 1988. "Values Deep in the Woods," *American Forests* 94/5 & 6: 66-69.
———. 1998. "Aesthetic Experience in Forests," *Journal of Aesthetics and Art Criticism* 56:157-166.
Varmints. 1998. Film Missoula: High Plains Films.
Wohl, Ellen. 2001. *Virtual Rivers: Lessons from the Mountain Rivers of the Colorado Front Range*. New Haven: Yale University Press.

EARTH 101[1]

Roger S. Gottlieb

Abstract
This paper is an account of a course called *Philosophy and the Environment*. The course responds to problems common in environmental education: that is, either leaving the audience unmoved, or, struck by the information and the analyses, but without emotional support or positive experiences, full of even more despair, cynicism and numbness than when they began. Many of us in higher education are seeking a different path, believing that it is possible to connect our bodies and our minds, our intellects and our emotions, our analytical intelligence and our spiritual hopes. *Philosophy and the Environment* attempts to do just this, providing a theoretical account of the crisis with an experience of its meaning.

Keywords: environmental education, environmental crisis, emotional intelligence, environmental philosophy, nature

> We continue to educate the young for the most part as if there were no planetary emergency.
>
> David Orr, *Earth in Mind*[2]

> If we can get attached to just one tree from spending 30-45 minutes a week with it, then imagine how attached we could get if we lived in the forest, or visited it every day for work or pleasure. Then we would realize just how important the environment really is and how much magic it holds. If everyone could only see this, then perhaps we wouldn't be in the environmental crisis we are in now.
>
> Ryan D., *Plant Journal*, (Student on *Philosophy and the Environment*)

Introduction

Why are we awash in pesticides, cautious of now dangerous sunlight, frightened for (and of) our breasts and prostates, and lonely for vanished species? Why, that is, do we live in an environmental crisis? Because, say many of us, there is something fundamentally amiss in the depths of our society, our culture, and our civilization. We suffer from a misguided economy, the shortsighted self-interest of governments, our own addiction to consumption, and the deep and destructive flaws that mark how we think about who we are and what it is to

Clare Palmer (Ed.), *Teaching Environmental Ethics*, 213-229.

be alive on this earth. We have mistakenly taken humanity to be the only species of value, privileged our minds over our bodies, discounted women as "natural" while exalting men as the source of intelligence and religious truth, and assumed that if we had scientific facts we could dispense with spirit. We have separated reason from emotion and all the fields of knowledge (sociology, biology, history, politics, ethics) from each other. We told ourselves (and everyone else who'd listen) that our technological brilliance would produce a safe and happy life, and that we'd progressed far beyond the accumulated wisdom of "primitive tribes" who (how silly can you get?) found wisdom in hawks and mountains.

For those of us who see the environmental crisis as a crisis of our entire civilization, the goal of environmental education is to raise students' awareness of the complexity of the problem, the depth of its causes, and the possibility for personal and collective change. Yet it's one thing to criticize our way of life, and another to figure out how to communicate that criticism in a way that leads anywhere. Sadly, the *manner* in which environmental values are taught may contradict *what* is being taught. Lectures about how mind-body dualism lead us to ignore our physical surroundings are given by an unmoving professor to slumped over, shallowly breathing students. Books are read about the importance of knowing our place in nature while students have no idea what is growing outside the classroom. Ecofeminist messages about empathizing with all of life are taught to students who never spend more than five seconds looking at any particular plant. The factual details of the environmental crisis are learned, while the emotions they arouse are ignored. Deep ecology bemoans our instrumental attitude towards nature and preaches that we cannot be fully human if we do not bond to something outside ourselves. Yet during a course in "Environmental Ethics" students bond only to books, words, papers, and screens.

Consequently, environmental education—not unlike environmental advocacy in the wider society—too often leaves its audiences unmoved. Or they may be struck by the information and the analyses, but without emotional support or positive experiences, they end up with even more despair, cynicism and numbness than when they began.

Many of us in higher education are seeking a different path.[3] We believe that it is possible to connect our bodies and our minds, our intellects and our emotions, our analytical intelligence and our spir-

itual hopes, a theoretical account of the crisis with an experience of
its meaning. In fact, we don't think students (or anyone else) will
learn very much about the environmental challenge until all these
dimensions are integrated.

What follows is an account of how I try to do this in a course
called "Philosophy and the Environment," taught at an engineering
college where virtually none of my students are philosophy majors
but most of whom have had at least an "Introduction to Philosophy
and Religion" course as background. The course satisfies distribution requirements for engineering and science majors all of whom
must do substantial work in some particular area of the Humanities.

Teaching the Course: the Eight Premises

Before the term starts, I email those registered to let them know that
"besides the usual reading, lectures and papers, there will be some
rather unusual experiential exercises and meditations in the course."
Thus when they come in on the first day, they've been warned.

Standing at the front of the class, I arrange on the small table before
me a folder with the class syllabus. Then I take out of my backpack
items that seem more fitted to geology or zoology than philosophy:
some rocks, a crystal or two, a feather, and a fossilized shell. Then
I light a large candle and ring an ornamental Tibetan bell.

From the beginning, then, I invoke two forces. By bringing in
actual pieces of the world I announce that our course will not be
confined to words. Nature, not just "nature," will be part of the
action. The candle and the bell—the students think they're strange,
and usually several giggle a bit—invoke a kind of ritualized seriousness which is not only particularly appropriate to a course on
the environmental crisis but also taps into cultural images of concentration and self-transcendence. After the initial nervous laughter,
I find, students pay close attention. And since each class is started
this way, before long the sound of the bell produces a hushed attention that I rarely find in the first moments of other courses.

The class has begun. As it unfolds over the next twenty-eight meet-
ings I am guided by eight premises about the environmental mess
we're all in. My goal is not only to explain and discuss these premises,
but also to help students personally experience them.

Premise 1. The environmental crisis is so universal and threatening that it inevitably provokes very strong emotions.

A well-intentioned colleague once told me: "I try to teach environmental material; I have students read the "World Watch" publications and study a mountain of details. But afterwards they have little or nothing to say. They just seem numb."

Indeed. What happens to our emotional life when we read, for instance, that of the 65,000 chemicals used in the U.S. only around 10% have been tested for their health effects? Or that toxic PCBs have been found in arctic seals (some so affected that their dead bodies have to be disposed of as 'hazardous waste')? Or that by age twenty students stand between a 35% and 45% chance of getting cancer? (Steingraber 1997; Groopman 2001). What happens over the long run when students—who now are commonly exposed to something "about the environment" as early as kindergarten—are rarely if ever asked what they *feel* about the situation?

What happens, I believe, is that people develop some extremely powerful—yet typically unacknowledged—emotional responses. Because they are largely unexpressed, they sap our psychic and intellectual vitality and mark our lives by a joyless numbing out or a frenetic search for stimulation. From the frighteningly high rate of alcohol use to Internet addiction, the consequences of unacknowledged feelings about the environmental crisis are a daily reality on college campuses and in broader society. Without a shred of empirical proof I believe that the prospects of environmental deterioration simply do darken the horizon of young people—as well as lead them to doubt the competence and wisdom of their elders. All this must take an emotional toll.

My response to this dilemma is not to turn the class into group therapy, but to encourage students to integrate the emotional dimensions of their responses to the situations by offering a view of rationality that does not exclude emotions, and thus does not reproduce the alienation of thought from feeling that is part of the crisis in the first place.

On that first day, after the candle is lit and the bell sounded, I sketch in extremely broad terms what the crisis is all about. (The depth of the problem is also brought home in the first reading assignment, which is to go through all of a mass market environmental magazine, such as *E*, *Sierra* or *The Ecologist*). I then make it clear that while I try to be objective about our planet, I am not—and have no desire to be—detached. I describe my own fear and grief, share my helpless anger over the threats to my daughters' health, acknowledge despair for the wilderness forever lost. I admit to years of avoiding information about just how bad things are, hoping to introduce the concepts of denial and avoidance and model the possibility of facing them. My goal is to demonstrate to students that awareness of my feelings in this setting is as important as my "expertise" about environmental ethics; and that *their* emotions deserve respectful attention rather than pseudo-rational dismissal. I suggest that the impact of the readings they will be doing may be felt in their emotional lives, and that at the least they should be aware of what is going on for them.

The value of their emotions is, among other things, to remind them that they can still love and grieve; and, as we see throughout the course, the emotions themselves convey information about our world. There are signs of connection to their surroundings and indications that something is deeply wrong.[4] I periodically raise this issue throughout the term, both in the class as a whole and in small discussion groups. Some people report that nothing is happening; others, however, talk about disquieting dreams, increased feelings of grief or anger, alienation from friends or family who think they are making a big deal out of nothing, or serious questions about career choices. The dominant message of the course is that these reactions are perfectly understandable and rational, and that the best response to them is patient, careful attention.

When I ask the students to speak about what they feel on that first day, they respond slowly and hesitantly, emboldened by my example but still somewhat unsure that a university classroom is the proper place for emotions. As the hour progresses, however, their statements become increasingly more revealing.

"I'm pissed off" one will say, "because the field where I used to hunt for grasshoppers was turned into a parking lot for a mall; and they hardly even use it. What a waste".

"I'm scared," a young woman admits. "Every time I go out in the sun in the summer I think about skin cancer. My aunt died from it".

Others toss off a kind of irritated shrug. "What does that mean?" I say, letting them know pretty quickly that I won't be satisfied with a mumbled "Nothing". Usually what surfaces after a few exchanges is that they are very angry, but that they are sure that their anger won't change anything. I ask them whether a deep anger that cannot change the world—and which for the most part cannot even be expressed—can lead anywhere but despair.

And then at times we find something lurking underneath the anger. Several young men tell me they don't see much use in thinking about all these problems. I ask one: "What would happen if you did think about it?"

"I don't know", he replies, "I'm not sure I could go on with what I'm supposed to do in this life. If I started to cry, I might never stop".

Premise 2. Meeting the emotional challenge of the environmental crisis requires spiritual resources.

Emotional responses to the environmental crisis are not neurotic feelings that need to be "cured." But we do need direct, intuitive, meditative practices as a source of calm, openness and connection to enable us to hold them. For want of a better word, I call such practices "spiritual."

To invoke spiritual resources in a college classroom—not unlike asking students to take their emotional lives seriously—is to resist the still dominant paradigms of scientism. (A paradigm widely shared at an engineering college!) In order to make this resistance comprehensible, we have to explore how the rise of science disenchanted the world and the cultural countertrends to that disenchantment that have arisen over the last few decades.[5] In contemporary society many people believe that scientific knowledge is inadequate as a total worldview or a way to respond to crucial personal problems. The seamless integration of scientific research and corporate and military technology have made many of us extremely skeptical about how "objective" or "value free" science is; and technological consequences from nuclear weapons to the hole in the ozone layer have made people suspicious of unmonitored scientific "progress." Further, the boundaries of psychology, biochemistry, and cognitive research have moved towards the notion of a "body-mind" medicine in which physical and emotional health are connected to psychic practices that have deep affinities to traditional meditation exercises.[6]

These and other developments have made people more open to what I am calling (rather broadly) "spiritual" practices: quieting the mind in meditation; using intuitive resources in visualizations; invoking ritualized forms of compassion, repentance and joy as ways to connect to other people and to the "more than human."[7]

In the first of the course's several lengthy sessions I begin with a full-body relaxation (some students lie on the floor, others lean back in their chairs). I then ask them to imagine some place of complete safety in nature—from their memory or their imagination— and in their mind's eye to see and feel that place in all its details. They are instructed to notice what other beings are there, the climate, the wind, sounds and smells and the position and appearance of their own body. They will return to this psychic spot a number of times during the course. In the second extended meditation I ask them if this place has a message or gift for them; or if they have something to give or communicate to it.

"Nick" was tall and thin, red-haired and thoughtful. Later I would get to know him well when he did lengthy projects under my direction and became one of "my" students. But this was the first course he took with me, and we were still feeling each other out. After the meditation in which I asked the class to listen to see if their special place had any message or teaching for them there was a long pause. I wasn't surprised, just a little disappointed. My students are smart, but not terribly expressive; a far cry from the "crunchy" types you get at Oberlin or Earlham. And this was the first time I had done this sort of thing in a classroom. Then, slowly and deliberately, Nick stood up and approached the candle in the center of the room. "I got a message", he said, and paused. I waited; the whole class waited. "Yes", I asked gently, "what did you hear?" "Stop it. Just stop it".

In another exercise students are each given two slices of apple. After going into a relaxation state they munch on the first one. Since this is towards the end of the class, they have already been exposed to the multiple roots of the crisis, from philosophical attitudes to economic structures; as well as the multiple types of beings whom the crisis affects, from plants, to indigenous tribes, to all of us. I then ask them to visualize the multitude of beings that make the apple possible: sun and water and earth and tree and microorganisms in the soil, and also farm laborers, truckers, supermarket workers, and, yes, pesticide manufacturers. They then eat the second piece of apple—which, some have said, tastes better than the first.

Another exercise focuses on the contrasting of the natural and the commercial environment. I can (and I do) lecture until I'm blue in the face about the effects of consumerism and our loneliness for nature. However, it is one thing to say it, and another to try to provide a context in which the ideas are directly experienced; to provide what Kierkegaard called a "subjective communication" aimed at conveying not a propositional claim but a felt experience. In this exercise I instruct students to spend fifteen minutes in a natural setting doing "nothing"—simply being aware of the sights and smells, sounds and feel of their surroundings. They are then to get themselves as quickly as possible to a mall, a supermarket, a large drugstore—and, once again, to do nothing for fifteen minutes while taking in their surroundings. If they do not learn the lesson by that immediate contrast, they probably will not learn it from my lectures. If they do learn it, than the intellectual critique of consumerism and the urban built environment begins to take on an importance it could never have for them without the experience. In this and in all the other exercises, the experiential does not replace or duplicate the intellectual content of the course, but (when it works) focuses their attention and deepens their understanding.

Premise 3. Students in classrooms have bodies.

It seems odd almost to the point of absurdity that the extended critique of Cartesian mind-body dualism, along with extended postmodern discussions of "the body" in feminism and Foucault, are communicated in classrooms that replicate exactly educational settings in which Descartes' premises were accepted. Therefore in *Philosophy and the Environment* certain simple yoga and chi kung postures and breathing exercises are used to promote relaxed and focused attention. Each class begins and ends with one minute of silent attention on the breath. If the energy lags in the middle of a class, I have students do a brief yoga posture to clear their minds. As our bodies are part of nature, and any destruction of nature will harm us, so we learn and think and feel with our bodies. If our bodies are ignored, our ability to learn and think and feel—even about the environment—will be diminished.

Premise 4. Intuitive experience of the world is essential in helping us understand it.

How do you teach students that all of nature is connected? That the world is deeply, meaningfully, alive? That not only human beings have value? Or that, at least, these ideas have some basis in intuitive experience as well as formal argument? The basic concepts involved in these questions are the bread and butter of a good deal of environmental philosophy (especially "Deep Ecology") and non-academic naturalism, and are repeatedly stressed in the course reading. And they are essential to the construction of a worldview that opposes our culture's dominant anthropocentrism. Is there any way to encourage students to experience these ideas directly?

An essential—and probably my looniest—course requirement is the "plant journal." Each student must pick some particular "plant"— from a blade of grass to a tree—and to sit with that plant three or four times a week, recording their experiences. I tell them to study the plant, talk to it, listen to it, touch it, and smell it. If the plant were to become extinct, they should be able to tell the world what has been lost. Any (legible!) record of this experience is acceptable— including writing over and over that they think the assignment is a waste of time and that their professor is an idiot. After years of this assignment, I have seen, time and again, a kind of magic unfold.

I remember one fellow in particular: tall and muscular, a football player-fraternity member-beer drinker type who usually dozed or fidgeted during meditations and clearly wasn't buying much of my deep-ecology-ecomarxist-ecofeminist-tree-hugger message. At the end of our seven week term I read his journal. For the first two weeks he did nothing but record his disdain for the plant, the plant journal, and his dopey professor. Then he began to notice the details of the small tree he had chosen. By the fifth week he had named the tree "George" and looked forward to visiting it. His final entry read: "All the other trees have their leaves and George doesn't. I'm really worried about him."

Other students have written:

> "I wish to thank nature for giving me peace and perspective in the middle of the city."
>
> "I don't think I am contributing to the environmental crisis. No, actually I am. I always drive my car everywhere when I am home in Boston. Sorry nature . . ."
>
> "Thank you for listening to my thinking and thoughts, grief and happiness."
>
> "My tree is actually blooming! And not just one or two buds. Many. It's like giving birth. I don't know why but it seemed the most dead tree around. But is has woken up!! It is saved."
>
> "The tulip is straightening back up. A proud survivor. Her immediate neighbor has an undignified floppiness. More moss has grown up around the base of the rhododendron where my tulip resides. Soon there will be the most fragrant ferns that grow there every summer."

"Honestly, I thought this was a dumb, immature assignment. But I'm glad I stuck with it. Having seen the slow process of nature in all its beauty, I will never look at trees the same."

What do students learn from these journals?

- That you can become emotionally attached to a plant. That love, in other words, doesn't stop with humans or even animals. One student began with "I feel kind of silly sitting out here writing about a tree; I don't think I can write much about it other than it's pretty dead looking." But then a week later she reflected: "Maybe I chose it because it looked lonely."
- How to be aware of the plant in the details of its existence— roots, bark, leaves, branches. Changes of budding and flowering. To notice the insects at its base, the birds that nest in its crown, the squirrels that jump from branch to branch. To see that plants are alive, changing, dynamic—and that their growth and change are astonishingly exciting. (Luckily, I've arranged always to teach this course in the spring.)
- To be aware of pollution in a visceral way. Students see the nails in their tree's bark, garbage or broken glass on the roots. They begin to care about how the plant faces acid rain, drought from global warming, threats from construction of new buildings.
- To remember encounters with plants when they were children and to recover a sense of magic pervading the natural world—a sense too easily paved over by "maturity". "I remember picking flowers for the church altar. I won't do that any more. They look better out here." "I think about all the things that concern and worry me. Then I look at the tree and it is just so peaceful. Nothing bothers it. I'm jealous!"
- To become aware of the guilt and shame they feel about their personal contribution to the environmental crisis. To realize that it is not some abstraction called "nature" that is threatened by our society and our culture, but particular entities: including this one with whom they've made friends. "I stop and think about how we as a society have afflicted nature with so many 'diseases'. And I wonder about the world my children will live in." "How will my future actions—where I work, what I eat, how I live—affect my tree?"
- That simply being with a plant can soothe them and make them happy; and therefore that nature has something to offer them that

is deeper and more personal than use-values or purely aesthetic pleasure. That, surprisingly, in a communion with nature they can feel their most human. "I have all these deadlines that are to be met and here I am "wasting" my time just sitting by a tree. But it makes me feel so much calmer." "My tree symbolizes my life, my growth, my wounds. It's grown as I have and it has been damaged as I have. It has a large broken branch. I have a broken heart."

• That in a world of scientific, technical and numerical "expertise" and "certainty" that there remains special joy in simply asking questions. "Are members of the natural world conscious? Do roaming deer watch their steps so as not to step on ants?"

Premise 5. No single discipline is adequate to the complexity of the environmental crisis.

Readings for the course come from philosophy, ecotheology, economics, natural history, and politics. If we are to understand the "causes" of the crisis, we must understand the role of religion and the rise of capitalism, the effects of modern science and the global market. We must learn to see the consequences of the current environmental practices for non-human nature (as in Bill McKibben's *The End of Nature*) and for people (as in our readings on environmental racism). If we are not to be left in despair, we must acquaint ourselves (as we do in the last week of the course) with resistance movements and success stories. This last is critical because even with the rise of campus activism in recent years the vast majority of my students do not relate to political action. When they hear about alliances between native and white activists to prevent destructive mining in northern Wisconsin, or about the sustainable growth of the city of Curitiba in Brazil, they realize that there are victories to celebrate and work to be done—work in which they, if they choose, can find a place.

Premise 6. Critical thought—including criticism of environmentalism—is essential to our response to the crisis.

The point of the course is not to privilege expressing feelings, intuition, or spiritual exercises over intellectual activity, but to integrate all of these together. As both the reading and my lectures are often deeply critical of contemporary society, so it is also necessary to encourage students to voice their own disagreements both to my position and to any particular environmentalist we are reading.

In the context of the environmental crisis, this is a somewhat complicated matter. As a moral being, I cannot (nor do I think I *should*) pretend to neutrality about these matters. Since I really do believe that we are on the civilizational equivalent of the Titanic, it would be unethical of me to pretend that I don't think the situation is dire in the extreme. As a person, a citizen, an educator, I have a responsibility to try to awaken other people to this belief. In doing so I cannot pretend that I believe the voices that deny the reality of the crisis have much to support their position. An absence of neutrality on basic questions, we should remember, is often present even in much more conventional courses: few classes on the Holocaust spend much time asking if the Nazis had good reasons to try to kill all the Jews; or on American history if black Africans were better off as slaves; or on physiology whether or not (as medical school textbooks of the late nineteenth century taught) higher education damages women's reproductive capacity. I do not take the environmental crisis as something about which we can cavalierly and cheerfully examine "competing narratives," since I view it as a practical problem of the greatest significance. This may strike some readers as uncritical and simple-minded. I would only respond that they ask themselves how much they would engage in the search for "competing narratives" after an initial cancer diagnosis were confirmed by a second and third opinion. One could at that point engage in a fascinating study of the history of science, the politics of medicine, and the cultural biases of the western technology. Yet I doubt if such efforts would really be high on the list of someone, even the most sophisticated intellectual, after they received the Bad News. Of course it is a matter of some debate whether the environmental crisis is as bad as all that. Support for that belief is offered throughout the course, both in lectures and reading.

At the same time, however, it is necessary for me to make a protected space for students who don't see things my way. Dissenting voices must be encouraged, praised for their willingness to disagree, and dealt with directly and respectfully. This is not always easy, especially when—to my irritation—I hear a student repeating some of the more vicious forms of conservative anti-environmentalist propaganda. Yet human respect can transcend ideological difference, especially since I believe that what is most important is that students come to grips with these issues, not parrot my own views. In my experience most people who seriously engage with the material— intellectually and emotionally—end up heading in (what I think is) the right direction. Serious criticism is itself a kind of engagement, and meets my purposes quite well.

We also spend some time examining tensions within environmentalism itself: notably, over the degree to which the concept of nature is historically constituted and in the relation between deep ecology's stress on the inherent value of nature and social ecology's concern with relations between social structures and ecology. Beyond their intellectual value, these debates have a moral and political value as well, for they reveal that environmentalism—no less than the environmental crisis itself—is a product of human thought and action, not a transcendentally-given reality. As a human product the environmental movement is something which these students can take part in shaping. To feel free to do so, they must be able to see that controversies, doubts, and difficulties are part of it.

Premise 7. The environmental crisis is a desecration of the holy and not only an economic or health problem.

This premise certainly does not imply that students must believe in God. Rather, I encourage those who wish it to articulate the profound feelings they have for at least some parts of nature; and to express their growing realization that the violation of nature is simultaneously a violation of themselves and of something that is sacred. That sense of the "sacred" can be theistic, pantheistic, or pagan. Or it may simply represent, as in Paul Tillich's phrase, a locus of "ultimate concern." The point is not to impose a view on them, but to allow those who indeed have this experience a place to express it. The key goal is provide a vocabulary for a sensibility—not to try to convince them that the sensibility exists where it does not. Typically a sizable number of these hard-headed, no-nonsense young engineers dismiss the notion of finding the sacred in nature altogether. Typically, however, a sizable number of just as hard-headed and no-nonsense types talk about experiences they had when hiking in the mountains, or of swamps they used to visit as kids, or—as happened just this past spring—of an encounter with squirrel in the park across the street. In describing these experiences, words like mystery, awe, and reverence, once legitimated by me, spring easily to their lips.

Premise 8. Students exist as moral beings in a morally complex world.

The environmental crisis makes our daily lives morally suspect. I raise the issue of our collective complicity in a crisis we want to alleviate: that all of us, including the tree-hugging professor who does a long commute to work by car, bear some responsibility. Again I do not, and I cannot, pretend to moral neutrality in this issue. In fact, it would be the height of irrationality to do so. And I make moral reflection on their own future choices—all the more significant because most of them will be engineers—an essential part of course discussion. They are confronted—directly but respectfully—with questions about what they would do in concrete situations: for whom will they work, what will they do, what risks and sacrifices will they make? Since morality is not separate from intelligence, I believe it is essential that they rehearse, if only for a few moments, possible responses to future moral dilemmas.

Conclusions

All these aspects of the course form (when they work) a synergistic whole. At times, a movement occurs: from the most personal and unspoken (the meditations and visualizations), through an intellectual understanding of the crisis (the readings, lectures and class discussions), through an "outer" experience of a particular plant, to our concluding studies of environmental resistance movements. The students begin to experience themselves and the entire world as related: by industry and commerce and science and spirituality and governments and political movements; by the way we pollute and the way we conserve; by what we see and what we ignore; by fear and greed, by love and care.

Notes

1. I am grateful to two anonymous reviewers for helpful comments on an earlier version of this paper.
2. See David Orr (1994: 2).
3. As I've learned from conversations with colleagues, many environmental faculty are expanding the sense of what is possible in a college course.
4. Our emotions, as a number of philosophers and psychologists are (finally) teaching, are in many cases rational responses of the human organism. In philosophy, see Nussbaum (2001); in psychology, Greenspan (2003).
5. This is a society-wide phenomenon. See, e.g., Ingelhart (1990) and Ray and Anderson (2000).
6. See Pert (1999) and Eisenberg (1985).
7. In David Abram's (1997) felicitous phrase.

REFERENCES

Abram, David. 1997. *The Spell of the Sensuous.* NY: Vintage Books.

Eisenberg, David. 1985. *Encounters With Qi: Exploring Chinese Medicine.* NY: Norton.

Greenspan, Miriam. 2003. *Healing Through the Dark Emotions: The Wisdom of Grief, Fear, and Despair.* Boston: Shambhala.

Groopman, Jerome. June 4, 2001. "The Thirty Years' War: Have we Been Fighting Cancer the Wrong Way?" *The New Yorker.*

Ingelhart, Ronald. 1990. *Culture Shift: In Advanced Industrial Society.* Princeton: Princeton University Press.

Kierkegaard, Soren. 1992. *Concluding Unscientific Postscript* Princeton: Princeton University Press.

Nussbaum, Martha C. 2001. *Upheavals of Thought: The Intelligence of Emotions.* NY: Cambridge University Press.

Orr, David W. 1994. *Earth in Mind: On Education, Environment, and the Human Prospect.* Washington, D.C.: Island Press.

Pert, Candace B. 1999. *Molecules Of Emotion: The Science Behind Mind-Body Medicine.* NY: Simon and Schuster.

Ray, Paul H. and Sherry Ruth Anderson. 2000. *The Cultural Creatives.* New York: Harmony Books.

Steingraber, Sandra. 1997. *Living Downstream: An Ecologist Looks at Cancer and the Environment.* Reading. MA: Addison-Wesley.

Appendix: Syllabus PY 2717 Philosophy and the Environment

This course is an introduction to the philosophical, spiritual, historical, and political dimensions of the environmental crisis. We will begin by trying to get some sense of the scope of the crisis and then focus on a variety of explanations for it. Throughout we will try to be aware of our own emotional reactions to the crisis and we will develop some psychological/spiritual resources to help us live with it. We will also explore some models of a social order that is destructive to neither the human nor the non-human world.

COURSE REQUIREMENTS:

Lectures and discussions are essential.
Reading: You must do a 300-400 word summary of the assigned reading once a week.
Papers: there will be a take-home mid-term and a final.
Group work: preparing a presentation on a particular book.
Plant journal:
Books: *The End of Nature* (Bill McKibben) and *Ecology* (ed. Carolyn Merchant). There will be group presentations on: *Hope Human and Wild, Monkey Wrench Gang, Confronting Environmental Racism, The New Resource Wars, Sustainable Planet.*

COURSE TOPICS, ASSIGNMENTS AND READING

I. *What is going on?*
   Read any *one* of the environmental magazines on reserve. Read: Bill McKibben: *The End of Nature.*

II. *Worldviews: Ethics, Philosophy, Religion, Science*
    David Abram, "Ecology and Magic" (*Finding Home, Spell of the Sensuous* and *Invitation to Environmental Philosophy* on reserve).
    Joanna Macy, "Toward a Healing of Self and World" (Merchant)
    Bill Devall, "The Deep Ecology Movement" (Merchant)
    Fritjof Capra, "Systems Theory and the New Paradigm" (Merchant)
    David Bohm, "Postmodern Science and a Postmodern World" (Merchant)
    Lynn White, "The Historical Roots of our Ecologic Crisis" (*This Sacred Earth*, on reserve)

Terry Williams, "The Clan of One-Breasted Women" (*This Sacred Earth*, on reserve)

III. *Tensions in Environmental Thought and the Transition to Social Ecology* (1 week)

Chapter 4 of Roger S. Gottlieb *A Spirituality of Resistance* (on reserve)

Roger S. Gottlieb "Spiritual Deep Ecology and the Left" (*This Sacred Earth*, and *Capitalism, Nature, Socialism*, on reserve)

IV. *Class, Race, Gender*

Mike Jacobs, Chapters 3 and 4 of *The Green Economy* (on reserve)

James O'Connor, "Socialism and Ecology" (Merchant)

Carol Christ, "Why Women Need the Goddess" (Merchant)

Ynestra King, "Feminism and the Revolt of Nature" (Merchant)

Robert Bullard, "Environmental Racism and the Environmental Justice Movement" (Merchant)

"Principles of Environmental Justice" (Merchant)

Winona Laduke, "From Resistance to Regeneration" (Merchant)

Vandana Shiva, "Development, Ecology, and Women" (Merchant)

V. *Group Presentations*

Hope Human and Wild

Monkey Wrench Gang

Confronting Environmental Racism

The New Resource Wars

Sustainable Planet

TEACHING ENVIRONMENTAL ETHICS
TO NON-SPECIALIST STUDENTS

Hugh Mason

Abstract
This paper outlines an approach to teaching environmental ethics to non-specialist students. The use of a "problem-solving" approach to ethical dilemmas is advocated as the most suitable vehicle for addressing the needs of non-specialists. This approach commences by considering the existence of ethical dilemmas and the different values that can account for the problems being contested. The approach then addresses the various methods by which such dilemmas can be appreciated and understood if not completely solved, drawing not merely on environmental ethics work but on approaches in cognate areas.

Keywords: environmental ethics, environmental values, ethical dilemmas, environmental education

Introduction

Many courses concerning the natural environment that form part of wider degree programmes in subjects such as geography or economics pay scant attention to matters of environmental ethics. But the omission leaves students ill equipped to address issues where the concerns of business or the exigencies of politics may appear to conflict with long term environmental benefit. In teaching students in the University of Portsmouth, UK, a university which, like so many, does not have a department of philosophy, students of geography and economics have little contact with the methods of philosophy and no background in the subject. When faced in their final year of the undergraduate programme with a unit that deals with ethics, many students initially question the relevance of the unit which they perceive as being abstract and arcane. The fact that the unit is taught by a lecturer who has previously lectured them in geography leads a few to assume that the lecturer is following a personal whim. The majority, however, while initially sceptical of the need for a substantial course on the matter, are none the less very aware that environmental issues are frequently contested on ethical grounds.

Clare Palmer (Ed.), *Teaching Environmental Ethics*, 230-236.

Constructing and Teaching a Course for Non-Specialist Students

The initial decision that has to be made in constructing a course for such students is how to approach the subject matter. The basic approach I have adopted is that the purpose of teaching environmental ethics is *neither* to inculcate a particular set of values *nor* to expound and propagate a well formulated, but rigid, moral code; but rather to enable people to recognise and understand the sources of their own values and to equip them to deal with ethical problems and dilemmas as they occur. Even where it is not possible to produce a solution to an ethical dilemma that will satisfy all interested parties, as for example where religious and animal rights views on slaughtering come into conflict, it is beneficial that people should have sufficient ethical education both to know the origins of their own position and to be able to justify the reasoning behind their own conclusions. In pursuing these purposes the teaching of environmental ethics is no different from any other area of practical or applied ethics, save that it may include distinct values related to environmental concerns.

Such an approach is bound to be contested, particularly by those who consider that the primary purpose of environmental ethics is advocacy. I adopted the problem-and-dilemma approach, however, on the grounds that it is more appropriate to the needs of students who, when later employed in business, commerce, or public service, are likely to be faced with wholly opposed arguments from trenchant advocates of different persuasions.

The starting point for the discussion of ethics is thus the recognition that complex problems exist. Although students are increasingly aware that there are values which may need to be considered when dealing with environmental problems, they usually perceive these in terms of a simple dichotomy between what is ethically desirable and what is economically practicable. Perhaps as a consequence many assume that their own understanding of what constitutes the ethical issues involved is self evident. The recognition of the complexity of most problems is therefore a pre-requisite before any discussion of the origins of values is undertaken. Situations such as the creation of national parks in poorer developing countries or access to countryside in more developed countries throw some of these complexities into high relief. In the former example the value of the development of a tourist economy for the well-being of the whole

country, the rights of pastoralists or land starved peasants, and the
value of conserving endangered species need to be prioritised with
respect to one another. In the latter case the supposed rights to enjoy
one's own property, to access countryside for recreation, to conserve
or to shoot wildlife, and the need to provide affordable housing for
local people may well come into conflict. Actual examples for discussion are quite easy to find. In any case chosen it is important to
show that all outcomes are value-laden and that to advocate the
most financially attractive outcome is not simply a negation of, nor
disregard for, values but is the placing of emphasis on economic values above those of environmental conservation.

The aim of this exercise is not merely to suggest to students that
there are few simple dichotomies and that most situations in environmental ethics are quite complex, requiring values to be prioritised, but also to demonstrate that a priority that is ethically justifiable
in one place may be quite different from that justifiable in an apparently similar situation in another place. This inevitably raises the
question of whether values and the strength with which they are
defended are not merely matters of personal inclination and preference. Indeed many students at this point question whether it is possible to achieve anything in the field of values that will not be the
predilections and preferences of the strong taking priority over the
values of the weak.

To address these questions it is necessary to discuss the origins and
nature of values. Although this is ideally done whilst wandering lazily
around the baths at Athens with a small group of argumentative students, in a modern university this usually involves throwing a few
questions to students in a large lecture theatre in the course of a
time-limited semi-formal lecture. Nonetheless, it is possible to consider
the extent to which values are innate or are matters related to, and
derived from, individual circumstances. In the latter case, in order
to develop a framework within which specific environmental issues
may be considered, it is useful to classify, or preferably ask the students to classify, the possible origins of values: divine revelation, stories at mother's knee, the social conditioning of school, work and
state, personal experiences, and many others. The importance of this
exercise is that it leads on to a number of other questions that will
be directly relevant to environmental questions. First and foremost
is the question whether values are absolute or whether values may
be different in different places and different times. If, as often happens

in a multi-cultural group of students, there are those who intelligently hold a fundamentalist religious position and those who are convinced pragmatists, the discussion of this matter can spill from the lecture theatre to the bar (coffee or alcohol). Such discussions can, of course, rapidly become unfocussed but a focus can be provided by directing the discussion towards such questions as whether Aldo Leopold's "land ethic" is something that is essentially new or whether it is a reformulation of traditional values (as for example in Leviticus Chapter 25) for a society that is both more complex and better able to destroy an environment than were pre-industrial societies.

At this point in the sequence, and preferably before the students have taken too hard-and-fast a stand, it proves useful to introduce them to a range of positions from simple absolutism to axiological relativism and to look at possible sources for such relativities, ranging from the exigencies of the physical environment to distance in space or time. Famine in a far off part of the world suffering from desertification provides a suitable vehicle for the discussion of the way in which distance, physical conditions, quality of government, historical responsibilities and economic organisation might impinge on a simple decision on what are the most important values. There are rarely years when such a famine is not occurring. Such discussion leads to a consideration of how values are to be prioritised and to the observation that even those who believe that their values are absolute throughout space and time may be faced with the decision of ranking one value above another.

A second matter which arises from consideration of the origins of values is whether the most important elements in environmental ethics are *principles* that can be stated in an abstract manner or *human virtues* that cannot be divorced from the whole personality. To contain this discussion within bounds it is useful to observe that most virtuous people and possibly even the most virtuous person would at some point have to wrestle with an ethical dilemma, and that this is more likely to be so when considering environmental issues which are constantly reappearing in new circumstances if not in new forms.

It is at this point that the need to read relevant material and not merely listen to and argue with the lecturer is reinforced, usually by the requirement to submit course work. The students are primarily directed towards basic texts in the field such as Robin Attfields's *The Ethics of the Global Environment* and the older *The Ethics of Environmental Concern,* and the books edited by David Cooper and Joy Palmer *Just*

Environments and *The Environment in Question*. The students are also encouraged to read more widely in related areas, partly because of the inevitable disparity between the number of students and the number of books in the university library but also to encourage them not to view problems in environmental ethics as being wholly discrete and unlike those in other areas. Books which have proved useful in recent years include Tom Beauchamp and James Childress' *Principles of Biomedical Ethics*, which deals with another area of life (and death) where ethics involves the making of hard decisions; Tom McEwan's *Managing Values and Beliefs in Organisations*, a very accessible book on ethical decision-making in the business environment; and David Smith's *Moral Geographies* which emphasises the ethical dimension of substantive issues with which the students will already be familiar.

From this point attention may be directed towards methods for making judgements. In this the course draws heavily upon educational material from biomedical and nursing ethics. This is partly because it is in these fields that some of the most acute ethical dilemmas are to be found but also because there are parallels to be found between medical and environmental matters. It is perhaps no accident that we use language in discussion such as the "health" of the environment; a "dying" ecosystem, and the "sickness" and "recovery" of elements of a natural landscape.

It may be argued that so lengthy a process before actually getting to grips with normative ethics severely limits the amount of time which can be given to the real issues of environmental ethics education. If, however, a short course is not merely to be regarded by the average student as yet another peripheral unit that must be passed in order to study their chosen subject matter it is essential that time be taken to demonstrate that their subject is more like dynamite than like porridge and could easily blow up in their face; and that there are no straightforward and simple ways of dealing with questions relating to values and containing the word "should".

Before considering methods for making judgements it has been found helpful to consider why we need to do so. It is usually concluded that if everyone agreed on a matter there would be no problem, and thus no *need* to develop means for coming to a judgement. All would agree that the mass slaughter of children on any pretext would be wrong and there is little need for a method to come to that decision. On the other hand the mass slaughter of badgers on the grounds that they carry bovine TB is an open ethical question and some method of coming to a reasoned conclusion, even if that conclusion is not shared by others, is required. The approaches to making judgements, following Beauchamp and Childress, are divided into "top-down" and "bottom-up" models. In the former case the students are introduced to the ideas of deontology and consequentialism and, in particular, they consider what consequences would be appropriate grounds for taking action in environmental matters (is the sum of human happiness wholly appropriate?). Of the "bottom-up" approaches, attention is primarily paid to the reworking of casuistry as proposed by Jonson and Toulmin in their book *The Abuse of Casuistry*, and to other case-based approaches.

From this point in the teaching programme the approach becomes more fluid and the students are presented with issues where a decision needs to be made. Unless the class is small, students are divided into small groups, since free discussion is inhibited by large numbers. Presented with a particular case, students are first asked to consider what are the significant matters which need to be taken into account. Usually all are agreed that the substantive facts of the environmental issue need to be known as fully as possible and not merely in general outline. It is also generally agreed that the values that might need to be taken into consideration also need to be detailed and weighed against each other or prioritised. The question is, though, how to do it? In the discussion that follows, frequently someone proposes (and if not they may be prompted to propose) that it is wasteful to reinvent the wheel; rather, it is useful to try to establish what people have done in similar previous situations. From this it is but a short step to the conclusion that making decisions in ethical dilemmas is more like decision-making in common law than testing scientific hypotheses. Whereas in common law the facts of the case are considered alongside established laws and precedent cases, in ethical matters values, precedent and detailed facts need to be considered. While such an approach to decision-making cannot guarantee an agreed outcome, it will at least ensure that all parties know why the others have come to a different conclusion. Eventually as in real life it is usually, although surprisingly not always, the judgement of the most powerful or influential member of any group that will prevail.

In the process the most difficult problem which needs to be faced is that of prioritising values in relation to the matter under consideration and it is here that dissent frequently breaks out in a group. The use of a modification of McEwan's "moral compass", which attempts to present in a simple graphical form the perceived relevance of different ethical approaches to a particular problem (McEwan, 2000: 75), is often useful at this point, allowing people to recognise that the difference between their position and that of their neighbour is often not great and may actually be resolved by discussion.

The course usually concludes with a simple and short summing up of the concepts which have been introduced and a rather bland conclusion that one object of ethical analysis and argument is dissuading people from seeking to address their different conclusions by means closed to conciliation. In a university where those in charge of laboratories have received intimations of forthcoming harm from animal rights activists, conciliation should not to be seen as an undesirable or weak outcome.

Some Concluding Thoughts

This approach would clearly be quite inadequate for a course to be taken by those who were taking a diet of courses in environmental philosophy or even those who had any substantial background in philosophy. It is, rather, an approach that will provide some basic elements of understanding and some practical suggestions for dealing with problems to students whose background is not in philosophy and who expect every problem to have a simple and definite solution. It is thus of some utility to the students, not only when they find themselves facing ethical dilemmas, but also when faced with the realisation that even in science there may be no universally agreed outcomes.

REFERENCES

Attfield, Robin. 1983. *The Ethics of Environmental Concern.* Oxford: Blackwell.
———. 1999. *The Ethics of the Global Environment.* Edinburgh: Edinburgh University Press.
Beauchamp, Tom and James Childress. 2001. *Principles of Biomedical Ethics.* 5th edn. New York: Oxford University Press.
Cooper, David and Joy Palmer. 1992. *The Environment in Question.* London: Routledge.
———. 1995. *Just Environments.* London: Routledge.
Jonson, Albert and Stephen Toulmin. 1988. *The Abuse of Casuistry.* Berkeley: University of California Press.
Leopold, Aldo. 1966. *A Sand County Almanac with Other Essays on Conservation.* New York: Oxford University Press.
McEwan, Tom. 2001. *Managing Values and Beliefs in Organisations.* Harlow: Pearson.
Smith, David. 2000. *Moral Geographies.* Edinburgh: Edinburgh University Press.

INDEX